THE ART OF
POLISH COOKING

THE ART OF
POLISH
COOKING

By Alina Żerańska

ILLUSTRATED BY JANINA DOMANSKA

PELICAN PUBLISHING COMPANY
Gretna 2006

First published by Doubleday and Company, November 1968
First Pelican edition, January 1989
Second Pelican printing, June 1992
Third Pelican printing, May 1997
Fourth Pelican printing, September 1999
Fifth Pelican printing, January 2002
Sixth Pelican printing, March 2004
Seventh Pelican printing, July 2006

Library of Congress Cataloging-in-Publication Data

Żerańska, Alina.

The art of Polish cooking / by Alina Żerańska ;
illustrated by Janina Domanska.
p. cm.
Reprint. Originally published: Garden City, N.Y. :
Doubleday, 1968.
Includes index.
ISBN-13: 978-0-88289-709-7

1. Cookery, Polish. I. Title.
TX723.5.P6Z4   1988
641.59438--dc19

88-30375
CIP

Printed in the United States of America
Published by Pelican Publishing Company, Inc.
1000 Burmaster Street, Gretna, Louisiana 70053

To

ALL MY POLISH FRIENDS

who were willing to share with me
their favorite recipes,

with thanks,

A. Ż.

CONTENTS

Recipes followed by an asterisk (*) can be found
by consulting the Index.

INTRODUCTION

At the 10th International Gastronomic Festival of 1967 in Torquay, Great Britain, the Polish delegation—5 masters of cooking— won three gold medals, two gold cups, two bronze medals, and one honorable mention. In Poland, gourmet traditions are as old as Polish culture, which has a written testimony of a thousand years, and many centuries more proved by the latest excavations.

Since Poland is on the crossroads between the East and the West, between severe Scandinavia and sunny Italy—Polish cuisine consists of an unusual variety of dishes. On their way to Germany and France, the merchants from the Middle East exchanged gladly their exotic spices, dried fruits, and nuts for Polish amber from the Baltic Sea. The splendor of the Polish kings' court attracted many Italian artists, who brought with them the taste for vegetables. Close ties with France and many intermarriages between Polish and French nobility brought to the Polish cuisine a distinctive French flair, which in conglomeration with native dishes gave Polish cooking a refined originality.

In the Polish cuisine, the most interesting dishes are the endless hors d'oeuvres accompanied by delicious dressings; the tasty, refreshingly cold summer soups, sour or sweet, and an unusual variety of pastries. From the majestic kings' castles, opulent palaces of the aristocracy, and spacious country manors of the gentry— the art of cooking spread to the city dwellers and to the peasants' huts.

I was brought up in the traditions of a high Polish cuisine. My mother and my grandmother were excellent cooks. I was learning my way around the stove helping often in the kitchen of our home in Warsaw before parties and holidays. I remember so well how the hundreds of dishes looked, I remember their smell and their taste. Polish cooking is not overly hot and spicy, but very fragrant because of an old tradition of cultivating herbs in each home garden, and drying them with care for the winter. The favorite seasonings are dill leaves, green parsley, and horseradish. Onions are used in almost every dish, but never in large amounts; garlic —seldom and sparingly. Sour cream is an important ingredient for all sauces and soups.

Polish sausage, which gained such fame in America, is only one of many kinds of delicious smoked meats prepared in Poland. In old times, due to the lack of proper refrigeration for fresh meats, Polish peasants would make sausage from their hogs. Sausage and cabbage have become mostly peasants' food, and because of their comparatively low price, the food of the poor in the cities. However cabbage and sauerkraut were always appreciated for special dishes like Cabbage Rolls* or Hunters' Stew*. The latter was for centuries a delicacy of people enjoying the excitement of the outdoor life.

The following excerpt from the 130-year-old epic *Pan Tadeusz* by one of the greatest Polish poets, Adam Mickiewicz, describes the values of the most national of Polish dishes—the Hunters' Stew*—*Bigos*.

Bigos was being cooked in every kettle.
In human language it is hard to settle
The marvels of its odor, hue and taste;
In poetry's description one has traced
Only the clinking words and clanging rhymes.
                    . . . .
This bigos is no ordinary dish,
For it is aptly framed to meet your wish.
Founded upon good cabbage, sliced and sour,
Which, as men say, by its own zest and power
Melts in one's mouth, it settles in a pot
And its dewy bosom folds a lot
Of the best portions of selected meats;
Scullions parboil it then, until heat
Draws from its substance all the living juices,
And, from the pot's edge, boiling fluid sluices
And all the air is fragrant with the scent.

Translated by Watson Kirkconnell

POLISH CUSTOMS
and
FAVORITE MENUS

POLISH CHRISTMAS

Polish Christmas celebrations were always simple, and no one sang Christmas carols until Christmas Eve. But it was easy to feel that something important was approaching.

In Poland the stores are busy and crowded before Christmas just as they are here. On city squares arise enchanted forests of Christmas trees, stretching proudly on their wooden stands. At every corner street vendors offer silver strings, shiny bulbs, sparklers, and all kinds of decorations. Warsaw is full of their merry shouts. On the steps of old churches, flocks of children are running, looking for the most beautiful crèche.

There is an excitement in the air which keeps growing and growing. On the day before Christmas, the wide Warsaw avenues vibrate with life. Happily smiling women rush from the bakers to the florists, and back home with arms filled with packages. Gentlemen emerge from numerous cafés, chatting and checking their last shopping lists.

But when the afternoon starts to sink into the early darkness of the winter evening, everything stops almost at once. Stores close in a hurry, a belated shopper runs to his destination, all the cars vanish somewhere, here and there passes an empty bus. And it becomes so quiet that it is almost possible to hear the snowflakes dancing in the frosty air.

Through shining windows of each home, one can see families clad in their best, gathering around the dining room table for the unique Polish ceremony—the quintessence of the Polish Christmas—the breaking of the bread.

The white, almost transparent communion wafer in the mother's hand is a symbol of love, friendship, and forgiveness. One does not approach the Christmas Eve table without forgiving and forgetting, without being able to wish everybody well with a whole heart.

The supper that follows is a delicious display of traditional dishes, but it is not a feast. After the whole day's fast it tastes wonderful, but it is meatless, as a remembrance that one must always give something up in the goal of gaining.

The old tradition requires one to invite to the Christmas Eve supper not only the people one likes, but primarily those who are lonely, unhappy, or sick. It used to be the only meal of the year shared by the servants with their master and his family at the same table.

It is customary to set an extra place ready and waiting for any lonely traveler who may knock that night on the door, or for the loved ones who are far away, but may join their families in spirit.

In the old times peasants used to set a sheaf of wheat in a corner of their huts. In the country as well as in the city, it was customary to spread some hay under the tablecloth as a remembrance of the manger.

A white tablecloth is always used for the Christmas Eve supper and no one is supposed to leave the table during the meal. It adds dignity to the evening. Twelve dishes were usually served because of the twelve apostles. It is not done any more. But poppy seeds are always included as a symbol of peaceful sleep, and honey for sweetness and contentment.

Christmas Eve supper menus vary according to the number of guests. More dishes are served for a larger group than for a small family gathering. But it is practical to choose less time-consuming ones when a greater amount of food is necessary.

CHRISTMAS EVE SUPPER MENUS FOR A FAMILY OF SIX

I

Herring in Sour Cream* on lettuce leaves
Christmas Barshch* with Mushroom Pockets*
Carp or Pike Polish Style* in butter sauce
with hard-cooked eggs and boiled potatoes
Stewed Sauerkraut with Mushrooms*
Dried Fruit Compote*
Poppy Seed Rolls*, Honey Cake*, Almond Cookies*

II

Dried Mushroom Soup* with barley
Fish au Gratin* with potatoes and Stewed Sauerkraut*
Noodles with Poppy Seeds*
Dried Prune Compote*
Baba* and Christmas Honey Cookies*

CHRISTMAS EVE SUPPER MENUS FOR TEN OR MORE

I
Pike in Aspic* and Yeast Fingers*
Mushroom Consommé* and Kulebiak with Cabbage*
Carp or White Fish in Gray Sauce* with egg noodles,
Carrots and Peas*
Cookies and Poppy Seeds*
Dried Fruit Compote*
Nut Rolls*, Honey Kisses*, Light Fruit Cake from Warsaw*

II
Fish in Greek Sauce*
Stewed Sauerkraut with Mushrooms* and Yeast Fingers*
Pike Polish Style* in butter sauce
with hard-boiled eggs and boiled potatoes
Almond Soup*
Dried Fruit Compote*
Baba with Raisins*, Poppy Seed Rolls*, Honey Cake Hearts*

III
Potato Herring Salad* on lettuce leaves
Christmas Barshch* and Kulebiak with Cabbage*
Fish au Gratin with Mushrooms*, egg noodles, carrots
Cookies and Poppy Seeds*
Dried Fruit Compote*
Nut Rolls*, Honey Cake*, Apple Raisin Cake*

CHRISTMAS DAY DINNER

Christmas Day is very peaceful in Poland. People rest, visit relatives and friends. Not much cooking is done. Meals are served cold or reheated.

Christmas dinner consists usually of cold turkey with cranberry sauce, and Vegetable Potato Salad*. A clear, hot barshch in cups follows with Yeast Fingers* or patties.

Sometimes it is a goose with cabbage and baked potatoes.

If company is expected, there will be an elegant torte, Honey Cake* and cookies. Coffee is made very strong and served in demitasse cups. Bowls of nuts and dishes with candies are placed on tables.

On the second day of Christmas a Hunters' Stew* would be prepared from sausage and leftover meats.

NEW YEAR'S EVE PARTY

It is nice to start the New Year in a jovial mood and among friends. Restaurants are overcrowded; what can be better than a private party, especially when given by a hostess who knows the art of cooking.

Polish people love to dress. They do not favor casual wear. It is the everyday necessity. How pleasant it is to shed it off together with all the worries and to put on evening clothes, sparkling party dresses! Polish parties are dress-up parties, and on New Year's Eve more so than ever.

It is customary to bring flowers or a box of candy to the hostess. When the party happens to be a first visit, it is a must.

Otherwise it is done just once in a while. It is nice to bring a bottle of champagne, some other wine or liqueur on New Year's Eve.

For a small group (6–8), a late dinner is usually planned. After the dessert and the coffee, sweet champagne is served around midnight. Timing is very important. Everyone should be served before the clock strikes, but not too soon, otherwise waiting becomes awkward and the mood is gone.

It is more practical to prepare a buffet consisting of various hors d'oeuvres for a large party. People arrive late, around ten o'clock. Drinks and tiny canapés are offered. At midnight the party salutes the New Year with dry champagne. Soon afterward a buffet supper is served.

Not only the people but also the table looks best dressed up for the festive occasion. A centerpiece of flowers or fruits (please, no plastic!) tastefully arranged makes the food more attractive and tempting.

After the guests have helped themselves and eaten, the table is cleared for coffee, tea, and cakes.

BUFFET SUPPER MENUS

I

Ham and Egg Rolls*
Fish in Aspic*
Vegetable Potato Salad*
Pork Pâté*
Cold Roast Beef*
Horseradish Sauce*
Dill Pickles*
Hunters' Stew*
Rye bread
Butter

Favors*
Walnut Torte*

II
Eggs with Anchovies*
Chicken in Aspic*
Tomato Cucumber Salad*
Potato Salad*
Pancakes with Mushrooms*
Tripe with Dumplings*
Hot rolls
Butter

Cheese Cake*
Torte Provence*

III
Eggs in Green Onion Dressing*
Pike Jewish Style*
Pig's Feet in Aspic*
Vegetable Salad*
Cold Ham*
Red Beets with Horseradish*
Hunters' Stew from Warsaw*
French bread
Butter

Sand Baba*
Date Torte*

IV
Eggs in Horseradish Dressing*
Fish in Greek Sauce*
Chicken in Mayonnaise*
Red Cabbage with Apples*
Cold Pork Loin Roast*
Mustard Sauce*
Pancakes with Meat*
Pumpernickel
Butter

Polish Doughnuts*
Poppy Seed Torte*

V
Flybanes*
Fish in Mayonnaise*
Ham with Horseradish*
Turkey Pâté* ✽
Vegetable Potato Salad*
Dill Pickles*
Asparagus and Brains au Gratin*
Rye bread
Butter

Chocolate Roll*
Almond Torte*

VI
Eggs with Ham in Aspic*
Cold turkey breast
Cranberry sauce
Vegetable Salad*
Cabbage Rolls*
Rye bread
Butter

Apple Squares*
Torte Stephanie*

POLISH EASTER OF
MY CHILDHOOD

Poland is a predominately Catholic country, and Lent was always observed seriously. Two or three meatless days a week were a common practice. As Polish people prefer fish on canapés or in other forms of cold hors d'oeuvres, the few popular hot fish dishes were lavishly supplemented with entrées prepared from flour, rice, eggs, vegetables, cheese, or fruits.

The last week of Lent was dedicated to prayer, spring cleaning, and preparation of the biggest feast of the year—Easter Luncheon. With women so busy, and the whole household in a terrible turmoil, husbands loved to sneak out with friends to one of the numerous excellent Polish restaurants "for a little fish." But as the old saying points out "a fish loves to swim"; the opportunity was provided by generously washing it down with vodka. This unholy practice helped the last sad days of Lent pass by.

Polish children love Easter no less than Christmas, and by no means is it a smaller holiday. There is a tradition of visiting several churches on Good Friday. Each church presents a tomb with a figure of Jesus Christ lying among thousands of sweet-smelling hyacinths and tulips. Canaries hidden in the greenery chirp their delicate songs. Little maids in white veils, boy scouts, and soldiers keep guard at the tomb. The scene, artistically arranged by professional decorators, is enveloped by a mysterious green and blue light.

After seeing tombs in at least five churches, wet and cold from the slush (spring comes late in Poland), we were greeted at home by the delicious aromas of delicacies prepared in the kitchen. We were welcome to help, but nothing more than licking the bowl could be gained. Dinner on Good Friday consisted of just herring with boiled potatoes or vegetable barley soup. The evening was spent in coloring eggs. In the Polish countryside it was customary to decorate them with beautiful flowery designs.

Easter dishes were not tasted even on Saturday, but the house already cleaned, smelling of fresh wax and hyacinths, the traditional Polish Easter flower. Pussy willows in tall vases decorated each room. Samples of Easter food were put in a basket: a few eggs, salt, butter, sausage, a piece of a pâté, a few slices of babka and mazurkas (Easter cakes). Covered with a white napkin, it was taken to the church for blessing.

In old times the priests of the parish visited many neighborhood homes and blessed the house, the family, and the food displayed on the dining room table.

Saturday afternoon everything was ready. The table was covered with a large white tablecloth, hanging almost to the floor, and decorated with garlands of ground pine. At the middle of the table a little, white sugar lamb was placed, the symbol of Jesus, with a little red banner and sugar flowers on the stand. Next to the lamb stood a bowl of colored eggs and hyacinths. In the countryside the lamb was often made of butter or baked from the yeast baba dough.

The dishes of cold meats and relishes occupied the front of the table: a huge home baked ham, rolls of sausages in the company of numerous sauces and dressings, a little roast pig, a turkey or a goose, large pieces of roast beef, pork loin, or veal. The traditional Easter relish called *ćwikła** is prepared from red beets and horse-radish.

At the other end of the table stood tall Easter babas silvery with sweet icing, a rich cheese cake with raisins, and endless varieties of thin squares of mazurkas. Each dish was garnished with green boxwood. The display was adorned by crystal bottles of home-flavored vodka and sweet liqueurs shimmering like amber, rubies, and emeralds.

The food waited untouched until Sunday, around noon, when the family returned from the church usually in the company of many friends. Before everybody was seated, mother took a plate with quartered Easter eggs blessed in church, and approached everyone in the room offering a piece, wishing good health and happiness.

The Easter luncheon was an endless affair. It had to be pre-pared in advance, therefore it was always cold with the exception of the clear barshch, which could be reheated in a few minutes. Some guests left soon while others were arriving. The table was not cleared till evening. The next day, a delicious Hunters' Stew* was cooked from the leftover meats.

Easter Monday is a holiday in Poland. People are tired from too much festivity and food. But a refreshing surprise, a splash of cold water may wait for them at every city corner, or even a sprinkle in their own beds. This old tradition called *Śmigus* or *Dyngus* provides plenty of fun for the young, but worries the housewives who waxed the floors with such dedication. How would you like a shower from the nearest balcony over your Easter bonnet?

EASTER LUNCHEON MENUS

I

Hard-boiled eggs
Baked ham
Polish sausage
Cold Turkey*
Cold Roast Pork Loin*
Red Beets with Horseradish*
Mustard Sauce*
Tartar Sauce*
Potato Salad*

Easter Baba with Icing*
Cheese Cake*
Mazurkas: Royal*
Gypsy*
Walnut*

II

Hard-boiled eggs
Baked ham
Polish sausage
Cold Roast Beef*
Pig's Feet in Aspic*
Red Beets with Horseradish*
Green Onion Sauce*
Dill Pickles*
Vegetable Potato Salad*

Easter Baba*
Mazurkas: Cheese*
Chocolate*
All Fruit*

THE DINNER PARTY

Nothing can compare with the charm of a conversation of a small group (6–8) sitting around the table.

In the Polish countryside the place at the head of the table was reserved for the father of the family. The cities were more gallant toward the women. It was customary to offer it to the oldest and the most respectable lady in the company. But today the world worships youth. If the lady is not really old and not much older than the rest of the guests—she may not feel honored, but embarrassed and angry.

To avoid an awkward situation, the hostess often sits at the head. A round table solves the problem well, and so does the American custom of the host and the hostess sitting at both ends of the table.

It is practical to place small separate plates with hors d'oeuvres at each setting before the guests are called to the table. The soup may be poured in the kitchen. Each entrée dish goes round the table, and if the dishes were warmed, the food is not cold before people can start eating. In general, Poles do not eat bread with dinner. Vodka is served with the hors d'oeuvres, wine with the entrée. Cold beer in small tumblers goes well with a heavier meal on a hot summer day.

DINNER PARTY MENUS

I

Herring in Oil*, lettuce canapés
Barshch with Beans*
Beef à la Nelson* (with mushrooms and potatoes)
Asparagus Polonaise*
Tomato salad
Peach Meringue*

II

Fish in Mayonnaise*
Sorrel Soup* with rice
Duck with Apples*
Baked potatoes
Winter Salad*
Quick Fruit Cake*

III

Toasted Liver Sausage Canapés*
Tomato Soup*
Roast Turkey* with Polish stuffing
Cranberry sauce
Cabbage and Apple Salad*
Brussels Sprouts Polonaise*
Orange Cake*

IV

Stuffed Eggs*
Mushroom Consommé* with Croutons*
Roast Beef*
Red Beets with Apples*
Noodles
Sweet Sauerkraut Salad*
Strawberry Cream* with cookies

V

Herring in Sour Cream*
Red Beet Barshch* with Meat Patties*
Pork Loin Roast*
Cabbage with Apples*
Boiled potatoes
Tomato salad
Baba with Raisins*

VI
Toasted Sardine Canapés*
Crayfish Soup*
Roast Veal*
Carrots and Peas*
Rice
Cucumbers with Sour Cream*
Date Torte*

OTHER MENUS

GOURMET DINNERS

I
Pancakes with Brains*
Lemon Soup* with rice
Hunters' Stew*
Yeast Fingers* with Dill Butter*
Brazil Nut Torte*

II
Pig's Feet in Aspic*
Sorrel Soup* with eggs
Brains au Gratin*
Asparagus Polonaise*
Honey Cake from Warsaw*

III
Shrimp Salad*
Cauliflower Soup*
Cabbage Rolls*
Sweet Cheese Dumplings*
Favors*

IV

Eggs with Anchovies*
Veal with Paprika*
Buckwheat Groats*
Prune Soup* with Croutons*
Cheese cake

V

Quick Barshch* and
Kulebiak with Meat*
Fish in Greek Sauce*, hot
Potato Dumplings*
Pears in Vanilla Sauce*
Royal Mazurka*

VI

Fish and Mushrooms in Sea Shells*
French bread
Pierogi with Meat*
Young Carrots Polonaise*
Apple Soup*
Nut Roll

FAMILY DINNERS

I

Barshch from Eastern Poland*
Pork Chops Sauté*
Boiled potatoes with parsley
Red Cabbage with Apples*
Cranberry Pudding*

II

Sauerkraut Soup* with potatoes
Meat Loaf* with Mushroom Sauce*
Cauliflower Polonaise*
Cucumbers with Sour Cream*
Rice and Apple Casserole*

III
Potato Soup*
Chicken Polish Style*
Carrots and Peas*
Lettuce with Green Onions*
Pancakes with Cheese*

IV
Cabbage Soup*
Beef Pot Roast*
Macaroni
Red Beets with Sour Cream*
Apple Cake*

V
Beef Broth* with Dumplings*
Hamburgers Polish Style*
Mashed potatoes
Summer Salad*
Summer Compote*

VI
Tomato Soup* with rice
Ham and Noodles Casserole*
Stewed Sauerkraut*
Strawberry Dessert*

VII
Asparagus Soup*
Ham Pot Roast*
Baked potatoes
Brussels Sprouts Polonaise*
Sweet Sauerkraut Salad*
Bread and Apple Baba*

VIII
Sorrel Soup* with Croutons*
Chicken Fricassee*
Rice
Green Beans Polonaise*
Tomato Sour Cream Salad*
Almond Squares*

MIDNIGHT SNACKS OR LUNCHEONS

I
Ham with Horseradish*
Vegetable Potato Salad*
Hot rolls
Rosé wine
Charlotte*

II
Pancakes with Mushrooms*
Dill Pickles*
Tomato and Pea Salad*
Chianti
Sand Baba*

III
Stuffed Mushrooms*
Lettuce and Egg Salad*
Cinnamon Cake*

IV
Stuffed Eggs*
Asparagus Polonaise*
Hot rolls
Polish Doughnuts*

V
Toasted Mushroom Canapés*
Omelet with Spinach*
Apple Cake*

VI
Kidneys*
Hot rolls
Lettuce with Green Onions*
White wine
Poppy Seed Torte*

VII
Kulebiak with Cabbage*
Mushroom Sauce*
Cucumbers with Sour Cream*
Cheese Bread*

VIII
Pancakes with Meat*
Red Cabbage with Apples*
Chianti
Summer Compote* and cookies

BANQUETS

I
Vegetable Salad* and hard-cooked eggs in Mayonnaise*
Hunters' Stew*
Mashed potatoes
Tomato salad
Lemon Torte*

II
Flybanes* on lettuce
Meatballs with Mushroom Sauce*
Shell macaroni
Cabbage with Apples*
Grandmother's Cheese Cake*

III
Fish in Mayonnaise* on lettuce
Pork Loin Roast*
Stewed Sauerkraut*
Baked potatoes
Favors*

IV
Pig's Feet in Aspic*
Veal with Vegetables*
Buckwheat Groats*
Lettuce
Ice cream and Chocolate Sandwiches*

V
Turkey Pâté* on lettuce
Hot rolls
Cauliflower with Ham au Gratin*
Rice
Polish Doughnuts*

VI
Chicken Salad* on lettuce
French bread
Roast Beef*
Baked potatoes
Green Beans Polonaise*
Pumpernickel Torte*

LIGHT SUMMER MEALS

I
Spring Barshch* with vegetables
Cheese Dumplings*

II
Cold Sorrel Soup* with eggs
Baked chicken
Mashed potatoes
Cucumber with Sour Cream*

III
Roast Veal*
Young potatoes with dill
Young Carrots Polonaise*
Blueberry Soup* with noodles

IV
Sour Milk, Cultured*, and potatoes
Omelet with Mushrooms*
Fresh fruit

V
Stuffed Tomatoes* with meat and rice
Lettuce with sour cream
Cold Apple Soup* with Croutons*

VI
Cauliflower Soup*
Pierogi with Cherries* with sour cream

VII
Lemon Soup* with rice
Meat Loaf*
Vegetable Bouquet*
Ice cream

VIII
Dill Pickle Soup*
Veal Chops Sauté*
Young potatoes
Asparagus Polonaise*
Strawberry Tarts*

IX
Lobster Soup* with rice
Pancakes with Cheese*

X
Green Bean Soup*
Hamburgers Polish Style*
Young potatoes
Tomato Sour Cream Salad*
Plum Tarts*

RECIPES

HORS D'OEUVRES
Zakąski

Hors d'oeuvres have a very important place in the Polish cuisine. This is what is prepared and served on all festive occasions.

Polish traditional hospitality never knew limitations. It was customary to greet important guests with bread and salt on a tray, indicating readiness to offer everything valuable. Friends were welcomed with a hearty embrace and the old saying: All that this home possesses—we will be happy to share.

Hospitality was always considered sacred in Poland. No harm could come to a guest because Slavs believed that "A guest in the house—is God in the house."

Even in the most difficult times, Polish people always loved to entertain. Friendship is valued highly, people like to visit, to be merry, and to feast. Being more often extravagant than thrifty, a Polish family would gladly limit itself to a modest table for days or even weeks, for the purpose of entertaining lavishly on a special occasion.

It is not customary to serve drinks before a meal in Poland. People prefer to have their vodka, their wine, or their beer with food. Therefore Polish cuisine provides endless variations of hors d'oeuvres appropriate to be served with alcoholic beverages.

An experienced Polish hostess knows that as long as there are several excellent hors d'oeuvres on artistically decorated dishes, and the vodka is cold and tasty—the party will be a success. The rest of the dinner is not too important. Not many would notice it, and almost nobody would have much room for it.

Entertaining a larger group, in the place of a formal dinner, a hostess would often present to her guests an attractive buffet loaded with cold and hot hors d'oeuvres.

Buffet entertaining is given often a French name *à la fourchette*, which means that every dish can be eaten with just a fork. This is practical because people help themselves, eat and drink standing.

It saves the trouble of setting a table and serving. There is a wider opportunity for conversation and more circulation among the guests. Sitting at a large table, one is limited to the company of his neighbors. In a household with a wide social life, this type of entertaining is favored more often.

Polish hors d'oeuvres consist of a variety of cold cuts, fish and poultry in aspic, mayonnaise; different salads, eggs in homemade dressings, relishes, the famous Polish pâtés and patties, and the king of all dishes—the traditional Hunters' Stew.

The mayonnaise sauce and the horseradish sauce are favorites. Some time ago the preparation was tedious and worrisome. It took at least half an hour of hard beating to produce a homemade mayonnaise, and there was a risk that it would be a flop. Nowadays it takes three minutes to make a mayonnaise with a mixer and it is always successful.

Grating horseradish is irritating to the eyes, and it was the cause of tears of many generations of Polish homemakers. Today we can buy a good prepared horseradish.

For a small, simpler party, instead of elaborate dishes, a tray of artistically garnished and arranged canapés would be served, usually with various drinks, and it would be followed with homemade delicious pastries.

COLD HORS D'OEUVRES

COLD HORS D'OEUVRES

Canapés
Liver Spread
Steak Tartare
Steak Tartare with Dill
    Pickles
Herring Spread
Cottage Cheese Sardine Spread
Spring Cottage Cheese Spread
Mustard Butter
Onion or Dill Butter

Ham and Egg Rolls
Eggs with Anchovies
Eggs in Green Onion, Mustard,
    or Horseradish Dressing

Eggs with Ham in Aspic
Flybanes
Pickled Mushrooms
Herring in Oil
Herring in Sour Cream
Fish in Greek Sauce
Fish in Horseradish Sauce
Fish in Mayonnaise
Fish in Aspic
Cold Roasts
Chicken in Aspic
Pig's Feet in Aspic
Ham with Horseradish
Pork Pâté
Veal Pâté
Turkey Pâté
Chicken in Mayonnaise
Roast Veal or Beef in
    Mayonnaise

ZIMNE ZAKĄSKI

Kanapki
Pasta z wątróbki
Befsztyk tatarski
Tatar z ogórkami

Pasta śledziowa
Awanturka
Twarożek wiosenny
Masło musztardowe
Masło szczypiorkowe lub
    koperkowe
Jajka zawijane w szynce
Jajka ze śledzikami
Jajka w sosie szczypiorkowym,
    musztardowym lub
    chrzanowym
Jajka z szynką w galarecie
Muchomorki
Grzybki marynowane
Śledź w oliwie
Śledź w śmietanie
Ryba po grecku
Ryba w sosie chrzanowym
Majoneziki z ryb
Ryba w galarecie
Zimne mięsa
Kura w galarecie
Galareta z nóżek wieprzowych
Szynka z chrzanem
Pasztet wieprzowy
Pasztet z cielęciny
Pasztet z indyka
Kura w majonezie
Cielęcina lub wołowina w
    majonezie

CANAPÉS
Kanapki

Rye bread or French bread is used for canapés. Butter each thin slice and cut it in four. Cover each little piece with several ingredients, garnish with vegetables and dressings to make them colorful, attractive, and tasty.

Suggested combinations:
1: sardines, Swiss cheese, tomato.
2: ham, sliced dill pickle, mayonnaise.
3: cottage cheese, sliced radishes, green onion.
4: ham, egg, horseradish-sour cream dressing.
5: sausage, beets with horseradish.
6: herring, egg, tomato.
7: herring, potato salad, sliced dill pickle.
8: vegetable salad in mayonnaise, pâté.
9: smoked salmon, lettuce, mayonnaise.
10: salami, cheese spread, sliced dill pickle.

All kinds of cold meats and different types of cheese may be used for canapés. Homemade spreads provide a pleasant variety as a base instead of butter.

LIVER SPREAD
Pasta z wątróbki

½ pound liver	*3 tablespoons grated*
2 tablespoons butter	*Parmesan cheese*
3 tablespoons water	*Salt and pepper*
2 slices bacon, diced	*1 bouillon cube*
1 medium onion, sliced	*¼ cup water*

Cut the liver in small pieces, remove skin and veins. Heat the butter in a skillet and brown the liver on both sides. Add 3 tablespoons water, reduce heat, and cook for 5 minutes. Fry the

bacon and the onions till golden. Put everything through meat grinder. Add the Parmesan cheese, season with salt and pepper, moisten with bouillon cube dissolved in ¼ cup water. Mix with a spoon until creamy.
Yields 1¾ cups.

STEAK TARTARE
Befsztyk tatarski

2 *pounds top round, trimmed of all fat, ground twice*
2 *teaspoons salt*
½ *teaspoon pepper, freshly ground*
¼ *cup minced onions*
3 *egg yolks, white threads removed*
6 *slices buttered rye toast*

Mix all the ingredients well. Chill ½ hour. Form 6 thin steaks. Place on 6 buttered rye toasts. Cut each toast in quarters.
Serve with drinks.
Steak Tartare has become very fashionable in Poland during the last 10 years.
Serves 6.

STEAK TARTARE WITH DILL PICKLES
Tatar z ogórkami

1½ *pounds top round, trimmed of all fat, ground twice*
1½ *teaspoons salt*
¼ *teaspoon pepper, freshly ground*
¼ *teaspoon paprika*
¼ *cup finely chopped dill pickles*
1 *teaspoon chopped green parsley*
Crackers

Mix all the ingredients well. Chill ½ hour. Spread on crackers. Serve with drinks.
Serves 6.

HERRING SPREAD
Pasta śledziowa

½ pound salt herring
2 hard-cooked egg yolks
½ cup soft butter

Soak the herring overnight in cold water. Remove skin and bones. Grind the fish fillets and the egg yolks. Add butter and mix with a spoon until creamy.
Smoked fish, which does not require soaking, may be substituted for herring.
Serve on canapés or on baked potatoes.
Yields 1¾ cups.

COTTAGE CHEESE SARDINE SPREAD
Awanturka

¾ cup cottage cheese   ½ cup sour cream
¾ cup sardines   Salt
2 hard-cooked eggs

Strain the cottage cheese, the sardines, and the eggs. Add sour cream and salt to taste. Mix until creamy.
This is a favorite spread from Kraków. Delicious on rye bread.
Yields 2 cups.

SPRING COTTAGE CHEESE SPREAD
Twarożek wiosenny

1½ cups cottage cheese   Lettuce leaves
½ cup sour cream   8 radishes, sliced
½ teaspoon salt   Rye or French bread
3 tablespoons chopped
  green onions

Mix the cottage cheese with sour cream; add salt and onions.

Arrange on lettuce leaves. Garnish with radishes.
Serve on rye or French bread. Excellent on a spring day with
Sour Milk, Cultured*.
Serves 8.

MUSTARD BUTTER
Masło musztardowe

½ cup soft butter
½ cup mustard

Mix the butter with the mustard until creamy. Use for canapés
and sandwiches.
Yields 1 cup.

ONION OR DILL BUTTER
Masło szczypiorkowe lub koperkowe

1 tablespoon chopped green onions or dill leaves
½ cup soft butter

Mix the onions or the dill leaves with the butter. Form a roll and
chill. Cut into small disks.
Serve on canapés, on baked potatoes, on steaks and cutlets.
Yields ½ cup.

HAM AND EGG ROLLS
Jajka zawijane w szynce

4 hard-cooked eggs   *Lettuce leaves*
8 slices ham   *Mayonnaise*

Shell the eggs and cut in halves. Roll each half in a slice of ham.
Arrange on lettuce leaves, decorate with mayonnaise.
Serves 8.

EGGS WITH ANCHOVIES
Jajka ze śledzikami

4 hard-cooked eggs
Lettuce leaves
16 anchovy fillets
2 tablespoons mayonnaise
1 dill pickle, sliced
1 tomato, sliced

Shell the eggs and cut in halves. Arrange them on a dish covered with lettuce leaves, egg yolks up. Cover the eggs with the anchovy fillets. Decorate with mayonnaise, pickle, and tomato slices. Serves 8.

EGGS IN GREEN ONION, MUSTARD, OR HORSERADISH DRESSING
Jajka w sosie szczypiorkowym, musztardowym lub chrzanowym

Shell 4 hard-cooked eggs and cut in halves. Arrange on lettuce leaves, cover with the dressing. Serves 8.

GREEN ONION DRESSING

Mix well: ½ cup sour cream, 2 tablespoons chopped green onions, 1 raw egg yolk, 2 tablespoons mustard, 1 teaspoon lemon juice, ½ teaspoon sugar, salt.

MUSTARD DRESSING

Mix well: ½ cup sour cream, 3 tablespoons prepared mustard, ½ teaspoon sugar, and salt. Decorate with tomato slices.

HORSERADISH DRESSING

Mix well: ½ cup sour cream, ½ cup prepared horseradish, 1 teaspoon prepared mustard, ½ teaspoon sugar, and salt. Decorate with dill pickle slices.

EGGS WITH HAM IN ASPIC
Jajka z szynką w galarecie

4 hard-cooked eggs
1 tablespoon gelatin
¼ cup cold water
2 beef bouillon cubes
1¾ cups hot water

Lettuce leaves
½ *pound ham, diced*
2 *dill pickles, chopped*
*Tartar Sauce**

Shell the eggs and cut in halves. Soften the gelatin in ¼ cup cold water. Dissolve bouillon cubes in 1¾ cups hot water, add the gelatin, mix well. Chill until mixture thickens slightly.
Use a Teflon-coated mold or rub the mold with salad oil. Put lettuce leaves on the bottom. Pour in ½ cup aspic, chill until set. Arrange the egg halves in the mold, cover with ham. Mix the rest of the aspic with pickles, pour in the mold. Chill until set.
Unmold by loosening edges with a paring knife and shaking onto chilled serving plate. Serve with Tartar Sauce*.
Serves 8.

FLYBANES
Muchomorki

8 hard-cooked eggs
4 small tomatoes
Salt

Pepper
Mayonnaise
Lettuce

Shell the eggs and cut off both ends. Arrange the eggs standing on a small tray; they will serve for mushroom stems. Cut the tomatoes in halves lengthwise. Put each half over an egg as a mushroom cup. Sprinkle with salt and pepper. Dot the flybanes' cups with mayonnaise. Decorate the tray with lettuce.
Serves 8.

PICKLED MUSHROOMS
Grzybki marynowane

4 pounds small mushrooms
4 cups boiling water
1½ tablespoons salt

MARINADE

1¾ cups water
15 peppercorns
2 bay leaves

2½ tablespoons salt
¾ cup sugar
¾ cup vinegar

Cut the mushroom stems off at the cap level. Place the heads in boiling salted water. Simmer till they sink to the bottom. Strain. Boil the marinade water with peppercorns and bay leaves for 30 minutes. Add salt and sugar. Stir till dissolved. Add the vinegar, bring to a boil.

Place the mushrooms in small jars. Cover with hot marinade. Close the jars. Keep refrigerated.

Use for canapés and salads, or as appetizers.

Yields 4 1-fluid-pint jars.

HERRING IN OIL
Śledź w oliwie

1 pound salt herring
2 tablespoons prepared mustard
½ cup salad oil
Green parsley

Soak the herring for 24 hours, changing water several times. Dry off, skin, cut open, clean, bone. Cut out long fillets. Spread each fillet on one side with mustard and roll. Put in a jar, cover with the salad oil. Refrigerate for 24 hours. Cut inch wide pieces. Arrange on a small dish. Stick a toothpick into each piece of herring. Decorate with green parsley.

Serves 8.

HERRING IN SOUR CREAM
Śledź w śmietanie

1 pound salt herring
1 medium apple, peeled and coarsely shredded
1 medium onion, chopped
½ cup sour cream
1 teaspoon lemon juice
½ teaspoon sugar
Dash salt
1 teaspoon chopped green parsley

Soak and clean the herring (as in Herring in Oil*). Cut inch wide pieces, arrange on a dish. Mix the apple and the onion with sour cream. Season with lemon juice, sugar, and salt. Pour the sauce over the herring. Sprinkle with parsley.
Serves 8.

FISH IN GREEK SAUCE
Ryba po grecku

1 pound carp, white fish, or flounder fillets
2 tablespoons salad oil
Salt
Greek Sauce
Green parsley

GREEK SAUCE

2 tablespoons salad oil
½ cup sliced celery
2 carrots, coarsely shredded
1 parsley root, coarsely
    shredded
2 onions, diced
3 tablespoons water

Salt
½ cup tomato paste
Pepper
½ teaspoon sugar
1 tablespoon lemon juice
½ teaspoon paprika

Cut the fish fillets in 2-inch pieces. Fry in hot oil, sprinkle with salt. Arrange in a long dish. Make the Greek Sauce.
Heat the oil in a small skillet. Fry the celery, the carrots, and the

parsley. Add the onions, 3 tablespoons water, and salt. Cover, cook over low heat for 15 minutes. Add tomato paste. Season with salt, pepper, sugar, lemon juice, and paprika. Remove from heat, chill. Pour the sauce over fish. Decorate with green parsley. May be served hot for a change.
Serves 4.

FISH IN HORSERADISH SAUCE
Ryba w sosie chrzanowym

2 *carrots*	*Salt*
2 *celery stalks*	6 *cups water*
1 *parsley root*	1 *pound carp, sole,*
1 *onion, quartered*	*or pike fillets*
1 *bay leaf*	*Horseradish Sauce*
3 *peppercorns*	*Lettuce*

HORSERADISH SAUCE

2 *tablespoons butter*	¼ *teaspoon salt*
2 *tablespoons instant flour*	½ *cup sour cream*
½ *cup cold fish stock*	½ *teaspoon sugar*
¾ *cup prepared horseradish*	2 *hard-cooked eggs, chopped*

Cook the vegetables and spices in the water for 20 minutes. Cook the fish fillets in strained vegetable stock for 15 minutes. Chill.
To make the Horseradish Sauce: Melt the butter in a saucepan, blend with the flour until smooth. Stir in the cold fish stock gradually and cook stirring until the sauce boils and becomes thick and smooth. A lumped sauce may be restored by rubbing through a sieve. Add the horseradish, salt, sour cream, sugar, and mix. Add eggs.
Remove cold fish from the stock, place carefully on a dish. Pour over the Horseradish Sauce. Decorate with finely shredded lettuce.
Serves 4.

FISH IN MAYONNAISE
Majoneziki z ryb

2 carrots	Salt
2 celery stalks	6 cups water
1 parsley root	1½ pounds fish fillets
1 onion, quartered	¾ cup Mayonnaise*
1 bay leaf	2 cups Vegetable Salad*
3 peppercorns	Lettuce

Cook the vegetables and spices in the water for 20 minutes. Cook the fish in the strained vegetable stock for 15 minutes. Cut the fish in small pieces and mix with 2 tablespoons Mayonnaise*. Arrange the Vegetable Salad* on a dish. Spoon the fish over it in egg-sized portions. Pour over the rest of the Mayonnaise*. Garnish with shredded lettuce.
Serves 8.

FISH IN ASPIC
Ryba w galarecie

2 carrots
2 celery stalks
1 parsley root
1 onion, quartered
1 bay leaf
3 peppercorns
Salt
6 cups water
1½ pounds carp, pike, sole, or white fish
1½ tablespoons gelatin
1 tablespoon vinegar
Egg, tomato, and cucumber slices

Cook the vegetables and the spices in the water for ½ hour. Put the fish in a saucepan, add strained vegetable stock. Cook over low heat for 15 minutes. Cool the fish in the stock. Remove, place on a long dish.

Soak the gelatin in ½ cup fish stock for 5 minutes. Add 2½ cups hot stock, stir till dissolved, add vinegar. Chill till thickens slightly. Pour half of the aspic over the fish, chill until set. Pour the rest of the aspic over the fish, chill. Garnish with egg slices, tomato, and cucumber.

Serve with vinegar or cold sauces.

Serves 8.

COLD ROASTS
Zimne mięsa

All kinds of cold meats are used for hors d'oeuvres. Most delicious is a cold Roast Pork*, Beef*, or Veal*. It is best to prepare the roast in advance, and to refrigerate overnight before cutting.

Cut large, thin slices with a long, thin, sharp knife. Arrange attractively on a flat dish or tray covering half of each slice with another. Garnish with green parsley and slices of carrots, tomatoes, and pickles. Cover each dish tightly with plastic wrap, and keep refrigerated until serving time.

Tasty and attractive are cold cuts of meat in aspic. A homemade stock may be used for this purpose or canned bouillon, with added gelatin.

CHICKEN IN ASPIC
Kura w galarecie

3–4-pound chicken, cut up	*1 parsley root*
2 teaspoons salt	*1 onion, quartered*
4 cups water	*1½ tablespoons gelatin*
1 bay leaf	*½ tablespoon vinegar*
4 peppercorns	*Canned fruits*
2 celery stalks	*Lettuce*
2 carrots	

Wash the chicken and peel off the excess fat. Fit pieces compactly into a kettle, sprinkle with salt. Add 4 cups water and spices. Cover closely, heat to boiling then reduce heat, and cook until tender, 2–2½ hours. For the last ½ hour add vegetables. Remove from heat, cool slightly. Remove the chicken from the kettle, skin and bone.

Soak the gelatin in ½ cup cold bouillon for 5 minutes. Add 2½ cups hot, strained bouillon, stir until dissolved. Add vinegar and chill until slightly thickened.

Use a Teflon-coated mold or rub the mold with salad oil. Pour ½ cup cold aspic in the mold, chill until set. Arrange the chicken in the mold, garnish with canned fruits. Pour carefully the rest of the aspic. Chill.

Unmold by loosening edges with paring knife and shaking onto chilled serving plate. Garnish with lettuce.

Serves 8.

PIG'S FEET IN ASPIC
Galareta z nóżek wieprzowych

1½ pounds pig's feet	*2 bay leaves*
½ pound lean pork	*5 peppercorns*
2 carrots	*¼ teaspoon minced garlic*
1 onion	*Salt to taste*
1 parsley root	*Green parsley*
2 celery stalks	*Lemon juice or vinegar*

Have the butcher skin and split the pig's feet. Cook the pig's feet, the pork, the vegetables, and the spices for 4 hours on low heat. In the middle of cooking add salt.

Strain. Remove the bones. Dice the meat.

Use a Teflon-coated mold or rub the mold with salad oil. Arrange on the bottom carrot slices and meat. Pour over the cold stock. Chill until set. Remove fat.

Unmold by loosening edges with a knife and shaking onto chilled serving plate. Garnish with green parsley. Serve with lemon juice or vinegar.

Use the same recipe for calves' feet.

Serves 8.

HAM WITH HORSERADISH
Szynka z chrzanem

⅓ cup prepared horseradish   ½ teaspoon sugar
4 tablespoons sour cream   8 slices ham
¼ teaspoon salt   Green parsley

Mix the horseradish with sour cream, salt, and sugar. Spread each slice of ham with horseradish dressing and roll. Arrange attractively on a flat dish or tray. Garnish with green parsley. Serves 8.

PORK PÂTÉ
Pasztet wieprzowy

½ pound salt pork, sliced
3 pounds fresh shoulder pork
5 medium onions, quartered
2 pounds pork liver, trimmed
2 eggs
Salt
Freshly ground black pepper
1 teaspoon marjoram
½ teaspoon nutmeg
Pinch allspice
1 tablespoon cube bouillon concentrate
½ pound sliced bacon

Roast the salt pork and the shoulder of pork in an open pan for 3 hours in slow 300° F. oven. When the pork is half done, add the onions. Remove the pork and add the liver to the onions in the pan. Raise the oven temperature to 350° F. and roast 15 minutes.

Remove the bones from the pork and grind the meat and liver twice. Sieve the onions and pan juices into meats. Add the eggs, salt and pepper to taste, marjoram, nutmeg, allspice, and bouillon concentrate. Mix well.

Line a bread pan with bacon and fill it ¾ full with the pâté mixture. Bake 40 minutes at 300° F. Chill, slice, and serve with Horseradish Sauce*.
Yields 1 loaf. Serves 20.

VEAL PÂTÉ
Pasztet z cielęciny

5 *dried mushrooms or*
    4 *ounces fresh mushrooms*
1 *large onion, quartered*
2 *bay leaves*
5 *peppercorns*
1 *pound veal, cut up*
1 *pound bacon*

1 *cup cube bouillon*
1 *pound pork liver, cut up*
3 *slices white bread*
3 *eggs*
Salt and pepper
Pinch allspice
½ *teaspoon nutmeg*

Scrub the dried mushrooms with a brush.
Simmer: dried mushrooms, onions, bay leaves, peppercorns, veal, and bacon in the bouillon for 2 hours.
Add the liver and fresh mushrooms (if used) ½ hour before it is done.
Strain the bouillon and soak the bread in it.
Grind twice: mushrooms, onions, veal, ¾ of the bacon, liver, and bread.
Add the eggs, season with salt, pepper, allspice, and nutmeg. Mix very well.
Line the bread pan with the rest of the bacon. Fill it ¾ full with the meat mixture. Cover with foil.
Bake in a moderate 350° F. oven for 1 hour.
Chill, remove from the pan. Refrigerate overnight. Slice.
Serve with Horseradish Sauce*, or Red Beets with Horseradish*.
Yields 1 loaf. Serves 12.

TURKEY PÂTÉ
Pasztet z indyka

1 large onion, quartered
½ bay leaf
8 slices bacon
10 ounces chicken livers
½ pound mushrooms
2 cups chicken cube bouillon mixed with turkey drippings
5 slices white bread
6 cups leftover turkey meat
4 eggs
Salt and pepper
½ teaspoon nutmeg

Cook the onion, the bay leaf, the bacon, the livers, and the mushrooms in the bouillon for 10 minutes.
Strain the bouillon and soak the bread in it.
Line 2 loaf pans with wax paper.
Grind twice: onions, bacon, livers, mushrooms, turkey meat, and bread. Add eggs, salt, pepper, and nutmeg. Mix very well. Fill the pans ¾ full. Cover with foil.
Bake in a slow 325° F. oven for 1½ hours. Remove from the pan when slightly warm.
Serve cold, sliced, with Mustard Sauce* or Horseradish Sauce*.
Yields 2 loaves. Serves 16.

CHICKEN IN MAYONNAISE
Kura w majonezie

3–4-pound chicken, boiled, skinned, boned
*2 cups Vegetable Salad**
*1 cup Mayonnaise**
Lettuce leaves

Arrange the chicken meat over the salad on a large serving platter.
Pour over the Mayonnaise*. Garnish with lettuce leaves.
Serves 8.

ROAST VEAL OR BEEF IN MAYONNAISE
Cielęcina lub wołowina w majonezie

4 cups leftover roast
1 cup Mayonnaise*
4 cups Vegetable Salad*
1 tablespoon dill leaves

Chop leftover roast and mix with ½ cup Mayonnaise*. Spread Vegetable Salad* on a large flat dish. Spoon over the meat in egg-sized portions. Pour over the rest of the Mayonnaise*, sprinkle with dill leaves.
Serves 10.

HOT HORS D'OEUVRES *and* LUNCHEON DISHES

HOT HORS D'OEUVRES *and* LUNCHEON DISHES	GORĄCE ZAKĄSKI DANIA ŚNIADANIOWE
Toasted Ham Canapés	*Grzanki z szynką*
Toasted Sausage and Horse-radish Canapés	*Grzanki z kiełbasą i chrzanem*
Toasted Liver Sausage Canapés	*Grzanki z pasztetówką*
Toasted Liver Canapés	*Grzanki z wątróbką*
Toasted Brain Canapés	*Grzanki z móżdżkiem*
Toasted Sardine Canapés	*Grzanki z sardynkami*
Toasted Mushroom Canapés	*Grzanki z pieczarkami*
Toasted Ham, Tomato, and Cheese Canapés	*Grzanki z szynką, pomidorem i serem*
Yeast Fingers	*Drożdżowe paluszki*
Patties with Sausage or Mushrooms	*Paszteciki z kiełbasą lub grzybami*
Meat Patties	*Paszteciki z mięsem*
Quick Patties	*Paszteciki szybkie*
French Shells with Brains	*Paszteciki z mózgiem*
Meat Torte	*Biszkopt z mięsem*
Ham Pudding	*Budyń z szynki*
Kulebiak with Cabbage	*Kulebiak z kapustą*
Kulebiak with Meat	*Kulebiak z mięsem*
Hunters' Stew	*Bigos myśliwski*
Hunters' Stew from Warsaw	*Bigos warszawski*
Kidneys	*Smażone cynaderki*
Fried Calf's Feet	*Nóżki cielęce w cieście*
Fried Ham	*Szynką w cieście*
Tripe Warsaw Style	*Flaki warszawskie*
Dumplings for the Tripe	*Pulpety*
Omelet with Frankfurters	*Omlet z parówkami*
Omelet with Ham	*Omlet z szynką*
Omelet with Croutons	*Omlet z grzankami*
Omelet with Mushrooms	*Omlet z pieczarkami*

Omelet with Asparagus	*Omlet ze szparagami*
Omelet with Spinach	*Omlet ze szpinakiem*
Omelet with Tomatoes	*Omlet z pomidorami*
Stuffed Eggs	*Faszerowane jajka*
Eggs in Sea Shells	*Jajka w muszelkach*
Eggs au Gratin	*Jajka zapiekane*
Eggs and Macaroni in Tomato Sauce	*Jajka zapiekane z makaronem*
Asparagus and Brains au Gratin	*Szparagi zapiekane z mózgiem*
Brains in Sea Shells	*Móżdżek w muszelkach*
Fish and Mushrooms in Sea Shells	*Ryba w muszelkach*
Cauliflower with Ham au Gratin	*Kalafior zapiekany z szynką*
Macaroni, Sausage, and Peas au Gratin	*Muszelki zapiekane z szynką i groszkiem*
Pancakes	*Naleśniki*
Pancakes with Brains	*Naleśniki z móżdżkiem*
Pancakes with Sauerkraut	*Naleśniki z kapustą*
Pancakes with Meat	*Naleśniki z mięsem*
Pancakes with Mushrooms	*Naleśniki z grzybami*
Pancakes with Spinach	*Naleśniki ze szpinakiem*
Cabbage Rolls	*Gołąbki*

TOASTED HAM CANAPÉS
Grzanki z szynką

8 slices white bread
¼ cup soft butter
½ pound ham, finely chopped
¼ cup grated cheese
4 tablespoons sour cream

Use two-day-old bread. Spread each slice on both sides with butter. Cut each one in half. Mix the ham with the cheese and sour cream. Spread canapés on one side. Put into a hot 450° F. oven for 10 minutes.

All kinds of leftover cold cuts may be used instead of ham. Serve with tea or coffee. A tasty snack for an unexpected guest. Yields 16 canapés.

TOASTED SAUSAGE AND HORSERADISH CANAPÉS
Grzanki z kiełbasą i chrzanem

8 slices white bread
¼ cup soft butter
½ pound sausage, skinned and chopped
4 tablespoons sour cream
¼ cup prepared horseradish
1 teaspoon flour
1 tablespoon sour cream

Use two-day-old bread. Spread each slice on both sides with butter. Cut each one in half.
Mix the sausage with sour cream, spread the canapés. Mix the horseradish with the flour and sour cream. Spread over the sausage. Put into a hot 450° F. oven for 10 minutes.
Yields 16 canapés.

TOASTED LIVER SAUSAGE CANAPÉS
Grzanki z pasztetówką

8 slices white bread
¼ cup soft butter
8 slices liver sausage

3 tablespoons Mayonnaise*
3 tablespoons grated cheese

Use two-day-old bread. Spread each slice on both sides with butter. Spread with the liver sausage on one side. Cut each slice in quarters. Mix the mayonnaise with the grated cheese. Spread over the sausage. Put into a hot 450° F. oven for 10 minutes. An excellent bridge snack.
Yields 32 canapés.

TOASTED LIVER CANAPÉS
Grzanki z wątróbką

½ pound calf liver	*Salt and pepper*
4 slices bacon, diced	*8 slices white bread*
1 small onion, sliced	*¼ cup butter*
3 tablespoons water	*¼ cup grated cheese*

Cut the liver in small pieces, remove skin and veins. Heat the bacon in a skillet. Add the onions, fry for few minutes, add the liver and 3 tablespoons water. Cover, reduce heat, simmer for 10 minutes. Chop everything finely, season with salt and pepper. Spread each slice of bread with butter on both sides. Cut each one in half. Spread with liver, sprinkle with grated cheese. Place on a cookie sheet in a hot 450° F. oven for 10 minutes.
Yields 16 canapés.

TOASTED BRAIN CANAPÉS
Grzanki z móżdżkiem

8 slices white bread	*1 onion, chopped*
¼ cup soft butter	*1 egg*
10 ounces brains	*Salt and pepper*
2 tablespoons vinegar	*¼ cup grated cheese*
1½ tablespoons butter	*3 tablespoons bread crumbs*

Spread each slice of bread with butter on both sides. Cut each one in half.
Clean the brains and cook in salted water with vinegar for 2 minutes. Drain, dice.
Heat the butter in a skillet, add onions and fry until golden. Add brains, fry for 3 minutes. Remove from heat, add the egg, season with salt and pepper.
Spread canapés with brains, sprinkle with cheese and bread crumbs. Place on a cookie sheet in a hot 450° F. oven for 10 minutes.
Yields 16 canapés.

TOASTED SARDINE CANAPÉS
Grzanki z sardynkami

8 slices white bread
¼ cup soft butter
6 ounces sardines, boneless and skinless
¼ cup grated cheese
¼ cup bread crumbs

Spread each slice of bread with butter on both sides. Cut each one in half. Arrange the drained sardines on the canapés. Sprinkle with grated cheese and bread crumbs.
Place on a cookie sheet in a hot 450° F. oven for 10 minutes.
A tasty appetizer for a gourmet dinner.
Yields 16 canapés. Serves 8.

TOASTED MUSHROOM CANAPÉS
Grzanki z pieczarkami

2 tablespoons butter
1 onion, sliced
½ pound mushrooms, chopped
1 tablespoon instant flour
1 tablespoon cold water
3 tablespoons sour cream
Salt and pepper
1 tablespoon butter
4 eggs, beaten
1 tablespoon dill leaves
8 slices white bread, toasted

Heat the butter in a skillet, add the onions, fry for 3 minutes. Add mushrooms, fry for 5 minutes.
Mix the flour with 1 tablespoon cold water, add to the mushrooms, fry for 1 minute. Remove from heat, add sour cream, season with salt and pepper.
Heat butter and scramble eggs, add dill.

Spread the toasts with mushrooms, spoon eggs in the middle, serve immediately.
An elegant midnight snack.
Yields 8 canapés. Serves 8.

TOASTED HAM, TOMATO, AND CHEESE CANAPÉS
Grzanki z szynką, pomidorem i serem

8 slices white bread	*8 slices tomato*
¼ cup soft butter	*1 tablespoon green onions*
8 slices ham	*8 slices American cheese*

Spread each slice of bread with butter on both sides. Cover each slice with ham and tomato. Sprinkle with green onions. Top with cheese.
Place on a cookie sheet in a hot 450° F. oven for 10 minutes. A quick family luncheon.
Yields 8 canapés. Serves 8.

YEAST FINGERS
Drożdżowe paluszki

½ cup butter
2¼ cups flour, sifted
1 ounce fresh yeast
1 teaspoon sugar
½ teaspoon salt
1 egg
2 egg yolks
2 tablespoons sour cream
1 egg white
2 tablespoons caraway seeds or poppy seeds

Cut the butter into the flour with a knife and rub in with finger-tips. Add yeast combined with sugar. Add salt, egg, egg yolks, and sour cream. Knead the dough for few minutes.

Form long, thin rolls. Place on a buttered cookie sheet and let rise in a warm place. When doubled in size, brush with egg white, sprinkle with caraway seeds. Bake in moderate 375° F. oven for 15 minutes. Remove immediately from the cookie sheet. Serve with drinks or with clear soups.
Yields 40 fingers.

PATTIES WITH SAUSAGE OR MUSHROOMS
Paszteciki z kiełbasą lub grzybami

*Prepare dough as for Yeast Fingers**

STUFFING

10 ounces Polish sausage, skinned, chopped
  OR
10 ounces mushrooms, chopped, sautéed in 2 tablespoons butter
½ cup grated cheese
¼ cup bread crumbs
1 egg

SPREAD

1 egg white

Mix the ingredients of the stuffing.
Roll out the dough ¼ inch thick. Cut into long 2-inch-wide strips. Place the stuffing on one side of each strip. Fold the dough over lengthwise and seal the ends. Cut into small 1-inch-wide patties. Brush with the egg white.
Place on a buttered cookie sheet in the oven heated to 100° F. Cover with a towel. Leave the oven door half open. Let stand till doubled in size.
Bake in a moderate 375° F. oven for 20 minutes.
Excellent for luncheons, buffet suppers, and with clear soups.
Yields about 60 patties.

MEAT PATTIES
Paszteciki z mięsem

STUFFING	DOUGH
2 tablespoons fat	⅔ cup butter
1 pound veal or **pork**, diced	2½ cups flour
3 tablespoons water	2 teaspoons baking powder
1 onion, sliced	2 egg yolks
¼ pound mushrooms, sliced	1 egg
Salt and pepper	3 tablespoons sour cream
1 tablespoon dill leaves	1 egg white

Heat fat in the skillet and brown meat on both sides. Remove to a saucepan. Add 3 tablespoons water and onions. Cook on low heat for 2 hours. For the last ½ hour add mushrooms. Grind everything. Add seasoning, and mix well.

To make dough: Cut the butter into the flour with a knife and rub in with fingertips. Add baking powder, egg yolks, egg, and sour cream. Knead the dough for few minutes.

Roll out 2 rectangles 18×6 inches. Form a line of stuffing 1 inch off one long side of each rectangle. Fold the dough over the stuffing, brush with the egg white. Cut into 26 patties. Place on a buttered cookie sheet. Bake in a moderate 350° F. oven for 35 minutes. All kinds of leftover meats may be used for stuffing.

Serve with drinks and with clear soups.

Yields 26 patties.

QUICK PATTIES
Paszteciki szybkie

8 slices ham or any meat, chopped
2 tablespoons Mayonnaise*
1 roll frozen crescent dough

1. Sprinkle the meat with mayonnaise, stuff the crescents, and bake as directed on the dough package.

Serve hot with soups and salads.

Yields 8 crescents.

2. Cut each crescent dough into 3 triangles. Stuff, roll, and bake, allowing 5 minutes less than directed on the package.

Serve with drinks as an appetizer.

Yields 24 tiny crescents.

FRENCH SHELLS WITH BRAINS
Paszteciki z mózgiem

DOUGH	STUFFING
1 cup butter	*1 pound brains*
2¼ cups flour, sifted	*3 tablespoons butter*
1 egg	*1 onion, sliced*
2 egg yolks	*1 egg*
5 tablespoons sour cream	*3 tablespoons sour cream*
Dash salt	*Salt*

To make dough: Cut the butter into the flour with a knife, and rub in with fingertips. Add all ingredients. Knead for few minutes. Refrigerate in a covered dish overnight.

Soak the brains for ½ hour in water. Clean and dice. Heat the butter in a small saucepan, and fry the onions until golden. Add brains and fry 10 minutes. Remove from heat, and combine with other ingredients.

Roll out the dough ¼ inch thick. Cut out circles with a glass. Brush off ½ of the circles with egg white. Cut out small circles from the rest of large circles with a juice glass. Put cut out rings on the circles that have been brushed with egg white. Bake for 15 minutes in 400° F. oven.

Reheat before serving, stuff with brains. Serve immediately.

The same shells are delicious stuffed with diced meat, fish, or mushrooms in Béchamel Sauce*.

Serves 15.

MEAT TORTE
Biszkopt z mięsem

Meat stuffing	*Salt to taste*
5 eggs, separated	*1 tablespoon butter*
1 cup flour	*Tomato Sauce**
8 tablespoons sour cream	

Use the same stuffing as for Meat Patties* or any kind of left-over meat.

Beat egg yolks on high speed. Add flour and sour cream by spoon-fuls alternately; add dash of salt. Beat egg whites until stiff. Fold in half of the egg whites, mix gently with a spatula. Add the rest of the egg whites, mix slightly.

Fold half of the batter into a well-buttered spring pan. Fold in the meat stuffing evenly. Cover with the rest of the batter. Bake in 375° F. oven for 50 minutes. Turn off the heat, open the oven doors slightly. Leave the Meat Torte in the oven for another 10 minutes. Remove from the oven gently. Cool slightly. Serve warm with Tomato Sauce*.

Serves 8.

HAM PUDDING
Budyń z szynki

2 cups ground ham
2 cups cooked and ground potatoes
2 tablespoons butter
4 eggs, separated
Salt and pepper to taste
1 tablespoon butter
1 tablespoon bread crumbs
Mustard Sauce* or Horseradish Sauce*

Mix the ham and the potatoes well. Beat the butter with egg yolks until creamy. Add to ham mixture, add salt and pepper. Beat the

egg whites until stiff. Fold half of egg whites into the ham mixture, stir gently and fold in the rest of the egg whites.
Bake for 1 hour at 350° F. in a covered baking dish that has been well buttered and sprinkled with bread crumbs.
Serve with Mustard Sauce* or Horseradish Sauce*.
Serves 6.

KULEBIAK WITH CABBAGE
Kulebiak z kapustą

*Prepare dough as for Yeast Fingers**

STUFFING

2-pound head cabbage
4 tablespoons water
1 large onion, sliced
4 ounces mushrooms, sliced
3 tablespoons fat
Salt and pepper
2 hard-boiled eggs, chopped
1 egg white

Chop the cabbage finely and place in a kettle. Add 4 tablespoons water, onions, mushrooms, and fat. Cook on low heat until tender, about 30 minutes. Add salt, pepper, and chopped eggs.
Roll out the dough ½ inch thick. Form a rectangle. Form a roll of stuffing in the middle of the dough. Fold over both long sides and seal the ends. Place carefully on a buttered cookie sheet and let rise in a warm place. Brush with the egg white. Bake in a moderate 375° F. oven for 1 hour.
Serve with Tomato Sauce* or Mushroom Sauce* for luncheons or buffet suppers or with clear soups.
Serves 10.

KULEBIAK WITH MEAT
Kulebiak z mięsem

Prepare dough as for Yeast Fingers*

STUFFING

2 tablespoons fat
1 large onion, sliced
1¾ cups ground leftover roast
¾ cup cooked rice
2 bouillon cubes
3 tablespoons hot water
Salt and pepper to taste
1 tablespoon chopped green parsley
1 egg white
Tomato Sauce* or Mushroom Sauce*

Heat the fat in a skillet, add the onions and fry until golden. Add the meat and the rice, mix. Add bouillon cubes dissolved in 3 tablespoons hot water, season with salt, pepper, and green parsley. Roll, stuff, and bake as in Kulebiak with Cabbage*. Serve with Tomato Sauce* or Mushroom Sauce*.
Serves 10.

HUNTERS' STEW
Bigos myśliwski

4 dried mushrooms
¼ cup water
2 pounds sauerkraut
1 large apple, peeled, cored, sliced
1 (20-ounce) can tomatoes
5 peppercorns
1 bay leaf
2 cups diced Polish sausage or leftover meat
1 cup coarsely chopped bacon
Steamed potatoes or rye bread

Soak the mushrooms in ¼ cup water for 2 hours. Bring to boil and simmer for ½ hour. Slice.

Wash the sauerkraut and squeeze it. Add mushrooms and the liquid in which they were cooked. Add the apples, the tomatoes, peppercorns, and bay leaf. Cover and simmer for 1 hour and 15 minutes.

Add the meat and the bacon, simmer 1 hour longer.

It is best reheated. Serve with steamed potatoes or rye bread.

It is one of the oldest traditional Polish dishes. Excellent for banquets and buffet entertaining.

Serves 5.

HUNTERS' STEW FROM WARSAW
Bigos warszawski

4 dried mushrooms, or ½ pound fresh mushrooms, sliced
¼ cup water
½ pound pork or 1 cup leftover meat
1 tablespoon bacon drippings
1 pound sauerkraut, washed
1 cup cube bouillon
1 cup diced Polish sausage
1 pound cabbage, finely sliced
¾ cup diced bacon
1 large onion, sliced
2 tablespoons instant flour
2 tablespoons water
3 tablespoons tomato paste
Salt and pepper
½ cup red table wine
Potatoes or rye bread

Soak the dried mushrooms in ¼ cup water for 2 hours.

Brown the pork in hot drippings on all sides. Place in a kettle. Add sauerkraut, bouillon, sausage, and dried mushrooms with their liquid. Simmer for 2 hours. Take out and slice the pork. Cook the cabbage in a separate saucepan for 20 minutes, drain. Fry the bacon with the onions until golden. Add the flour mixed with 2 tablespoons water, fry few more minutes, stirring.

Add to the sauerkraut stew: the cabbage, bacon and onion mixture, fresh mushrooms (if they are being used), tomato paste, pork, salt and pepper. Simmer for 5 minutes.

Prepare a day ahead. It is best reheated. Reheat in a moderate 375° F. oven for 1 hour. Add wine before serving.

Serve with potatoes or rye bread.

Serves 5.

KIDNEYS
Smażone cynaderki

4 veal kidneys
Salt
2 tablespoons flour
2 tablespoons fat
1 teaspoon chopped green parsley

Remove most of the fat from the kidneys. Soak in water for 1 hour, rinse very well, dry. Cut into diagonal slices ¼ inch thick, sprinkle with salt and flour. Heat the fat in a skillet and fry the kidneys, browning evenly on all sides. Lower the heat and fry 4 more minutes. Sprinkle with green parsley and serve.

Serves 6.

FRIED CALF'S FEET
Nóżki cielęce w cieście

4 calf's feet   *Salt and pepper*
1 cup beef cube bouillon   *Green parsley*

DOUGH

1¾ cups flour   *2 tablespoons salad oil*
2 small eggs, separated   *¼ cup fat for frying*
8 tablepoons water

Have the butcher skin and split the calf's feet. Simmer them covered in the bouillon for 4 hours. In the middle of cooking add salt and pepper. Strain. Remove the bones. From each foot form 2 small rectangles. Cover with wooden board and leave until cold. Mix flour with egg yolks, water, and oil. Beat egg whites until stiff, add to the dough. Dip each serving in the dough and fry on both sides until golden.

Serve on a warmed dish garnished with green parsley. It is best with raw vegetable salad.

Serves 8.

FRIED HAM
Szynką w cieście

Prepare dough as for Fried Calf's Feet*
8 slices ham
¼ cup fat

Dip each slice of ham in the dough and fry on both sides in fat until golden.

Serve with Horseradish Sauce* and lettuce.

Serves 8.

TRIPE WARSAW STYLE
Flaki warszawskie

1½ pounds honeycomb tripe
1 can beef bouillon
2 carrots, coarsely shredded
1 parsley root, coarsely shredded
1 onion, sliced
2 tablespoons fat
2 tablespoons instant flour
Salt and pepper
½ teaspoon paprika
¼ teaspoon nutmeg
1 teaspoon grated ginger
½ teaspoon marjoram
3 tablespoons grated cheese
2 tablespoons bread crumbs

Soak the tripe in cold water for several hours; wash very well, rinse in a colander. Cover with boiling water, heat to boiling, drain. Repeat the boiling. After the second draining add beef bouillon and simmer 3–4 hours.

Prepare the Dumplings*.

Cook the vegetables in small amount of water. Drain the tripe, cut very finely in 1½-inch-long strings. Add to the vegetables. Melt the fat, combine with flour, stir until smooth, add to the pot. Add all the spices, add the dumplings. Pour in 5 separate heat-proof serving dishes. Sprinkle with cheese and bread crumbs. Place in a hot 400° F. oven for 30 minutes.

Serves 5.

DUMPLINGS FOR THE TRIPE
Pulpety

¼ pound beef suet, ground
1 egg
Salt and pepper
Dash marjoram, paprika, ginger, nutmeg
1 tablespoon chopped green parsley
3–4 tablespoons bread crumbs
1 tablespoon flour

Cream the beef suet with the egg, spices, parsley, and bread crumbs. Shape into small balls, roll in flour, and cook in boiling water for 30 minutes. They are done when they rise to the surface. Serves 5.

OMELET WITH FRANKFURTERS
Omlet z parówkami

4 eggs
4 teaspoons instant flour
8 tablespoons milk
Salt

2 tablespoons butter
4 frankfurters, sliced
2 tablespoons sour cream

Beat the eggs in a mixer at medium speed adding flour and milk by spoonfuls. Add salt to taste.

Heat the butter in a large skillet. Pour in the egg mixture, do not stir. When the eggs begin to set, carefully lift the edges of the omelet with a knife, and allow some of the runny egg to flow under. The omelet should be golden underneath and soft inside. Place the frankfurters mixed with sour cream in the middle of the omelet. Fold over both sides. Put a plate over the omelet and reverse quickly.

Serves 3.

OMELET WITH HAM
Omlet z szynką

1 tablespoon butter
½ pound ham, diced
1 tablespoon water
Prepare omelet as for Omelet with Frankfurters*
Green parsley

Heat the butter in a skillet, add ham and water. Cover and heat for few minutes.
Place the ham in the middle of the omelet. Fold over both sides. Slide off to a warmed dish. Garnish with green parsley.
Serves 3.

OMELET WITH CROUTONS
Omlet z grzankami

4 slices white bread
2 tablespoons salad oil
2 tablespoons butter
2 eggs
1 cup milk
7 tablespoons grated cheese
1 tablespoon chopped green onion
Salt to taste

Dice the bread. Heat the oil and the butter in a large skillet. Fry the croutons on high heat.

Mix the eggs, milk, cheese, and onions, add salt to taste. Pour the mixture over the croutons. Cover and bake in moderate 350° F. oven for 10 minutes.
Serve with lettuce salad. A quick lunch for two.
Serves 2.

OMELET WITH MUSHROOMS
Omlet z pieczarkami

1½ cups chopped mushrooms
1 onion, sliced
2 tablespoons water
1 tablespoon instant flour
3 tablespoons cube bouillon
Salt and pepper to taste
1 tablespoon dill leaves
4 tablespoons sour cream
6 eggs
2 tablespoons water
Salt to taste
2 tablespoons butter

Put the mushrooms and the onions in a saucepan. Add water and cook for 5 minutes.
Mix the flour with cold bouillon. Add to the mushrooms, heat to boiling. Remove from heat, season with salt and pepper. Add dill leaves and sour cream.
Beat the eggs with water and salt. Heat the butter in a large skillet. Pour in the eggs, fry on a low heat. When the eggs begin to set, carefully lift the edges of the omelet with a knife, and allow some of the runny egg to flow under. Place the mushrooms in the middle of the omelet. Fold over both sides. Put a plate over the omelet and reverse quickly.
Serve with Tomato Cucumber Salad*. A delicious lunch for a small group.
Serves 4.

OMELET WITH ASPARAGUS
Omlet ze szparagami

1½ pounds asparagus
Salted water
Dash sugar
Prepare omelet as for Omelet with Mushrooms*
1 teaspoon butter

Cook the asparagus in a small amount of salted water, add a dash of sugar. Drain.
Prepare the omelet. Place the asparagus in the middle, dot with butter. Fold over both sides. Put a plate over the omelet and reverse quickly. Serve with a tomato salad.
Serves 4.

OMELET WITH SPINACH
Omlet ze szpinakiem

1½ pounds spinach
1 tablespoon butter
1 tablespoon instant flour
¾ cup milk
Salt to taste
Dash garlic powder
Prepare omelet as for Omelet with Mushrooms*

Wash the spinach very well. Place in a kettle, cover with boiling salted water. Cook for 5 minutes. Drain well. Chop and press through a sieve.
Melt the butter, blend with the flour. Add the milk and stir until smooth. Add the spinach; mix, season, and heat.
Prepare the omelet. Place the spinach in the middle. Fold over both sides. Put a plate over the omelet and reverse quickly.
Serve with Red Cabbage with Apples*.
Serves 4.

OMELET WITH TOMATOES
Omlet z pomidorami

3 medium tomatoes
2 tablespoons butter
Salt to taste
Prepare omelet as for Omelet with Mushrooms*
1 tablespoon chopped green onion

Wash the tomatoes and cut into thick slices. Heat half of the butter and fry half of the tomatoes. Repeat. Sprinkle with salt. Prepare the omelet. Place the tomatoes in the middle. Sprinkle with green onions. Fold over both sides. Slide off.
Serve with green salad.
Serves 4.

STUFFED EGGS
Faszerowane jajka

7 eggs
3 tablespoons bread crumbs
4 tablespoons sour cream
1 tablespoon dill leaves
1 tablespoon chopped green onion
Salt and pepper
2 tablespoons butter

Wash the eggs, place in a kettle, cover with cold water, heat until water boils. Cook on low heat for 10 minutes. Remove from the kettle, place in cold water.
Cut cold eggs lengthwise using a sharp knife. Avoid crushing the shells. Scoop out the eggs and chop fine. Mix with 1 tablespoon bread crumbs, sour cream, dill, onions, salt and pepper. Return the mixture to the shells, cover with the rest of the bread crumbs, flatten with a knife.

Heat the butter in a large skillet. Fry the eggs (stuffing down) till golden.
Serve with green salad or with Sorrel Soup*.
Serves 7.

EGGS IN SEA SHELLS
Jajka w muszelkach

Butter	*½ cup grated cheese*
8 eggs	*¼ cup butter, melted*
Salt to taste	*3 tablespoons bread crumbs*

Spread each sea shell or individual baking dish with butter. Drop 1 egg in each shell. Sprinkle with salt and with cheese. Pour over the butter and sprinkle with bread crumbs. Bake in hot 450° F. oven for 8–10 minutes.
It can be done in one dish.
Serves 8.

EGGS AU GRATIN
Jajka zapiekane

1 tablespoon butter
8 hard-cooked eggs
*1¾ cups Béchamel Sauce**
½ cup grated Parmesan cheese

Spread the baking dish with butter. Shell the eggs and cut in halves. Place them in the baking dish. Cover with Béchamel Sauce*, sprinkle with cheese. Put under broiler for a few minutes. When the cheese starts to brown, remove from the oven. Serve with tomato salad.
Serves 8.

EGGS AND MACARONI IN TOMATO SAUCE
Jajka zapiekane z makaronem

2 tablespoons butter
8 eggs
4 cups cooked macaroni
1½ cups Tomato Sauce*
½ cup grated Parmesan cheese

Heat the butter in a large skillet, fry the eggs. Spread a baking dish with butter, arrange the macaroni on the bottom. Remove carefully each egg separately from the skillet and place on macaroni. Cover with Tomato Sauce*, sprinkle with cheese.
Bake in a hot 400° F. oven for 10 minutes. Serve with a green salad.
Serves 8.

ASPARAGUS AND BRAINS AU GRATIN
Szparagi zapiekane z mózgiem

6 ounces asparagus, frozen
Salt to taste
¼ teaspoon sugar
6 ounces brains
1 tablespoon vinegar

1 bay leaf
3 peppercorns
1¾ cups Béchamel Sauce*
2 tablespoons butter, melted
2 tablespoons bread crumbs

Cook the asparagus in a small amount of salted water and with sugar. Drain. Place in the middle of a baking dish.
Clean brains and cook in salted water with vinegar and spices for 5 minutes; drain. Place the brains on both sides of the asparagus. Cover with Béchamel Sauce*. Mix the butter with the bread crumbs, sprinkle over the sauce. Bake in a hot 400° F. oven for 15 minutes.
Serves 4.

BRAINS IN SEA SHELLS
Móżdżek w muszelkach

1 *pound brains*
1 *bay leaf*
3 *peppercorns*
1 *tablespoon vinegar*
1 *cup Béchamel Sauce**
½ *cup grated Parmesan cheese*
2 *tablespoons bread crumbs*
2 *tablespoons butter, melted*

Prepare brains as in Asparagus and Brains au Gratin*. Dice the brains and mix with Béchamel Sauce*. Place in 4 sea shells or small baking dishes. Sprinkle with cheese and bread crumbs mixed with butter. Place in hot 400° F. oven for 10 minutes, or until crumbs are golden.
Serve with a bowl of salad and hot rolls. It is a gourmet midnight snack.
Serves 4.

FISH AND MUSHROOMS IN SEA SHELLS
Ryba w muszelkach

1 *pound mushrooms, sliced*
5 *tablespoons butter*
3 *tablespoons lemon juice*
1 *cup dry white wine*
¼ *teaspoon thyme*
1 *bay leaf*
½ *teaspoon salt*

⅛ *teaspoon pepper*
1 *pound fish fillets, diced*
3 *tablespoons instant flour*
1 *cup coffee cream*
¾ *cup buttered bread crumbs*

Cook mushrooms in 2 tablespoons butter and lemon juice until golden brown, stirring often. Combine wine, thyme, bay leaf, salt, and pepper in a saucepan. Add fish. Cover and cook over medium heat for 10 minutes. Drain, saving 1 cup broth.
Melt remaining butter in saucepan. Stir in flour and blend. Stir in the broth and cream. Cook over moderate heat, stirring until the

sauce is smooth and thickened. Add the fish and the mushrooms. Mix well. Spoon into 6 shells. Top with buttered crumbs. Bake in preheated 400° F. oven about 10 minutes, or until crumbs are golden.

A delicious entrée for a gourmet dinner.

Serves 6.

CAULIFLOWER WITH HAM AU GRATIN
Kalafior zapiekany z szynką

1 medium cauliflower	*¾ cup milk*
½ pound ham, diced	*3 eggs, separated*
3 tablespoons butter	*Salt*
3 tablespoons instant flour	*1 tablespoon dill leaves*

Cook the cauliflower in salted water until tender, about 20 minutes. Drain and divide into small parts. Arrange in a buttered baking dish, add the ham.

Heat the butter, stir in the flour and blend. Stir in the milk. Cook over moderate heat, stirring until the sauce is smooth and thickened. Remove from the heat, add egg yolks, salt, and mix. Beat egg whites until stiff, add to the sauce. Pour the sauce into the baking dish. Sprinkle with dill. Bake in hot 400° F. oven for 30 minutes.

Serves 4.

MACARONI, SAUSAGE, AND PEAS AU GRATIN
Muszelki zapiekane z szynką i groszkiem

2 cups cooked shell macaroni
1 cup canned peas, drained
1 pound Polish sausage, skinned and diced
1¾ cups Béchamel Sauce*
½ cup grated Parmesan cheese

Mix the shells with the peas and the sausage. Place in a buttered baking dish. Cover with Béchamel Sauce*. Sprinkle with cheese.

Bake in a hot 400° F. oven for 20–30 minutes or until cheese is golden.

A hearty luncheon dish.

Serves 6.

PANCAKES
Naleśniki

6 tablespoons flour, sifted	1 teaspoon sugar
2 eggs	½ teaspoon salt
2 egg yolks	¼ cup butter, melted
2 cups milk	

Mix the flour, eggs, and egg yolks. Add the milk, sugar, and salt; beat with mixer at low speed for 2 minutes.

Heat a skillet 4 inches in diameter and brush with butter. Pour in 1 tablespoon of the batter and tilt the pan immediately so the batter will spread over entire bottom of pan. Cook the pancake on both sides. Repeat until all the pancakes are cooked, stacking them on a plate.

Yields 12 pancakes. Serves 4.

PANCAKES WITH BRAINS
Naleśniki z móżdżkiem

1 pair fresh brains
Salt and freshly ground black pepper to taste
1 bay leaf
⅓ cup finely chopped onion
3 tablespoons butter
1 egg yolk
12 Pancakes*

Clean the brains and place in a saucepan with water to cover, salt, pepper, and bay leaf. Bring to a boil and cook 3 minutes. Drain and dry the brains.

Cook the onions in the butter until golden. Add the brains and stir to mix well. Cook 2 minutes. Stir the egg yolk into the mixture and blend well. Season with salt and a generous amount of black pepper.

Spoon a little of the mixture into the center of a pancake and fold the pancake envelope fashion to completely encase the stuffing. Fry each stuffed pancake in a little hot butter until golden on both sides.

Yields 12 pancakes. Serves 6.

PANCAKES WITH SAUERKRAUT
Naleśniki z kapustą

BATTER

1 cup milk	*½ cup water*
2 eggs	*½ teaspoon salt*
1 cup flour	*3 tablespoons salad oil*

STUFFING

½ pound sauerkraut	*1 hard-cooked egg, chopped*
2 tablespoons fat	*2 tablespoons sour cream*
1 onion, chopped	
4 ounces mushrooms, sliced	*1 egg, beaten*
Salt and pepper	*½ cup bread crumbs*
	3 tablespoons butter

To make batter: Mix the milk with the eggs. Add the flour, beat with mixer for 1 minute. Add water and salt, beat another minute.

Heat a skillet 6–7 inches in diameter, and brush with oil. Pour in 1 tablespoon of the batter and tilt the pan immediately so the batter will spread over entire bottom of pan. Cook the pancake on both sides. Repeat until all the pancakes are cooked, stacking them on a plate.

Wash the sauerkraut and squeeze. Place in a saucepan. Cover with small amount of boiling water. Cook for 20 minutes, drain. Heat the fat in a skillet, fry the onions until golden. Add the mushrooms, fry 3 minutes. Mix with sauerkraut, salt, and pepper. Fry until the sauerkraut becomes golden. Remove from heat, add the egg and sour cream. Mix well.

Stuff and fold the pancakes as in Pancakes with Brains*. Roll each stuffed pancake in egg and then in bread crumbs. Fry in butter until golden on both sides.

Yields 15 pancakes. Serves 7.

PANCAKES WITH MEAT
Naleśniki z mięsem

BATTER

*Prepare pancakes as for Pancakes with Sauerkraut**

STUFFING

1 onion, chopped
1 tablespoon butter
2 cups ground leftover roast
Salt and pepper to taste
¼ cup cube bouillon

Fry the onions in butter. Add the meat, salt, and pepper. Mix well. Add the bouillon, mix.

Spoon a little of meat stuffing into the center of each pancake and fold the pancake envelope fashion to encase the stuffing completely. Fry each pancake in a little hot butter until golden on both sides.

Yields 15 pancakes. Serves 7.

PANCAKES WITH MUSHROOMS
Naleśniki z grzybami

BATTER

*Prepare pancakes as for Pancakes with Sauerkraut**
Save 3 tablespoons batter

STUFFING

2 tablespoons butter
1 onion, sliced
10 ounces mushrooms, sliced
2 tablespoons water
2 slices white bread

Salt and pepper

3 tablespoons bread crumbs
2 tablespoons butter

Heat the butter in a skillet, add onions, and fry until golden. Add mushrooms and 2 tablespoons water, cover and cook on low heat for 5 minutes. Soak the bread in water, squeeze. Put everything through a grinder, season with salt and pepper. Mix until creamy.

Spoon a little of the stuffing into the center of each pancake and fold the pancakes envelope fashion to encase the stuffing completely. Roll each stuffed pancake in leftover batter and in bread crumbs. Fry in hot butter until golden on both sides.

Yields 15 pancakes. Serves 7.

PANCAKES WITH SPINACH
Naleśniki ze szpinakiem

BATTER

Prepare and stuff pancakes as for Pancakes with Sauerkraut*

STUFFING

1½ pounds spinach
1 onion, chopped
1 tablespoon butter
2 tablespoons grated Parmesan cheese
1 tablespoon bread crumbs
Salt

Wash the spinach very well. Place in a kettle, cover with boiling salted water. Cook for 5 minutes. Drain well. Chop and press through a sieve. Fry the onions in butter until golden. Mix the spinach, onions, cheese, and bread crumbs. Season with salt to taste. Prepare and stuff the pancakes. Fold envelope fashion.

Yields 15 pancakes. Serves 5.

CABBAGE ROLLS
Gołąbki

1 onion, chopped
1 tablespoon fat
1 cup cooked rice
¼ pound ground beef
¼ pound ground pork
Salt and pepper
1 head cabbage (about 3 pounds)
2 beef bouillon cubes
1 cup hot water
1 can cream of tomato soup, undiluted

Fry the onions in the fat until golden. Mix the onions with the rice and the meat (do not use precooked rice), season with salt and pepper.

Place the whole head of cabbage in a large kettle with boiling water. Cover and cook for 5 minutes. Remove the cabbage from the kettle. Separate the soft leaves from the surface. Return the rest of the cabbage to the kettle and cook for another 5 minutes. Repeat until all the leaves are separated easily. Cut out the hard part of the stem of each leaf.

Place a spoonful of the stuffing on each cabbage leaf. Wrap the stuffing in each leaf. Place the rolled stuffed cabbage leaves one next to the other in a baking dish. Dissolve the beef bouillon cubes in hot water, pour the bouillon over the cabbage rolls.

Bake uncovered cabbage rolls in a hot 450° F. oven for 1 hour. Pour the undiluted cream of tomato soup over the cabbage rolls. Cover the baking dish. Reduce the oven temperature to 350° F. Bake for another hour.

Cabbage rolls are best reheated.

Mushroom Sauce* may be used for a change instead of cream of tomato soup.

Serves 10.

SALADS

Tossed salad is not as popular in the Polish cuisine as in America, but there is a variety of definitely Polish ones. Usually a raw vegetable salad accompanies each dinner. Salads consisting of cooked or mixed ingredients take an important part in any buffet supper.

The favorite seasonings are dill leaves, chopped green parsley, and green onions. Lemon juice, mayonnaise, or sour cream is usually used for dressings.

Dry dill leaves (sometimes called dillweed) are sold in the spice departments of larger supermarkets and gourmet shops. It serves the purpose, but fresh dill is always better. One can purchase it in larger Canadian and some American cities, but it is not found easily.

As dill is so important in the Polish cuisine, used generously for hors d'oeuvres, salads, soups, and sauces, it is worth the effort of growing it. Seed it early in the spring, and by the end of May it will be 1 foot high, ready to cut, as only the young leaves and tender stems are used.

Divide the twigs into dinner portions. Wrap each portion in plastic, forming small cigarette-like rolls. Place them in a plastic box, and store in the freezer. Several months later the dill will be almost as fragrant as on the day it was cut.

Parsley poses no problems, one can find it in most stores the year round. Use it fresh, or in an emergency frozen, but not the dry one, which resembles hay.

SALADS

SAŁATKI

Radish and Cottage Cheese Salad	*Sałatka z rzodkiewki i twarogu*
Tomato Cucumber Salad	*Surówka z pomidorów i ogórków*
Cucumbers with Vinegar	*Mizeria z octem*
Cabbage and Dill Pickle Salad	*Surówka z kapusty i kiszonego ogórka*
Cabbage and Apple Salad	*Surówka z kapusty z jabłkami*
Sauerkraut and Onion Salad	*Surówka z kiszonej kapusty i cebuli*
Sauerkraut, Carrot, and Apple Salad	*Surówka z kiszonej kapusty z marchwią i jabłkami*
Sauerkraut and Tomato Salad	*Surówka z kiszonej kapusty i pomidorów*
September Salad	*Sałatka wrześniowa*
Green Pepper Salad	*Surówka z zielonego pieprzu*
Carrot, Apple, and Horseradish Salad	*Surówka z jabłek, marchwi i chrzanu*
Radishes with Sour Cream	*Surówka z rzodkiewki*
Cucumbers with Sour Cream	*Mizeria ze śmietaną*
Tomato Sour Cream Salad	*Sałatka z pomidorów w śmietanie*
Carrot and Rhubard Salad	*Sałatka z marchwi i rabarbaru*
Summer Salad	*Sałatka letnia*

Lettuce and Egg Salad	*Sałata z jajami*
Lettuce with Green Onions	*Sałata ze szczypiorkiem*
Cabbage in Mayonnaise	*Kapusta w majonezie*
Tomato and Pea Salad	*Pomidory z groszkiem w majonezie*
Lettuce with Mayonnaise	*Sałata w majonezie*
Leek and Apple Salad	*Surówka z porów i jabłek*
Red Cabbage with Apples	*Czerwona kapusta z jabłkami*
Winter Salad	*Sałatka zimowa*
Sweet Sauerkraut Salad	*Kiszona kapusta na słodko*
Potato Salad	*Sałatka kartoflana*
Potato Bean Salad	*Sałatka z ziemniaków z fasolą*
Vegetable Salad	*Sałatka jarzynowa*
Vegetable Potato Salad	*Sałatka kartoflano-jarzynowa*
Meat or Poultry Salad	*Sałatka z mięsa lub drobiu*
Chicken Salad	*Sałatka z kury*
Shrimp Salad	*Sałatka z krewetek*
Herring Salad	*Sałatka śledziowa*
Potato Herring Salad	*Sałatka kartoflano-śledziowa*
Tomato Frankfurter Salad	*Sałatka z pomidorów i parówek*
Potato Frankfurter Salad	*Sałatka z parówek i kartofli*
Tomato Egg Salad	*Sałatka z pomidorów i jaj*
Cucumber Egg Salad	*Sałatka z ogórków i jaj*

RADISH AND COTTAGE CHEESE SALAD
Sałatka z rzodkiewki i twarogu

1 bunch radishes, thinly sliced
1 cup creamed cottage cheese
1 tablespoon chopped green onion
Salt
Lettuce leaves

Mix the radishes with cottage cheese. Add green onions and salt.
Chill for ½ hour. Serve on lettuce leaves.
Serves 4.

TOMATO CUCUMBER SALAD
Surówka z pomidorów i ogórków

1 medium cucumber, peeled and sliced
4 medium tomatoes, sliced
Salt
¼ teaspoon sugar
1 tablespoon chopped green onion
1 teaspoon dill leaves
1 teaspoon vinegar

Arrange cucumber and tomato slices alternately on a long dish.
Sprinkle with salt, sugar, green onions, and dill. Sprinkle with
vinegar.
Serves 6.

CUCUMBERS WITH VINEGAR
Mizeria z octem

2 cucumbers, peeled and thinly sliced
Salt
½ teaspoon sugar
2 teaspoons dill leaves
2 teaspoons vinegar

Arrange cucumber slices on a long dish. Sprinkle with salt, sugar, dill, and vinegar. Serve immediately.
Serves 6.

CABBAGE AND DILL PICKLE SALAD
Surówka z kapusty i kiszonego ogórka

2 cups shredded cabbage
2 medium dill pickles, coarsely shredded
Salt
½ teaspoon sugar
2 tablespoons pickle juice
2 tablespoons salad oil
1 small tomato, sliced

Mix the cabbage with pickles. Season with salt, sugar, juice from the pickle jar, and oil. Arrange on a dish, garnish with tomato slices. Chill for ½ hour.
Serves 6.

CABBAGE AND APPLE SALAD
Surówka z kapusty z jabłkami

2 cups savoy cabbage, shredded
Salt
1 medium dill pickle, coarsely shredded
1 large apple, peeled and coarsely shredded
3 tablespoons salad oil
¼ teaspoon sugar
1 tablespoon lemon juice
Parsley

Sprinkle the cabbage with salt. Mix with all other ingredients. Arrange in a dish. Chill for 1 hour. Garnish with parsley.
Serves 6.

SAUERKRAUT AND ONION SALAD
Surówka z kiszonej kapusty i cebuli

⅔ pound sauerkraut	*3 tablespoons salad oil*
1 tablespoon sugar	*1 teaspoon chopped parsley*
1 medium onion, chopped	*1 small onion, sliced*

Rinse the sauerkraut, squeeze, and chop finely. Sprinkle with sugar. Combine with the chopped onions and oil.
Arrange in a dish and chill for 1 hour. Sprinkle with parsley and garnish with onion slices.
Serves 4.

SAUERKRAUT, CARROT, AND APPLE SALAD
Surówka z kiszonej kapusty z marchwią i jabłkami

½ pound sauerkraut
2 medium carrots, peeled and shredded
1 large apple, shredded
1 tablespoon sugar
3 tablespoons salad oil

Rinse the sauerkraut, squeeze, and chop. Add the carrots, the apple, sugar, and oil. Chill for 1 hour.
Serves 4.

SAUERKRAUT AND TOMATO SALAD
Surówka z kiszonej kapusty i pomidorów

⅔ pound sauerkraut
1 tablespoon sugar
3 tablespoons salad oil
1 medium onion, chopped
3 tablespoons tomato paste
2 tablespoons chopped green onion

Rinse the sauerkraut, squeeze, and chop. Add sugar, oil, onions, and tomato paste. Place in a dish, chill for 1 hour. Sprinkle with green onion.
Serves 4.

SEPTEMBER SALAD
Sałatka wrześniowa

4 medium tomatoes, thinly sliced
2 apples, peeled, coarsely shredded
1 cucumber, peeled, thinly sliced
4 peaches, peeled, sliced
3 tablespoons salad oil
½ teaspoon sugar
1 tablespoon lemon juice
¼ teaspoon salt
Lettuce leaves

Combine all ingredients, leaving a few peach and tomato slices for decoration. Serve immediately on lettuce leaves.
Serves 8.

GREEN PEPPER SALAD
Surówka z zielonego pieprzu

5 green peppers, cored, thinly sliced
4 tomatoes, coarsely chopped
2 pears, peeled, cored, sliced
3 tablespoons salad oil
¼ teaspoon salt
½ teaspoon sugar
1 tablespoon lemon juice

Combine the peppers, tomatoes, and pears. Season with oil, salt, sugar, and lemon juice. Chill for ½ hour.
Serves 8.

CARROT, APPLE, AND HORSERADISH SALAD
Surówka z jabłek, marchwi i chrzanu

6 medium carrots, peeled and finely shredded
2 apples, peeled, cored, and coarsely shredded
2 tablespoons grated horseradish
Salt and sugar
⅔ cup sour cream
Green parsley

Combine the carrots with apples and horseradish. Season with salt and sugar, add sour cream. Chill for 15 minutes and serve garnished with green parsley.
Serves 4.

RADISHES WITH SOUR CREAM
Surówka z rzodkiewki

3 bunches radishes, sliced or coarsely shredded
½ teaspoon salt
1 cup sour cream
Lettuce leaves
1 tablespoon dill leaves

Sprinkle the radishes with salt. Combine with sour cream. Arrange on lettuce leaves, sprinkle with dill.
Serves 5.

CUCUMBERS WITH SOUR CREAM
Mizeria ze śmietaną

2 cucumbers, peeled and thinly sliced
1 cup sour cream
Salt and sugar
1 tablespoon dill leaves

Combine cucumbers with sour cream, season with salt and sugar. Sprinkle with dill. Serve immediately.
Serves 4.

TOMATO SOUR CREAM SALAD
Sałatka z pomidorów w śmietanie

5 *tomatoes, sliced*	*Salt*
2 *medium dill pickles, sliced*	1 *cup sour cream*
1 *onion, sliced*	*Green parsley*

Arrange tomato and pickle slices on a long dish, garnish with onion. Sprinkle with salt, cover with sour cream. Garnish with parsley and serve.
Serves 8.

CARROT AND RHUBARB SALAD
Sałatka z marchwi i rabarbaru

4 *medium carrots, peeled, coarsely shredded*
2 *stalks rhubarb, finely sliced*
1 *tablespoon sugar*
½ *teaspoon salt*
3 *tablespoons sour cream*
Lettuce leaves
1 *tablespoon chopped green parsley*

Mix the carrots with sweetened rhubarb. Season with salt, add sour cream. Arrange on lettuce leaves. Sprinkle with parsley.
Serves 4.

SUMMER SALAD
Sałatka letnia

2 *heads butter lettuce*
1 *bunch radishes, sliced*
1 *large cucumber, peeled, sliced*
1 *cup sour cream*
Salt and sugar
1 *tablespoon chopped green onion*

Wash the lettuce and separate the leaves. Combine with the

radishes and cucumber. Season sour cream with salt and sugar, pour over the vegetables. Sprinkle with green onions and serve immediately.

Serves 6.

LETTUCE AND EGG SALAD
Sałata z jajami

3 heads butter lettuce	*Salt and sugar*
1 cup sour cream	*2 hard-boiled eggs, quartered*

Wash the lettuce and separate the leaves. Arrange on a dish. Season sour cream with salt and sugar, pour over the lettuce. Garnish with the egg and serve.

Serves 6.

LETTUCE WITH GREEN ONIONS
Sałata ze szczypiorkiem

3 heads butter lettuce	*2 tablespoons chopped*
1 cup sour cream	*green onion*
Salt and sugar	*1 tablespoon dill leaves*

Wash the lettuce and separate the leaves. Arrange on a dish. Season sour cream with salt and sugar. Pour over the lettuce. Sprinkle with green onions and dill.

Serves 6.

CABBAGE IN MAYONNAISE
Kapusta w majonezie

4 cups finely shredded cabbage
3 medium carrots, peeled, finely shredded
1 cup Mayonnaise*
Salt and sugar

Combine the cabbage with carrots and mayonnaise. Season with salt and sugar. Chill for 1 hour.

Serves 8.

TOMATO AND PEA SALAD
Pomidory z groszkiem w majonezie

4 medium tomatoes, diced   *Lettuce leaves*
1 medium can peas, drained   *Green parsley*
¾ cup Mayonnaise*

Combine tomatoes with peas. Pour the mayonnaise over. Serve on lettuce leaves, garnish with parsley.
Serves 6.

LETTUCE WITH MAYONNAISE
Sałata w majonezie

3 heads butter lettuce
*¾ cup Mayonnaise**
Radishes

Wash the lettuce and separate the leaves. Arrange on a dish, pour the mayonnaise over. Garnish with radishes.
Serves 6.

LEEK AND APPLE SALAD
Surówka z porów i jabłek

4 leeks
2 apples, peeled, coarsely shredded
*¾ cup Mayonnaise**
Lettuce leaves

Slice the yellow part and finely chop the green part of leeks. Combine sliced leeks with apples and mayonnaise. Arrange on lettuce leaves. Sprinkle with green leeks.
Serves 6.

RED CABBAGE WITH APPLES
Czerwona kapusta z jabłkami

1 small head red cabbage, shredded
Salt
2 large apples, peeled, shredded
Juice 1 lemon
2 tablespoons sugar

Cook the cabbage in salted water for 15 minutes. Drain, cool.
Combine with the rest of the ingredients. Refrigerate for 1 hour.
Serve with roasts and fried meats.
Serves 5.

WINTER SALAD
Sałatka zimowa

Dash garlic powder
¼ teaspoon pepper
½ teaspoon paprika
1 teaspoon salt
¼ teaspoon dry mustard
¼ cup vinegar

½ cup salad oil
1 onion, sliced
½ head lettuce, well chilled
½ pound spinach, washed,
  drained, sliced
1 bunch radishes

Sprinkle the salad bowl with garlic powder. Add pepper, paprika,
salt, mustard, vinegar, and oil. Mix well.
Add onions, lettuce in small pieces, and spinach. Mix slightly.
Garnish with radishes. Serve immediately.
Serves 6.

SWEET SAUERKRAUT SALAD
Kiszona kapusta na słodko

2 cups sauerkraut
1 large apple, peeled, coarsely shredded
2 tablespoons sugar

Rinse sauerkraut, squeeze, and chop finely. Add the apple and sugar. Mix well. Chill for ½ hour.
Serves 4.

POTATO SALAD
Sałatka kartoflana

6 *medium potatoes*
2 *onions, sliced*
Salt and pepper
Vinegar to taste

4 *tablespoons salad oil*
1 *tablespoon chopped*
   green onion

Wash potatoes with a brush. Cook until tender. Chill well. Peel and slice, add the onions. Season, add vinegar and oil, mix, and sprinkle with green onions.
Serves 4.

POTATO BEAN SALAD
Sałatka z ziemniaków z fasolą

4 *potatoes*
1 *cup canned baked beans*
1 *onion, sliced*
¾ *cup sour cream*
Salt
Sugar
Vinegar
2 *tablespoons prepared mustard*
Lettuce leaves
1 *tablespoon chopped green onion*

Wash potatoes with a brush. Cook until tender, chill well. Peel and dice.
Drain and rinse the beans. Add to the potatoes. Add the onions, mix with sour cream. Season with salt, sugar, and vinegar, add mustard. Arrange on lettuce leaves, sprinkle with green onions. Green beans may be used instead of baked beans for a change.
Serves 4.

VEGETABLE SALAD
Sałatka jarzynowa

2 packages frozen mixed vegetables, cooked and drained
1 package frozen peas, cooked and drained
2 dill pickles, diced
1 apple, peeled, cored, diced
2 tablespoons pickled mushrooms, diced
¾ cup Mayonnaise*
Salt
1 tablespoon prepared mustard
Lettuce leaves
2 hard-boiled eggs, sliced

Mix the vegetables with the pickles, the apple, and the mushrooms. Combine with the mayonnaise. Season with salt and mustard. Arrange on lettuce leaves, garnish with egg slices. Serves 6.

VEGETABLE POTATO SALAD
Sałatka kartoflano-jarzynowa

4 cups cooked, diced potatoes
2 packages frozen mixed vegetables, cooked and drained
1 package frozen peas, cooked and drained
3 large dill pickles, diced
½ cup chopped green onion
2 tablespoons dill leaves
Salt and pepper
¾ cup Mayonnaise*
¾ cup sour cream
2 tablespoons prepared mustard
2 hard-boiled eggs, chopped
Lettuce leaves
Radishes

Mix the potatoes with the vegetables, pickles, onions, and dill. Season with salt and pepper.
Mix mayonnaise with sour cream and mustard, add to the salad. Chill for 2 hours.
Put into a dish, sprinkle with the egg, garnish with lettuce and radishes.
Serves 10.

MEAT OR POULTRY SALAD
Sałatka z mięsa lub drobiu

2 cups cooked, diced potatoes
2 cups diced veal, beef, or poultry meat
2 dill pickles, diced
1 apple, peeled, shredded
1 medium can peas, drained
2 hard-boiled eggs, coarsely chopped
½ cup Mayonnaise*
½ cup sour cream
1 tablespoon prepared mustard
Salt and pepper
1 tablespoon chopped green parsley
Lettuce

Mix potatoes with meat, pickles, apple, peas, and eggs.
Mix the mayonnaise with sour cream and mustard. Combine half of the sauce with the salad. Season with salt and pepper.
Place the salad in a dish, chill for 2 hours.
Pour the rest of the sauce over the salad, sprinkle with parsley. Garnish with lettuce.
Serves 8.

CHICKEN SALAD
Sałatka z kury

2 cups cut-up cold cooked chicken
1 cup canned peas, drained
1 tablespoon dill leaves
1 tablespoon lemon juice
Salt and pepper
½ cup Mayonnaise*
Lettuce leaves

Blend all the ingredients except lettuce. Season to taste. Chill thoroughly. Serve on crisp salad leaves.
Serves 6.

SHRIMP SALAD
Sałatka z krewetek

Shrimp can be successfully substituted for the crayfish in the original recipe.

20 jumbo shrimp, cooked, diced
1 package frozen asparagus, cooked, diced
4-ounce can peas, drained
1 cucumber, peeled, finely diced
2 cups cooked, finely diced potatoes, chilled
2 stalks celery, finely diced
1 large apple, peeled, cored, finely diced
Salt to taste
½ teaspoon sugar
¾ cup Mayonnaise*
Lettuce, finely shredded

Combine the shrimp with asparagus, peas, cucumbers, potatoes, celery, and apple. Season with salt and sugar. Blend with mayonnaise. Decorate with lettuce. Serve immediately.
Serves 8.

HERRING SALAD
Sałatka śledziowa

4 herring fillets, boned, skinned, finely sliced
5 medium potatoes, boiled in skins, chilled, peeled, diced
1 medium can mixed vegetables, drained
2 onions, finely diced
2 apples, peeled, cored, finely diced
1 large dill pickle, peeled, finely diced
1 hard-boiled egg
½ cup sour cream
1 teaspoon prepared mustard
Lettuce leaves

Combine herring fillets with potatoes, vegetables, onions, apples, pickle, and chopped egg white.
Blend the egg yolk with sour cream and mustard. Add to the salad, mix well. Chill for 2 hours. Serve on lettuce leaves.
Serves 8.

POTATO HERRING SALAD
Sałatka kartoflano-śledziowa

5 medium potatoes, boiled, chilled, peeled, sliced
Salt and pepper to taste
2 hard-boiled eggs
4 herring fillets, boned, skinned, cut in ½-inch slices
2 onions, finely diced
¼ cup Mayonnaise*
½ cup sour cream
1 tablespoon prepared mustard
1 small dill pickle, sliced
Green parsley

Arrange the ingredients in a dish in layers. First ⅓ of the potatoes. Sprinkle with salt, pepper, and ⅓ of chopped egg whites. Then

half of herring and onions; then second layer of potatoes. Sprinkle with salt, pepper, and egg whites. Then the rest of the herring, onions, and potatoes. Sprinkle with salt, pepper, and egg whites. Blend the mayonnaise with egg yolks, add sour cream and mustard. Pour over the salad. Chill for 1 hour. Decorate with pickle slices and parsley.
Serves 8.

TOMATO FRANKFURTER SALAD
Sałatka z pomidorów i parówek

8 cooked frankfurters, diced	Salt and pepper
4 large tomatoes, diced	Sugar
1 onion, finely diced	Vinegar

Mix the frankfurters with tomatoes and onions. Season with salt, pepper, sugar, and vinegar. Chill well.
Serves 8.

POTATO FRANKFURTER SALAD
Sałatka z parówek i kartofli

8 cooked frankfurters, diced
4 large potatoes, cooked, chilled, diced
1 onion, diced
Salt and pepper
½ cup Mayonnaise*
Lettuce leaves

Mix the frankfurters with potatoes and onions. Season with salt and pepper, chill. Combine with the mayonnaise, serve on lettuce leaves.
Serves 8.

TOMATO EGG SALAD
Sałatka z pomidorów i jaj

4 hard-boiled eggs, sliced
5 tomatoes, sliced
1 large dill pickle, sliced
½ cucumber, sliced
1 tablespoon chopped
* green onion*

¼ teaspoon garlic powder
¼ teaspoon sugar
Salt to taste
½ cup sour cream
Lettuce leaves

Combine gently the eggs with tomatoes, pickle, cucumber, and half of the green onions. Sprinkle with garlic powder, sugar, and salt. Mix carefully. Pour sour cream over, sprinkle with the rest of green onions. Garnish with lettuce. Serve immediately. Serves 5.

CUCUMBER EGG SALAD
Sałatka z ogórków i jaj

3 cucumbers, peeled, coarsely shredded
4 hard-boiled eggs, finely sliced
1 large onion, finely sliced
½ cup sour cream
Salt, pepper, and sugar to taste
1 tablespoon chopped green onion

Combine the cucumbers with the eggs, the onions, and sour cream. Season. Sprinkle with green onions. Serve immediately. Serves 5.

SOUPS and SOUP GARNISHES

Soup is a fundamental part of a Polish dinner. In everyday family life, appetizers are not popular, it is the soup that begins the meal. Usually it is thick, fragrant, creamy, and nourishing; served in large, deep plates. Or, for a change, a clear consommé, drunk from cups without using a spoon, and accompanied by croutons, tiny puffs, or patties stuffed with meat, cabbage, and mushrooms. Bread is not necessarily served with a Polish dinner.

Before coffee and tea invaded Europe, it was customary in Poland to start each day with a steamy bowl of soup. In the country the entire peasants' dinner consists sometimes of just the cabbage, potato, or milk soup. However, on festive occasions, when a lot of delicious food is planned, and many guests are invited—just golden bouillon or clear burgundy barshch may be served.

The Crayfish (lobsters can be substituted) Soup* is a real delicacy of the Polish cuisine. Most original, and a real gourmet treat, are Sorrel Soup* and Lemon Soup*, served hot during the winter, and cold on a summer day. Easy to prepare and also delicious are the fruit soups. In general, however, the cooking of soups is time consuming. A modern housewife can take shortcuts, combining fresh ingredients with canned or frozen foods. This method is applied in this book on a large scale.

Most soup recipes yield 6–10 servings, which is not practical for a small family. Fortunately we have freezers nowadays, and soups in plastic containers freeze well. It is best to put aside the amount for freezing before sour cream and fresh greens are added.

Instant flour is recommended for thickening soups as it does not easily turn into ugly lumps.

Sour cream is an important ingredient. It is a safe method to add soup liquids to sour cream by spoonfuls, until it doubles its volume, mixing thoroughly. Then, add it to the soup. Soups with sour cream added may be reheated, but never to the point of boiling.

SOUPS *and* SOUP GARNISHES

ZUPY *i* DODATKI DO ZUP

Beef Broth	*Rosół wołowy*
Chicken Broth	*Rosół z kury*
Vegetable Beef Soup	*Zupa jarzynowa*
Fish Broth	*Rosół z ryby*
Red Beet Barshch	*Czerwony barszcz*
Christmas Barshch	*Barszcz Wigilijny*
Quick Barshch	*Barszczyk na prędce*
Barshch with Beans	*Barszcz z fasolką*
Barshch from Eastern Poland	*Barszcz ze wschodnich ziem*
Spring Barshch	*Boćwinka*
Cold Summer Barshch	*Chłodnik*
Summer Barshch with Pickles	*Chłodnik ogórkowy*
Summer Soup	*Chłodnik z kwaśnym mlekiem*
Dried Mushroom Soup	*Zupa z suszonych grzybów*
Mushroom Consommé	*Bulion grzybowy*
Mushroom Soup	*Zupa grzybowa*
Tomato Consommé	*Bulion pomidorowy*
Tomato Soup	*Zupa pomidorowa*

Polish Barley Soup	*Krupnik polski*
Giblet Barley Soup	*Krupnik na podróbkach*
Cream of Wheat Soup	*Rosół z manną*
Leek Soup	*Zupa z porów*
Pea Soup with Barley	*Grochówka z pęczakiem*
Pea Soup	*Grochówka*
All Vegetable Soup	*Zupa jarzynowa postna*
Sauerkraut Soup	*Kapuśniak*
Cabbage Soup	*Kapuśniak ze świeżej kapusty*
Solferino Soup	*Zupa solferino*
Onion Soup	*Zupa cebulowa*
Green Bean Soup	*Zupa z fasolki szparagowej*
Lemon Soup	*Zupa cytrynowa*
Cauliflower Soup	*Zupa kalafiorowa*
Cream of Vegetable Soup	*Zupa jarzynowa przecierana*
Kohlrabi Soup	*Zupa z kalarepy*
Asparagus Soup	*Zupa szparagowa*
Sorrel (sourgrass) Soup	*Zupa szczawiowa*
Dill Soup	*Zupa koprowa*
Dill Pickle Soup	*Zupa ogórkowa*
Crayfish or Lobster Soup	*Zupa rakowa*
Fish Soup	*Zupa rybna*
Neapolitan Soup	*Zupa neapolitańska*
Potato Soup	*Zupa ziemniaczana*
Potato Soup with Bacon	*Kartoflanka z boczkiem*
Cream of Potato Soup	*Kartoflanka przecierana*
"Nothing" Soup	*Zupa "Nic"*
Almond Soup	*Zupa migdałowa*
Cream of Wheat Milk Soup	*Zupa mleczna z manną*
Milk Soup with Rice	*Zupa mleczna z ryżem*
Oat Milk Soup	*Owsianka*
Milk Soup with String Dumplings	*Lane kluski na mleku*
Sour Milk, Cultured	*Kwaśne mleko*
Fruit Soup	*Chłodnik owocowy*
Raspberry Currant Soup	*Zupa porzeczkowo-malinowa*
Blueberry Soup	*Zupa jagodowa*
Strawberry Soup	*Zupa truskawkowa*
Cherry Soup	*Zupa wiśniowa*

September Plum Soup	*Jesienna zupa śliwkowa*
Prune Soup	*Zupa z suszonych śliwek*
Apple Soup	*Zupa jabłkowa*
String Dumplings	*Lane kluseczki*
Soup Dumplings	*Kluseczki kładzione*
French Dumplings	*Kluseczki francuskie*
Fish Dumplings	*Pulpeciki z ryby*
Dill Dumplings	*Kluski z koprem*
Mushroom Dumplings	*Kluski z grzybami*
Liver Dumplings	*Kluski z wątróbką*
Mushroom Pockets	*Uszka z grzybami*
Croutons	*Grzanki*
Cheese Croutons	*Grzanki z serem*
Tiny Puffs	*Groszek ptysiowy*

SOUPS

BEEF BROTH
Rosół wołowy

½ *pound bones*
2 *quarts water*
1 *pound beef*
Salt
2 *carrots*
2 *celery stalks*
1 *parsley root*
1 *large onion, quartered*
¼ *small head savoy cabbage*
5 *peppercorns*
1 *bay leaf*
1 *tablespoon chopped green parsley*
Noodles, macaroni, Patties*, or crackers

Cover the bones with cold water and cook for ½ hour. Add the beef and salt. Simmer for 2 hours.
Add carrots, celery, and parsley root. Brown the onions in a hot pan. Add to the broth together with cabbage, peppercorns, and bay leaf. Simmer for 15 minutes. Strain. Add green parsley.
Use as a foundation for different soups or serve with noodles, thin macaroni, Patties*, or crackers.
Serves 6.

CHICKEN BROTH
Rosół z kury

1 *chicken*
7 *cups boiling water*
Salt
2 *carrots*
2 *celery stalks*
1 *parsley root*

1 *large onion, quartered*
¼ *small head savoy cabbage*
4 *peppercorns*
1 *tablespoon chopped green parsley*
Patties* or crackers

Place the chicken in boiling water, add salt. Simmer for 2 hours. Add carrots, celery, and parsley root. Brown the onions in a hot pan. Add to the broth together with cabbage and peppercorns. Simmer for 20 minutes. Strain. Add green parsley.

Use as a foundation for various soups. Serve with noodles, dumplings, or thin macaroni. Serve clear in cups with Patties* or crackers.

Serves 6.

VEGETABLE BEEF SOUP
Zupa jarzynowa

2 *carrots, sliced*
1 *parsley root, diced*
2 *celery stalks, diced*
1 *leek, sliced*
¼ *small cauliflower, sliced*
½ *cup green beans, cut up*
2 *tablespoons butter*
1 *cup water*
6 *cups beef broth—homemade or canned*

Simmer the vegetables with butter in 1 cup water for 20 minutes. Add beef broth, simmer together 5 minutes.

Serves 8.

FISH BROTH
Rosół z ryby

2 carrots, cut up
2 celery stalks, cut up
1 parsley root, cut up
1 large onion, quartered, browned
¼ small head savoy cabbage
5 peppercorns
1 bay leaf
Salt to taste
2 quarts water
1½ pounds fish
¼ teaspoon nutmeg
Patties*
Crackers

Simmer the vegetables with peppercorns, bay leaf, and salt in water for 20 minutes.
Add fish, simmer another 20 minutes. Strain. Add nutmeg. Serve clear in cups with Patties* or crackers.
Serves 6.

RED BEET BARSHCH
Czerwony barszcz

6 medium beets
6 cups beef broth, homemade or canned
1 tablespoon vinegar
1 teaspoon sugar
⅛ teaspoon pepper
Dash garlic powder
Patties*, Kulebiak*, or crackers

Wash and bake the beets for ½ hour in moderate 350° F. oven. Peel, grate coarsely. Add to the broth, simmer for 5 minutes. Add vinegar and seasoning. Serve with Patties*, Kulebiak*, or crackers.
Serves 6.

CHRISTMAS BARSHCH
Barszcz Wigilijny

3 carrots, cut up
2 celery stalks
2 parsley roots
2 onions, quartered
¼ head savoy cabbage
5 peppercorns
Salt to taste

2 quarts water
8 medium beets
1 tablespoon lemon juice
1 teaspoon sugar
⅛ teaspoon pepper
Dash garlic powder

Simmer the vegetables with peppercorns and salt in water for 30 minutes. Strain.
Wash and bake the beets for ½ hour in moderate 350° F. oven. Peel, grate coarsely, and add to broth. Simmer 5 minutes. Add lemon juice. Season.
Serve with Mushroom Pockets* or Pancakes with Mushrooms* or Sauerkraut*.
Serves 6.

QUICK BARSHCH
Barszczyk na prędce

2 10½-ounce cans concentrate beef broth
2 1-pound cans red beets
1 cup water
1 tablespoon lemon juice
1 teaspoon sugar
⅛ teaspoon pepper
Dash garlic powder
Salt to taste
½ cup red table wine
Patties* or Kulebiak*

Dilute the broth using the juice from the red beets instead of water. Put aside the beets for the next day's vegetable or Red Beets with Horseradish*. Add 1 cup water.

Cook the barshch for 5 minutes. Season. Add wine. Serve in cups with Patties* or Kulebiak*.
Serves 6.

BARSHCH WITH BEANS
Barszcz z fasolką

2 10½-ounce cans concentrate beef broth
2 1-pound cans red beets
1 cup water
1 can (14 ounces) brown baked beans
1 tablespoon lemon juice
1 teaspoon sugar
Salt to taste
2 tablespoons sour cream
1 tablespoon dill leaves

Dilute the broth using the juice from red beets instead of water. Add ½ cup chopped beets, and 1 cup water.
Rinse the beans in a colander. Add to the soup. Cook for 5 minutes. Add lemon juice, seasonings. Add sour cream and dill.
Serves 6.

BARSHCH FROM EASTERN POLAND
Barszcz ze wschodnich ziem

1 carrot, sliced
1 celery stalk, sliced
¼ small head savoy cabbage, shredded
2 potatoes, diced
6 cups beef or chicken broth, homemade or canned
1 1-pound can beets
½ cup canned baked beans, rinsed with water
4 tomatoes, chopped
1 tablespoon instant flour
2 tablespoons cold water
Dash garlic powder
1 tablespoon lemon juice
½ teaspoon sugar
⅛ teaspoon pepper
Salt to taste
½ cup sour cream

Simmer the carrot, celery, cabbage, and potatoes for 20 minutes in the broth.

Add chopped beets with all the juice from the can. Add the beans and tomatoes. Cook for 5 minutes. Add the flour mixed with 2 tablespoons cold water. Cook for 5 minutes.

Remove from the heat. Season with garlic, lemon juice, sugar, pepper, and salt. Add sour cream.

Serves 10.

SPRING BARSHCH
Boćwinka

2 bunches young beets with leaves, washed and diced
2 cups water
1 teaspoon vinegar
4 cups beef or chicken broth, homemade or canned
2 tablespoons instant flour
¼ cup cold water
1 tablespoon lemon juice
1 teaspoon sugar
Salt to taste
1 tablespoon dill leaves
1 tablespoon chopped green parsley
1 tablespoon chopped green onion
1 tablespoon butter
½ cup sour cream
2 hard-boiled eggs, sliced

Cook the beets in water with vinegar for 20 minutes.

Add the broth, cook for 5 minutes. Add the flour mixed with ¼ cup cold water. Cook few minutes. Remove from heat.

Season with lemon juice, sugar, and salt. Add dill, parsley, green onions, butter, sour cream, and eggs.

Serves 8.

COLD SUMMER BARSHCH
Chłodnik

1 bunch young beets with tops, washed and sliced
1 cup water
1 teaspoon vinegar
4 cups beef broth, homemade or canned
1 cup beet juice from 1 can beets
2 tablespoons instant flour
¼ cup cold water
2 hard-boiled eggs, sliced
1 small cucumber, peeled, sliced
1 cup sliced roast veal
8 large shrimp, cooked, diced
Dash garlic powder
Salt to taste
½ teaspoon sugar
1 tablespoon lemon juice
1 cup sour cream
1 tablespoon dill leaves
1 tablespoon chopped green onion

Cook the beets in water with vinegar for 20 minutes.
Add the broth and beet juice. Cook for 5 minutes. Add the flour
mixed with ¼ cup cold water. Cook few minutes. Cool.
Add the rest of ingredients.
Chill for 2 hours. Serve very cold on hot summer days.
Serves 10.

SUMMER BARSHCH WITH PICKLES
Chłodnik ogórkowy

5 cups beef broth,
  homemade or canned
1 1-pound can beets,
  chopped
2 tablespoons instant flour
¼ cup cold water
2 large dill pickles, diced
1 cup juice from pickle jar

1 cup sour cream
3 hard-boiled eggs, quartered
1 tablespoon dill leaves
1 tablespoon chopped
  green onion
½ teaspoon sugar
Salt to taste

Combine the broth with beets and the juice from the can. Heat, add the flour mixed with ¼ cup cold water. Bring to boil, chill. Add the remaining ingredients. Serve very cold on hot summer days.
Serves 10.

SUMMER SOUP
Chłodnik z kwaśnym mlekiem

2 bunches young red beets with tops, sliced
2 cups water
1 tablespoon lemon juice
4 cups Sour Milk, Cultured* or thick buttermilk
⅔ cup sour cream
½ cup juice from canned beets
½ teaspoon sugar
Salt to taste
1 large cucumber, peeled, thinly sliced
2 hard-boiled eggs, sliced
1 tablespoon dill leaves
2 tablespoons chopped green onion

Cook the beets with the beet tops in water with lemon for 20 minutes. Cool thoroughly.
Add sour milk mixed with sour cream and beet juice. Season with sugar and salt. Add cucumber, eggs, dill, and green onions. Serve very cold.
Excellent on a hot summer day.
Serves 10.

DRIED MUSHROOM SOUP
Zupa z suszonych grzybów

1 ounce dried mushrooms	*Salt to taste*
1 cup water	*1 tablespoon instant flour*
6 cups water	*2 tablespoons butter*
1 large onion, diced	*3 tablespoons cold water*
2 carrots	*1 teaspoon dill leaves*
1 parsley root	*Dumplings*, macaroni,*
2 celery stalks	*or barley*

Wash the mushrooms very well with a brush. Soak in 1 cup water for 2 hours. Add 6 cups water and the onions. Simmer for 20 minutes.

Add the vegetables. Season with salt. Simmer for another 20 minutes. Strain. Slice the mushrooms finely.

Fry the flour with the butter until golden, dilute with 3 tablespoons cold water, add to the soup. Add the mushrooms, bring to boil. Add dill.

Serve with Dumplings*, macaroni, or barley.

Serves 8.

MUSHROOM CONSOMMÉ
Bulion grzybowy

1 ounce dried mushrooms
½ cup warm water
6 cups beef broth, homemade or canned
Salt and pepper to taste
1 tablespoon chopped green parsley
Patties*, Mushroom Pockets*, Kulebiak*, or noodles

Wash the mushrooms very well with a brush. Soak in ½ cup warm water for 2 hours. Add 1 cup broth, cook for 1 hour. Re-

move the mushrooms, add the rest of the broth, salt, pepper, and
parsley.
Serve in cups with Patties*, Mushroom Pockets*, or Kulebiak*. Or
serve with noodles in bowls.
Serves 6.

MUSHROOM SOUP
Zupa grzybowa

2 *carrots*
1 *parsley root*
2 *celery stalks*
2 *onions, sliced*
4 *cups salted water*
1 *pound mushrooms, washed very well, finely sliced*
1 *cup water*
Salt and pepper
2 *tablespoons instant flour*
¼ *cup cold water*
½ *cup sour cream*
1 *tablespoon dill leaves*
1 *tablespoon chopped green parsley*
Noodles, fine macaroni, or barley

Cook the carrots, parsley, celery, and 1 onion in 4 cups salted
water for 20 minutes. Strain.
Cook the mushrooms and the second onion in 1 cup water for 10
minutes. Add salt and pepper. Combine with the vegetable broth,
add the flour mixed with ¼ cup cold water. Boil.
Remove from heat. Add sour cream, dill, and parsley. Add noodles,
fine macaroni, or barley.
Serves 8.

TOMATO CONSOMMÉ
Bulion pomidorowy

4 tomatoes, cut up
1 onion, sliced
2 tablespoons butter
1 cup salted water
5 cups boiling beef or chicken broth, homemade or canned
½ teaspoon sugar
Salt to taste

Cook the tomatoes and the onions with butter in 1 cup salted water. Rub through a sieve. Add boiling broth, sugar, and salt. Serve with Patties*.
Serves 6.

TOMATO SOUP
Zupa pomidorowa

8 tomatoes
1 large onion, sliced
2 tablespoons butter
1 cup salted water
5 cups beef or chicken broth, homemade or canned
2 tablespoons instant flour
¼ cup cold water
Salt to taste
½ teaspoon sugar
½ cup sour cream
1 tablespoon dill leaves
*Rice or Croutons**

Cook the tomatoes and the onions with butter in 1 cup salted water. Rub through a sieve.
Add the broth, heat. Add the flour mixed with ¼ cup cold water. Boil. Remove from heat. Add salt, sugar, sour cream, and dill leaves. Add cooked rice, or serve Croutons* in separate dish.
Serves 8.

POLISH BARLEY SOUP
Krupnik polski

4 potatoes, sliced
2 carrots, sliced
1 parsley root, sliced
1 celery stalk, sliced
1 large onion, sliced
¼ pound mushrooms, sliced
6 cups boiling water
½ cup barley

2 tablespoons butter
2 bouillon cubes
2 cups water
1 tablespoon dill leaves
1 tablespoon chopped
  green parsley
Salt to taste

Cook the potatoes, carrots, parsley, celery, onions, and mushrooms in 6 cups boiling water for 20 minutes.
Simmer the barley with butter and bouillon cubes in 2 cups water until tender. Combine with the vegetable soup, cook for 10 minutes. Add dill and parsley. Season with salt.
Excellent on a winter day.
Serves 10.

GIBLET BARLEY SOUP
Krupnik na podróbkach

Chicken or turkey giblets
2 carrots
1 parsley root
2 celery stalks
1 large onion
3 dried or ¼ pound fresh mushrooms
4 cups salted water
½ cup barley
2 cups salted water
2 tablespoons butter
½ cup sour cream
1 tablespoon chopped green parsley
1 tablespoon dill leaves

Cook the giblets, with carrots, parsley, celery, onion, and mush-

rooms, in 4 cups salted water. (Soak dried mushrooms for 2 hours before cooking.) Slice the giblets and the vegetables.
Simmer the barley in 2 cups salted water and butter till tender. Combine with the soup. Simmer another 15 minutes. Remove from heat. Add sour cream, parsley, and dill.
Excellent for a snowy day.
Serves 8.

CREAM OF WHEAT SOUP
Rosół z manną

4 cups beef or chicken broth, homemade or canned
4 tablespoons cream of wheat (regular)
1 tablespoon butter
Salt to taste
1 tablespoon dill leaves
1 tablespoon chopped parsley leaves

Bring the broth to boil. Sprinkle the cream of wheat by spoonfuls slowly. Cover, reduce heat, simmer for 13 minutes. Add butter, salt, dill, and parsley. Serve immediately.
Serves 4.

LEEK SOUP
Zupa z porów

4 leeks, sliced
2 tablespoons butter
1 cup water
3 cups beef or chicken broth

4 potatoes, diced
1 tablespoon caraway seeds
Salt to taste

Cook the leeks with butter in 1 cup water for 20 minutes. Bring the broth to boil, add potatoes and caraway seeds. Simmer for 20 minutes. Add the leeks with the liquid, season with salt to taste. Serve with Croutons*.
Serves 6.

PEA SOUP WITH BARLEY
Grochówka z pęczakiem

½ cup barley
2 cups salted water
¼ pound bacon, diced

1 medium can green peas
4 cups beef broth

Add the barley to cold water, bring to boil, reduce heat. Simmer until tender.
Fry the bacon until golden. Add with the drippings to the cooking barley.
Rub the peas through a fine sieve. Combine the peas and their liquid with the barley. Add the broth, bring to boil.
Serves 8.

PEA SOUP
Grochówka

2 medium cans peas with the liquid
4 cups beef broth
¼ pound bacon, diced
1 large onion, diced
1 tablespoon instant flour
3 tablespoons cold water
Salt to taste
Dash garlic powder
½ teaspoon marjoram
Croutons*

Rub the peas through a fine sieve, combine with the broth. Bring to boil.
Fry the bacon with the onions till golden, add to the soup. Fry the flour with the bacon drippings, stirring all the time, until golden, dilute with 3 tablespoons cold water. Add to the soup.
Season with salt, garlic, and marjoram. Serve with Croutons*.
Serves 8.

ALL VEGETABLE SOUP
Zupa jarzynowa postna

STEP 1

    2 carrots
    1 parsley root
    2 celery stalks
    1 onion, quartered
    5 cups boiling, salted water

STEP 2

    ¼ head savoy cabbage, finely sliced
    ½ cup cut up green beans
    ½ cup cut up carrots
    ½ cup diced celery
    ½ cup small flowerets cauliflower
    1 leek, sliced
    1 potato, coarsely diced
    2 tablespoons butter
    1 tablespoon instant flour
    3 tablespoons cold water
    ½ tablespoon dill leaves
    ½ tablespoon chopped green parsley
    Salt to taste

STEP 1: Cook the vegetables for 30 minutes. Strain.

STEP 2: Add the cabbage, beans, carrots, celery, cauliflower, leek, and the potatoes to the boiling vegetable broth. Simmer for 20 minutes.

Heat the butter, add the flour, fry until golden, stirring all the time. Dilute with 3 tablespoons cold water. Add to the soup. Bring to boil. Add dill, parsley, and salt.

All Vegetable Soup may be prepared with canned or homemade beef broth.

Serves 10.

SAUERKRAUT SOUP
Kapuśniak

1 pound sauerkraut	*2 tablespoons instant flour*
6 cups beef broth	*3 tablespoons cold water*
¼ pound bacon, diced	*Salt and pepper*
1 large onion, diced	*Boiled potatoes*

Rinse the sauerkraut with cold water and cut up finely. Cook in a small amount of boiling water uncovered for few minutes. Cover, reduce heat, simmer 30 minutes. Add the broth.
Fry the bacon with the onions till golden. Sprinkle with flour, fry for few minutes stirring. Dilute with 3 tablespoons cold water. Add to the soup, bring to boil. Season with salt and pepper. Serve with boiled potatoes on individual small plates. Serves 10.

CABBAGE SOUP
Kapuśniak ze świeżej kapusty

¼ head (1 pound) cabbage, finely sliced
1 large onion, sliced
3 cups cold water
2 tomatoes, sliced
3 cups beef broth
2 tablespoons soft butter
1 tablespoon flour
½ teaspoon sugar
Salt to taste

Place the cabbage and the onions in a kettle with 3 cups cold water. Bring to boil and cook a few minutes uncovered. Reduce heat, cover. Simmer for 10 minutes. Add tomatoes, simmer another 10 minutes.

Bring the broth to a boil. Mix the butter with the flour. Add 4 tablespoons hot broth, one by one, mixing. Add to the broth, bring to boil. Add the broth to the cabbage. Season with sugar and salt.

Serves 8.

SOLFERINO SOUP
Zupa solferino

7 *cups chicken broth, homemade or canned*
1 *cup cut up green beans*
3 *potatoes, diced*
3 *medium tomatoes, diced*
2 *tablespoons soft butter*
1 *tablespoon instant flour*
Salt and pepper

Bring the broth to boil. Add green beans and potatoes. Simmer for 10 minutes. Add the tomatoes, simmer another 10 minutes. Mix the butter with the flour. Dilute with hot broth, adding spoonful by spoonful. Add to the soup. Bring to boil. Season with salt and pepper.

Serves 10.

ONION SOUP
Zupa cebulowa

1½ *cups onions, thinly sliced*
6 *cups chicken or beef broth*
1 *tablespoon instant flour*
3 *tablespoons cold water*
½ *teaspoon sugar*
Salt to taste
⅔ *cup sour cream*
1 *tablespoon chopped green parsley*

Simmer the onions in 1 cup broth until tender. Rub through a fine sieve, or use a blender. Add the rest of the broth.
Mix the flour with 3 tablespoons cold water, add to the soup, bring to boil. Remove from heat. Season with sugar and salt. Add sour cream and green parsley.
Serves 8.

GREEN BEAN SOUP
Zupa z fasolki szparagowej

1 pound green beans, cut up	*½ teaspoon sugar*
6 cups beef or chicken broth	*Salt to taste*
2 tablespoons instant flour	*½ cup sour cream*
¼ cup cold water	

Cook the beans in small amount of salted water for 20 minutes. Add the broth and the flour mixed with ¼ cup cold water. Bring to boil. Remove from heat. Season with sugar and salt. Add sour cream.
Serves 10.

LEMON SOUP
Zupa cytrynowa

7 cups chicken broth, homemade or canned
2 tablespoons instant flour
1 tablespoon soft butter
1 lemon, peeled and sliced very thinly
2 tablespoons lemon juice
3 cups cooked rice
½ cup sour cream

Bring the broth to boil. Mix the flour with butter, add few spoons of hot broth, mixing. Add to the broth, bring to boil. Remove from heat. Add the lemon, the juice, rice, and sour cream.
Serves 10.

CAULIFLOWER SOUP
Zupa kalafiorowa

7 *cups beef or chicken broth*
1 *small (1 pound) cauliflower, divided into small flowerets*
1½ *tablespoons instant flour*
1 *cup milk*
2 *egg yolks*
1 *tablespoon dill leaves*

Bring the broth to boil. Add cauliflower, simmer for 25 minutes. Add the flour mixed with ½ cup milk. Bring to boil. Remove from heat. Add egg yolks mixed with the rest of milk. Add dill. Serves 10.

CREAM OF VEGETABLE SOUP
Zupa jarzynowa przecierana

½ *pound bones*
6 *cups water, salted*
2 *carrots*
1 *parsley root*
1 *celery stalk*
1 *leek*
½ *cup green beans*
¼ *small head savoy cabbage*
3 *potatoes, peeled*
1 *tablespoon instant flour*
3 *tablespoons cold water*
½ *cup sour cream*
2 *egg yolks*
1 *tablespoon dill leaves*
1 *tablespoon chopped green parsley*

Place the bones in a kettle with cold water. Cook for 1 hour. Add the vegetables, simmer for 20 minutes. Rub the vegetables through a sieve, or use a blender.

Mix the flour with 3 tablespoons cold water, add to the soup, bring to boil. Remove from the heat.
Add sour cream mixed with egg yolks. Add dill and parsley.
Serves 10.

KOHLRABI SOUP
Zupa z kalarepy

6 cups beef broth, homemade or canned
1 pound kohlrabi, peeled, diced
1½ tablespoons instant flour
3 tablespoons water
1 tablespoon soft butter
2 egg yolks
Salt to taste
Croutons*

Bring to boil 2 cups broth, add kohlrabi. Simmer for 20 minutes. Rub half of the kohlrabi through a sieve, return to the soup. Add the rest of the broth and flour mixed with 3 tablespoons water. Bring to boil. Remove from heat.
Add butter mixed with egg yolks. Season with salt. Serve with Croutons*.
An original gourmet dish.
Serves 8.

ASPARAGUS SOUP
Zupa szparagowa

1½ pounds asparagus
6 cups beef or chicken broth
1½ tablespoons instant flour
3 tablespoons cold water

½ cup sour cream
2 egg yolks
Salt to taste
½ teaspoon sugar

Cut off the heads of asparagus and simmer in 1 cup of broth for 15 minutes.

Cook the rest of asparagus in the rest of the broth for 30 minutes. Rub through a sieve or use a blender.
Add the flour mixed with 3 tablespoons cold water. Bring to boil. Remove from heat.
Add the asparagus tips with their broth. Add sour cream mixed with egg yolks. Season with salt and sugar.
Serves 8.

SORREL (SOURGRASS) SOUP
Zupa szczawiowa

6 cups beef or chicken broth
4 tablespoons instant flour
⅔ cup milk
2 cups sorrel extract (from Jewish delicatessen)
  OR
*2 jars strained spinach (baby food) and 2 tablespoons lemon
    juice*
1 egg yolk
2 tablespoons soft butter
Salt to taste
Dumplings*, rice, hard-boiled eggs, Stuffed Eggs*, or Patties*

Heat the broth to boiling. Add the flour mixed with milk. Bring to boil. Remove from heat.
Add sorrel extract or spinach and lemon juice. Add egg yolk mixed with butter. Season with salt. Heat, but do not boil.
Serve hot or cold, with Dumplings*, rice, hard-boiled eggs, Stuffed Eggs*, or Patties*.
An original gourmet dish.
Serves 10.

DILL SOUP
Zupa koprowa

7 cups beef or chicken broth
2 tablespoons instant flour
¼ cup cold water
⅔ cup sour cream
2 egg yolks
3 tablespoons fresh dill leaves
Dumplings*

Bring the broth to boil. Add the flour mixed with ¼ cup cold water. Bring to boil. Remove from heat.
Add sour cream mixed with egg yolks. Add dill.
Serve with Dumplings*.
Serves 8.

DILL PICKLE SOUP
Zupa ogórkowa

6 cups beef broth, homemade or canned
2 tablespoons instant flour
1 cup milk
1 egg yolk
2 tablespoons soft butter
4 large dill pickles, shredded
⅔ cup liquid from pickle jar
2½ cups boiled, sliced potatoes

Bring the broth to boil. Add the flour mixed with milk. Bring to boil. Remove from heat.
Add egg yolk mixed with butter. Add the pickles, pickle liquid, and potatoes. Heat, but do not boil.
Serves 12.

CRAYFISH OR LOBSTER SOUP
Zupa rakowa

16 crayfish or 3 lobsters	*2 tablespoons cold water*
3 tablespoons dillweed	*Salt*
6 cups beef broth	*⅔ cup sour cream*
3 tablespoons butter	*2 cups cooked rice*
1 tablespoon instant flour	

Place the crayfish or lobsters in a kettle in boiling water with 2 tablespoons dill added. Strain, cool. Take out the meat from the tails and pincers. Place in a bowl, add just enough broth to cover. Grind all red parts of the shells. Add to butter boiling with 1 cup broth. Simmer till a red "crayfish butter" forms on top; add it, together with the broth from the shells, but without the ground shells, to the bowl.

Heat the rest of the beef broth, add the contents of the bowl. Add the flour mixed with 2 tablespoons cold water. Bring to boil. Remove from heat. Season with salt.

Add sour cream, hot rice, and 1 tablespoon dill.

This is a real Polish delicacy for special occasions.

Serves 8.

FISH SOUP
Zupa rybna

2 carrots	*1½ tablespoons instant flour*
1 parsley root	*3 tablespoons cold water*
2 celery stalks	*⅛ teaspoon nutmeg*
1 large onion, quartered	*⅛ teaspoon pepper*
1 bay leaf	*1 cup sour cream*
4 peppercorns	*Salt to taste*
8 cups salted water	*Fish Dumplings*, noodles,*
10 ounces pike or other fish	*or macaroni*

Cook the vegetables, the bay leaf, and peppercorns in salted water for 15 minutes. Add the fish, boil another 15 minutes. Strain.

Add the flour mixed with 3 tablespoons cold water. Bring to boil. Remove from heat. Add nutmeg, pepper, sour cream, and salt to taste.

Serve with Fish Dumplings*, noodles, or macaroni.

Excellent gourmet dish.

Serves 8.

NEAPOLITAN SOUP
Zupa neapolitańska

4 cups beef or chicken broth
1½ tablespoons instant flour
3 tablespoons cold water
2 cups cooked macaroni
⅔ cup sour cream
2 egg yolks
4 tablespoons grated Parmesan cheese

Bring the broth to boil. Add the flour mixed with 3 tablespoons cold water. Bring to boil, add macaroni. Remove from heat. Add sour cream mixed with egg yolks. Sprinkle with cheese. Serves 6.

POTATO SOUP
Zupa ziemniaczana

1½ pounds potatoes, peeled, sliced
2 dried mushrooms or 1 cup sliced fresh mushrooms
7 cups beef broth, homemade or canned
1 tablespoon instant flour
2 tablespoons cold water
Salt to taste
⅔ cup sour cream
1 tablespoon chopped green parsley
1 tablespoon dill leaves

Cook potatoes and dried mushrooms (scrubbed and soaked for 2 hours) or fresh mushrooms in the boiling broth for 30 minutes.

Add the flour mixed with 2 tablespoons cold water. Bring to boil.
Remove from heat. Season with salt.
Add sour cream, parsley, and dill.
Serves 10.

POTATO SOUP WITH BACON
Kartoflanka z boczkiem

1½ pounds potatoes, peeled, sliced
1 carrot, sliced
1 parsley root, sliced
7 cups beef broth
¼ pound bacon, sliced
1 onion, sliced
1 tablespoon instant flour
Salt to taste
1½ tablespoons chopped green parsley

Cook the potatoes, carrot, and parsley in boiling broth for 30
minutes.
Fry the bacon with the onions until golden. Add to the soup with
half of the drippings.
Add the flour to the rest of the drippings. Fry until golden, dilute
with soup liquid. Add to the kettle, bring to boil. Season with
salt, add green parsley.
Serves 10.

CREAM OF POTATO SOUP
Kartoflanka przecierana

Prepare the soup as in Potato Soup*. Before adding dill and
parsley, rub through a sieve, or mix in a blender. Heat, but do
not boil again.
Serve with Croutons*.
Serves 10.

"NOTHING" SOUP
Zupa "Nic"

5 cups milk	⅔ cup sugar
1 teaspoon vanilla	¼ cup cold milk
2 eggs, separated	Cooked rice or crackers

Bring the milk to boil, add vanilla.

Beat egg whites until stiff, add ½ cup sugar by spoonfuls still beating. Place the egg whites with a spoon on boiling milk, cook for few minutes, turn, cook again. Remove the egg whites from the milk into individual bowls. Remove the milk from heat.

Add the rest of the sugar to the milk, add egg yolks mixed with ¼ cup cold milk. Pour the milk over the egg whites in the bowls. Add cooked rice to each bowl and serve hot, or chill and serve with crackers on a hot day.

This is an all time children's favorite.

Serves 5.

ALMOND SOUP
Zupa migdałowa

5 cups milk
½ pound almonds, peeled, ground twice
1 teaspoon almond extract
2½ cups cooked rice
¼ cup sugar
½ cup small raisins

Heat the milk, add all the ingredients. Serve *after* the meat or fish course.

This is a very old traditional Christmas dish.

Serves 8.

CREAM OF WHEAT MILK SOUP
Zupa mleczna z manną

½ *cup cream of wheat* (*regular*)
½ *cup cold water*
2 *cups boiling milk*
Salt to taste

Mix the cream of wheat with water. Add 1 cup milk. Simmer for 5 minutes. Add the rest of milk, simmer 10 more minutes. Salt to taste.
This is a breakfast or luncheon soup.
Serves 3.

MILK SOUP WITH RICE
Zupa mleczna z ryżem

4 *cups milk*
2 *cups cooked rice*
Salt to taste

Heat the milk, add rice and salt. Simmer for 10 minutes.
Serves 5.

OAT MILK SOUP
Owsianka

4 *cups milk*   *Salt to taste*
2 *cups cooked oats*   *Crackers*

Heat the milk, add the oats and salt. Bring to boil, simmer for 5 minutes. Serve for breakfast or luncheon with crackers.
Serves 6.

MILK SOUP WITH STRING DUMPLINGS
Lane kluski na mleku

1 large egg
3½ tablespoons all purpose flour
Salt to taste
4 cups milk

Mix the egg with the flour in a cup, and beat with a teaspoon for 3 minutes. Add salt.
Bring the milk to boil, add the batter slowly, dripping from a teaspoon. Cook for 1 minute. Serve immediately.
Luncheon or supper soup.
Milk soups are good with French Dumplings* or macaroni.
Serves 4.

SOUR MILK, CULTURED
Kwaśne mleko

Pasteurized milk has to be cultured to become thick and sour. Add 1 teaspoon sour cream to milk, mix well. Pour into a bowl or individual serving plates. Keep at room temperature for 24 hours. Do not move. Refrigerate for 6 hours. Sour milk sets best on sunny summer days. Serve with young potatoes, sprinkled with melted butter and dill leaves, on separate plates.

FRUIT SOUP
Chłodnik owocowy

1 quart strawberries or raspberries
4 cups Sour Milk, Cultured or thick buttermilk*
⅔ cup sour cream
½ cup sugar
*Croutons**

Rub the berries through a sieve. Add Sour Milk mixed with sour cream. Add sugar, mix well. Chill thoroughly.

Serve with Croutons* after the meat course.
Excellent gourmet dish.
Serves 6.

RASPBERRY CURRANT SOUP
Zupa porzeczkowo-malinowa

1 pint raspberries	2 tablespoons water
1 pint currants	½ cup sugar
4 cups water	⅔ cup sour cream
1 teaspoon cornstarch	Croutons*

Crush the berries through a sieve. Save the juice.
Add the berries to boiling water, simmer 15 minutes. Strain. Add cornstarch mixed with 2 tablespoons water. Bring to boil. Add sugar. Chill thoroughly.
Add the saved juice, mixed with sour cream. Serve with Croutons* after the meat course.
Serves 6.

BLUEBERRY SOUP
Zupa jagodowa

1 quart blueberries	¼ teaspoon cloves
4 cups water	½ cup sugar
1 slice white bread	⅔ cup sour cream
½ teaspoon cinnamon	Noodles or Croutons*

Add the blueberries to boiling water. Add bread, cinnamon, cloves. Simmer for 15 minutes. Rub through a sieve. Add sugar, chill thoroughly.
Add sour cream. Serve with noodles or Croutons* after the meat course.
Original gourmet dish.
Serves 8.

STRAWBERRY SOUP
Zupa truskawkowa

1 quart strawberries	2 egg yolks
½ cup sugar	¾ cup sour cream
2 cups boiled, cold water	Croutons*

Rub the strawberries with sugar into a pulp. Mix with water.
Add egg yolks mixed with sour cream.
Serve very cold with Croutons* after the meat course.
Ideal dish for a hot day.
Serves 6.

CHERRY SOUP
Zupa wiśniowa

3 pints cherries	1 tablespoon cold water
½ teaspoon cinnamon	½ cup sugar
¼ teaspoon cloves	¾ cup sour cream
4 cups water	Noodles or Croutons*
1 teaspoon cornstarch	

Add the cherries, cinnamon, and cloves to the boiling water.
Bring to boil. Simmer for 15 minutes. Rub through a sieve. Add
the cornstarch mixed with 1 tablespoon cold water. Bring to boil.
Add the sugar. Cool thoroughly.
Add sour cream. Serve with noodles or Croutons* after the
meat course.
Serves 6.

SEPTEMBER PLUM SOUP
Jesienna zupa śliwkowa

1½ pounds plums, pitted, quartered	1 teaspoon cornstarch
	1 tablespoon cold water
½ teaspoon cinnamon	½ cup sugar
¼ teaspoon cloves	¾ cup sour cream, whipped
4 cups water	Macaroni or Croutons*

Add the plums, cinnamon, and cloves to the boiling water. Bring to boil. Simmer for 15 minutes. Rub through a sieve. Add the cornstarch mixed with 1 tablespoon cold water. Bring to boil, add sugar. Cool. Add sour cream.
Serve warm with macaroni or cold with Croutons*.
Serves 6.

PRUNE SOUP
Zupa z suszonych śliwek

½ *pound prunes, pitted*	⅔ *cup sugar*
2 *cups water*	1½ *tablespoons instant flour*
½ *pound rhubarb, cut up*	¼ *cup cold water*
2 *cups boiling water*	¾ *cup sour cream*
½ *teaspoon cinnamon*	*Macaroni or Croutons**
¼ *teaspoon cloves*	

Soak the prunes in 2 cups water overnight.
Cook in the same water for 30 minutes. Cook rhubarb in 2 cups boiling water for 10 minutes. Combine, rub through a sieve.
Add cinnamon, cloves, sugar, and flour mixed with ¼ cup cold water. Bring to boil. Remove from heat. Cool slightly, add sour cream.
Add macaroni or serve with Croutons* after the meat course.
This is an excellent mid-winter soup.
Serves 6.

APPLE SOUP
Zupa jabłkowa

1½ *pounds apples*	1 *teaspoon cinnamon*
4 *cups water*	⅓ *cup sugar*
1 *teaspoon cornstarch*	¾ *cup sour cream*
1 *tablespoon water*	*Macaroni or Croutons**

Cover ⅔ of apples, quartered, with boiling water and simmer for 15 minutes.

Rub through a sieve. Add cornstarch mixed with 1 tablespoon water. Bring to boil. Add cinnamon and sugar. Remove from the heat.

Add the rest of the apples, peeled and shredded, add sour cream. Serve warm or cold with macaroni or Croutons* after the meat course.

Serves 6.

SOUP GARNISHES

STRING DUMPLINGS
Lane kluseczki

1 large egg
3½ tablespoons flour
Dash salt
4 cups boiling milk, beef, chicken, or fish broth

Mix the egg with the flour and salt. Beat with a spoon for 2 minutes. Drip slowly from a spoon into 4 cups boiling milk, or beef, chicken, or fish broth. Cook for 1 minute. Serve immediately. Serves 4.

SOUP DUMPLINGS
Kluseczki kładzione

1½ cups flour   *¾ cup water*
1 large egg   *Dash salt*

Mix the flour with the egg, water, and salt. Beat with a spoon for 2 minutes. Drop small portions of the dough into boiling water from a teaspoon. Cook uncovered until dumplings float. Transfer to a hot soup with a colander spoon.
Serves 4.

FRENCH DUMPLINGS
Kluseczki francuskie

2 tablespoons soft butter   *¼ teaspoon salt*
2 medium eggs, separated   *⅔ cup flour*

Cream the butter with the egg yolks, add salt. Add small portions of whipped, stiff egg whites and flour alternately. Mix lightly. Drop small portions of the dough from a teaspoon into a boiling soup. Cook uncovered on high heat till dumplings float. Serves 4.

FISH DUMPLINGS
Pulpeciki z ryby

1 onion, sliced
1 tablespoon butter
1 slice white bread, soaked in water and squeezed
6 ounces fish fillets, cooked
2 eggs
Salt and pepper
1 teaspoon dill leaves
1 teaspoon chopped green parsley
2 tablespoons bread crumbs
2 tablespoons flour

Fry the onions in butter till golden. Grind together the onions, bread, and fish. Combine with the eggs. Season with salt and pepper. Add dill, parsley, and bread crumbs.
Form small balls (the size of walnuts). Roll in flour.
Cook in a kettle with boiling water for few minutes. Transfer with a colander spoon into the fish broth.
Serves 4.

DILL DUMPLINGS
Kluski z koprem

Prepare dough as for French Dumplings*
1 tablespoon dill leaves

Add dill to the dough. Cook and serve as for French Dumplings*.
Serves 4.

MUSHROOM DUMPLINGS
Kluski z grzybami

Prepare dough as for French Dumplings*
3 tablespoons chopped mushrooms
1 teaspoon butter

Sauté mushrooms in butter. Add to the dough.
Cook and serve as for French Dumplings*.
Serves 4.

LIVER DUMPLINGS
Kluski z wątróbką

2 tablespoons butter
2 eggs, separated
3 ounces chicken livers, chopped
Salt to taste
Dash pepper
½ cup flour

Cream the butter with egg yolks. Add the liver, salt, and pepper, mix well.
Beat the egg whites till stiff. Without mixing put the egg whites and flour in small parts alternately over the liver paste. Mix lightly.
Drop small portions of dough from a spoon into boiling water. Test first by boiling just 1 dumpling to make sure it does not fall apart. Add flour if needed.
Simmer 3 minutes. Strain. Add to the soup or serve as a separate dish.
Serves 4.

MUSHROOM POCKETS
Uszka z grzybami

STUFFING

2 ounces dried mushrooms
   OR
4 ounces fresh mushrooms, chopped
½ cup water
1 large onion, diced
2 tablespoons butter
1 slice white bread, soaked in water and squeezed
2 tablespoons bread crumbs
Salt and pepper

DOUGH

1½ cups sifted flour
Dash salt
1 egg
½ cup water

Wash dried mushrooms well. Soak in ½ cup water 4 hours. Bring to boil, simmer 1 hour, or fry fresh mushrooms in 1 tablespoon butter.

Fry the onions in butter till golden. Grind the mushrooms, onions, and bread. Add bread crumbs, salt, and pepper.

Combine the flour with salt and egg mixed with water. Knead into elastic, shiny dough. If needed add water or flour; it should roll out easily.

Roll out as thin as possible without tearing. Cut into 1½- or 2-inch squares. Lay 1 teaspoon stuffing in the center. Fold diagonally forming a triangle. Seal the edges with fingers. Lift the two long corners of the triangle up, and seal them together.

Cook in a large kettle of boiling water. Remove with colander spoon, add to the soup, and serve immediately.

Clear barshch or Mushroom Consommé* with Mushroom Pockets* are traditional Christmas Eve Supper soups.

Serves 6.

CROUTONS
Grzanki

Ready-made croutons are sold in most large supermarkets, but homemade are so much better that it is worth the work.

Spread 2-day-old white bread with butter on both sides. Cut into small cubes. Brown in a hot 450° F. oven for about 10 minutes. Serve warm with soups on a separate dish.
Count on 1 slice of bread per person.

CHEESE CROUTONS
Grzanki z serem

Spread 2-day-old white bread with butter on both sides. Sprinkle generously with grated cheese. Cut into small cubes. Brown in a hot 450° F. oven for about 10 minutes. Serve warm with soups on a separate dish.
Count on 1 slice bread per person.

TINY PUFFS
Groszek ptysiowy

½ cup water	1 cup flour
2 tablespoons butter	1 egg
Dash salt	1 egg yolk

Bring the water with butter and salt to boil. Add the flour, mix, reduce heat to simmer. Beat quickly with a spoon for a few minutes until the dough is smooth and shiny. Remove from heat, cool for few minutes, add the egg, mix, add the egg yolk. Beat with a spoon until cold.
Use a cookie gun or make a thin roll and cut up in small pieces. Bake on a buttered sheet in a hot 400° F. oven for 10 minutes. Reduce heat to 350° F. Bake another 10 minutes.
Serve with Tomato Consommé* and other clear soups.
Serves 6.

ENTRÉE DISHES

Polish cooking does not have to be time consuming. Using fast, modern methods, we can eat the delicacies of the Old World without toiling for hours in the kitchen. I do not ask you to roast a whole pig or rare game birds. Let's leave that to the country squires. Outside of a few more complicated, traditional, and gourmet dishes, I have chosen for this book practical, simple recipes for everyday use and holiday treats.

In a Polish dinner the main course is divided in equal proportions among the meat, the vegetables, and some potatoes, noodles, or groats. Steak was never considered the best of everything. Polish husbands favor variety and tender meats. They are glad to see pork on the table at least once a week.

For variety we have here 96 easy meat dishes and many casseroles. Meat will always be tender if you refrigerate it for 2–3 days before using. Do not be afraid to marinate, it is not time consuming or difficult. Do not skip the pounding, and do not overcook. Beef and lamb can be eaten half rare; veal and pork have to be cooked thoroughly. Braised beef is by no means inferior to rare roasts, if seasoned properly.

It is practical to boil a piece of chuck or shank once a week. That way we get an excellent stock for soups and sauces. Boiled beef in a good sauce can be delicious and money saving. Leftovers, chopped or ground, may be used for tasty casseroles or as stuffing for patties and pancakes. To prevent drying, never take boiled beef out of its broth before it cools. Refrigerate the broth and remove the fat before using it.

Polish recipes for fish are few but excellent. In spite of the abundance of fish in Polish rivers, lakes, and the Baltic Sea, Polish people are not great fish eaters. It has to be extremely fresh and carefully seasoned to be acceptable. Fish does not stand freezing and refrigeration well. Frozen fillets do not compare in taste with a fish that was still living an hour before cooking.

To have it really tasty, and to avoid the last minute shopping, Polish housewives like to buy their fish live. In my childhood the Christmas Eve carp or pike was carefully chosen two days in advance, and it splashed merrily in its new habitat—the family bathtub. Nobody minded skipping a shower, such were the delights of watching the strong beast swimming around, and of feeding it bits of bread.

Carp by no means is looked down upon in Poland. It is not cheaper than most other fish, and it is not caught in dirty bays, only reared with care in artificial ponds. When the carp reach the proper age and size, about 2 pounds, the water is drained and the fish are taken to the market.

Submitting to the rigors of numerous Catholic fasts, cooks substituted meat entrées with fish, and many sweet dishes were invented, delicious, but not too popular with weight watchers.

In the Polish cuisine there is also an abundance of casseroles, very tasty, handy budget stretchers. Nobody likes leftovers, but who can recognize them in a carefully prepared casserole?

Polish cooking has a characteristic seasoning for each dish. Sour cream is used often. The secret of combining it successfully with gravies and casseroles lies in its freshness. Use sour cream refrigerated for 2–3 days for salads and dressings, but it has to be dairy fresh for all the hot entrée dishes.

FISH

FISH	RYBY
Vegetable Fish Bouillon	*Wywar z włoszczyzny i ryby*
Pike Polish Style	*Sandacz po polsku*
Cod in Horseradish Sauce	*Drosz w sosie chrzanowym*
Salmon "from the Water"	*Łosoś z wody*
Boiled Lake or Stream Trout	*Pstrągi z wody*
Carp in Gray Sauce	*Karp w szarym sosie*
Pike Jewish Style	*Szczupak po żydowsku*
Pike Sauté with Mushrooms	*Sandacz z pieczarkami*
White Fish in Bread Crumbs	*Ryba smażona, panierowana*
Fish Cutlets	*Kotlety z ryby*
Herring in the Blanket	*Śledzie w cieście*
Fish Balls	*Pulpety z ryby*
Pike in Sour Cream	*Sandacz w śmietanie*
Fish with Tomatoes	*Ryba z pomidorami*
Fish with Cheese	*Ryba z serem*
Sole with Vegetables	*Sola z jarzynami*
Sole Stewed with Horseradish	*Sola duszona w chrzanie*
Carp with Beer	*Karp z piwem*
White Fish in Wine Sauce	*Ryba w winie*
Pike Goulash	*Gulasz ze szczupaka*
Flounder with Asparagus	*Flądra ze szparagami*
Baked Fish	*Ryba pieczona*
Fish au Gratin with Tomatoes	*Ryba zapiekana z pomidorami*
Fish à la Nelson	*Ryba po nelsońsku*
Fish au Gratin	*Ryba zapiekana w sosie beszamelowym*
Fish au Gratin with Mushrooms	*Ryba zapiekana z grzybami*
Fish au Gratin with Horseradish	*Ryba zapiekana w sosie 'chrzanowym*
Fish with Macaroni	*Ryba z makaronem*

VEGETABLE FISH BOUILLON
Wywar z włoszczyzny i ryby

Used for cooking fish and the sauces

1 onion, quartered　　　　　　*1 bay leaf*
1 large carrot, cut up　　　　　*Salt to taste*
1 stalk celery, cut up　　　　　*4 cups water*
1 parsley root, cut up　　　　　*Fish trimmings and head*
3 peppercorns

Place the vegetables and the spices in cold water. Add the fish trimmings and the head. Bring to a boil, then simmer for 30 minutes. Strain.
Yields 4 cups.

PIKE POLISH STYLE
Sandacz po polsku

1½ pounds whole pike, or any white fish fillets
3 cups Vegetable Fish Bouillon*
3 hard-boiled eggs, chopped
3 tablespoons butter, melted
Salt and white pepper
1 tablespoon chopped green parsley

Place the fish in boiling bouillon and cook on high heat for 25 minutes.
Remove fish gently from the kettle. Place on a warmed dish. Sprinkle with eggs, butter, salt, pepper, and parsley.
Serves 5.

COD IN HORSERADISH SAUCE
Dorsz w sosie chrzanowym

1½ pounds cod or any white fish fillets
3 cups Vegetable Fish Bouillon*
1 cup Horseradish Sauce*

Place the fish in boiling bouillon and cook on high heat for 25 minutes.
Remove fish gently from the kettle. Place on a warmed dish, pour Horseradish Sauce* over.
Serves 5.

SALMON "FROM THE WATER"
Łosoś z wody

1½ pounds salmon steaks
3 cups Vegetable Fish Bouillon*
2 tablespoons butter, melted
2 hard-boiled eggs, quartered
1 lemon, sliced
1 tablespoon chopped green parsley

Place salmon steaks in boiling bouillon and cook on low heat for 20 minutes.
Remove steaks gently from the kettle. Place on a warmed dish. Sprinkle with butter. Garnish with eggs, lemon slices, and green parsley. Serve with boiled potatoes and green peas.
Serve for a change with Mushroom Sauce*.
Serves 4.

BOILED LAKE OR STREAM TROUT
Pstrągi z wody

2–3 2-pound trouts	*A few green parsley twigs*
4 cups Vegetable Fish	*2 hard-boiled eggs, sliced*
Bouillon*	*1 lemon, sliced*
2 tablespoons butter, melted	*Lettuce leaves*

Place the trouts in boiling bouillon and cook on low heat for 15 minutes.

Remove fish gently from the kettle. Place on a warmed dish. Sprinkle with butter. Garnish with parsley, egg and lemon slices, and lettuce leaves.

Serve with boiled potatoes, sprinkled with melted butter and chopped green parsley.

Serves 6.

CARP IN GRAY SAUCE
Karp w szarym sosie

2 pounds carp, cut up into serving pieces
4 cups Vegetable Fish Bouillon*

GRAY SAUCE

1 cup honey
1 tablespoon instant flour
1 cup fish broth
¼ teaspoon cloves
½ teaspoon cinnamon
1 teaspoon grated lemon rind
Juice from half lemon
½ cup white table wine
2 tablespoons yellow raisins, steamed
2 tablespoons peeled, thinly sliced almonds
Salt to taste

Place the carp in boiling bouillon and cook on low heat for 25 minutes.
Prepare the Gray Sauce. Heat the honey, add the flour, bring to boil. Add the fish broth, spices, lemon rind and juice, wine, raisins, and almonds. Season with salt. Simmer for 10 minutes.
Remove the carp pieces gently from the kettle. Place on a warmed dish. Pour the sauce over.
Serve with potatoes or rice.
This is a traditional Christmas Eve dish.
Serves 6.

PIKE JEWISH STYLE
Szczupak po żydowsku

1 large onion, sliced
1 tablespoon butter
1½ pounds pike or any white fish fillets
2 slices white bread, soaked in milk and squeezed
2 egg yolks
Salt and pepper to taste
Dash nutmeg
3 cups Vegetable Fish Bouillon*
A few green parsley sprigs
1 tomato, sliced

Fry the onions with butter till golden. Grind the fish twice with onions and bread. Add egg yolks, season with salt, pepper, and nutmeg. Form a roll from the mixture, wrap in a cheese cloth. Place in a kettle, add warm bouillon. Simmer for 1 hour.
Serve warm or cold, garnish with parsley and tomato slices. Horseradish*, Mustard*, or Tomato Sauce* is recommended.
Serves 5.

PIKE SAUTÉ WITH MUSHROOMS
Sandacz z pieczarkami

6 ounces mushrooms, sliced
4 tablespoons butter
1 tablespoon water
2 pounds pike or any white fish fillets
1½ tablespoons flour
Salt to taste

Fry the mushrooms in half of the butter until golden. Add 1 table-spoon water, cover and simmer 5 minutes.
Roll the fish fillets in the flour, sprinkle with salt. Heat the remaining butter; fry fillets on both sides until golden. Cover with mushrooms. Place in moderate 350° F. oven for 10 minutes.
Serves 6.

WHITE FISH IN BREAD CRUMBS
Ryba smażona, panierowana

1½ pounds fish fillets, cut up in serving pieces
Salt to taste
2 tablespoons flour
1 egg
½ cup bread crumbs
3 tablespoons butter

Sprinkle the fish with salt and flour. Dip in egg, roll in bread crumbs.
Heat the butter. Fry the fish fillets on both sides till golden. Place in moderate 350° F. oven for 10 minutes.
Serve with potatoes and raw vegetable salad.
Serves 4.

FISH CUTLETS
Kotlety z ryby

1 onion, sliced
1 tablespoon butter
1½ pounds white fish fillets
2 slices white bread, soaked in milk and squeezed
1 egg
Salt and pepper
½ cup bread crumbs
3 tablespoons shortening

Fry the onions in hot butter until golden. Grind fish fillets with onions and bread twice. Add the egg, salt, and pepper. Mix very well. Form small cutlets, roll in bread crumbs.
Heat the shortening. Fry the cutlets on both sides till golden. Reduce the heat, fry 5 more minutes.
Serve with potatoes and salad.
Serves 5.

HERRING IN THE BLANKET
Śledzie w cieście

2 eggs, separated
2 tablespoons salad oil
5 tablespoons sour cream
1¼ cups flour
Salt to taste
1½ pounds salt herring fillets, soaked overnight
3 tablespoons shortening
*Tomato Sauce**

Mix the egg yolks with the oil, sour cream, and half of the flour. Beat the egg whites, till stiff. Add the egg whites and the rest of the flour to the dough alternately. Mix gently. Season with salt lightly.

Make small rolls from the herring fillets. Dip each roll (on a fork) in the dough and fry on both sides in hot shortening.
Serve with Tomato Sauce* and salad.
Serves 6.

FISH BALLS
Pulpety z ryby

1 onion, sliced
1 tablespoon butter
1½ pounds fish fillets
2 slices white bread, soaked in milk and squeezed
1 egg
Salt and pepper to taste
1½ tablespoons flour
*4 cups Vegetable Fish Bouillon**

Fry the onions in the butter till golden. Grind fish fillets with onions and bread twice. Add the egg, season with salt and pepper. Form egg-sized balls, roll in flour.
Cook in boiling bouillon for 10 minutes.
Serve with Dill Pickle Sauce*, potatoes or groats, and salad.
Serves 6.

PIKE IN SOUR CREAM
Sandacz w śmietanie

2 pounds pike or any fish
*   fillets*
1½ tablespoons flour
Salt to taste
1½ tablespoons shortening

1 cup water
2 bouillon cubes
½ cup sour cream
2 tablespoons dill leaves

Sprinkle the fish fillets with flour and salt. Fry in hot shortening on both sides till golden.
Place fish fillets in a kettle, add 1 cup water and bouillon cubes. Simmer for 20 minutes.

Remove from heat, add sour cream; transfer to a warmed dish, sprinkle with dill.
Serves 6.

FISH WITH TOMATOES
Ryba z pomidorami

1½ pounds fish fillets   *¼ cup chopped green parsley*
1 tablespoon lemon juice   *4 tomatoes, chopped*
Salt and pepper   *1 teaspoon dill leaves*
⅓ cup salad oil   *¼ cup white table wine*
2 onions, sliced   *4 thin slices lemon*
Dash garlic powder

Sprinkle fish fillets with lemon juice, salt, and pepper. Heat the oil. Fry the onions with garlic and parsley until golden. Add the tomatoes and dill. Cook a few minutes. Season with salt and pepper. Add wine.
Pour half of the sauce in a baking dish. Arrange the fish fillets in the dish. Pour on the rest of the sauce. Arrange the lemon on the top. Bake 35 minutes in moderate 350° F. oven.
Serves 6.

FISH WITH CHEESE
Ryba z serem

1½ pounds flounder or any white fish fillets
1 teaspoon salt
¼ teaspoon pepper
4 tablespoons butter
½ cup grated cheese
1 tablespoon lemon juice
1 teaspoon chopped green parsley

Sprinkle the fish with salt and pepper. Melt the butter in a small skillet. Stir in cheese and lemon juice, mix.

Place the fish on a foil-lined broiler rack. Spoon ⅓ of the cheese mixture over it. Put under preheated broiler for 10 minutes. Pour over the rest of the cheese mixture. Serve sprinkled with parsley. Serves 4.

SOLE WITH VEGETABLES
Sola z jarzynami

1½ tablespoons butter
1 large onion, chopped
¼ small head savoy cabbage, chopped
1 leek, finely sliced
1 large carrot, finely sliced
1 stalk celery, chopped
1 parsley root, finely sliced
3 tablespoons water
2 pounds sole or any white fish fillets
Salt

SAUCE

1½ tablespoons butter
1½ tablespoons instant flour
2 bouillon cubes
1 cup hot water
Salt and pepper
3 tablespoons sour cream

Heat the butter, add the vegetables and 3 tablespoons water. Simmer 5 minutes.

Sprinkle fish fillets with salt. Place on the vegetables. Simmer for 15 minutes.

To make the sauce: Heat the butter, add flour, fry for few minutes mixing. Add bouillon cubes dissolved in 1 cup hot water. Bring to boil.

Transfer the fish gently to a warmed dish. Add the sauce to the vegetables. Remove from heat. Season with salt and pepper, add sour cream. Pour over the fish.

Serve with Dumplings*.

Serves 6.

SOLE STEWED WITH HORSERADISH
Sola duszona w chrzanie

1½ pounds sole, divided into serving pieces
Salt
1½ tablespoons flour
2 tablespoons shortening
½ cup water
3 tablespoons grated prepared horseradish
½ cup sour cream
A few green parsley sprigs

Sprinkle the fish with salt and flour. Fry fish in hot shortening on both sides until golden. Add ½ cup water. Cover and simmer for 20 minutes.
Spoon the horseradish mixed with sour cream over the fish. Heat for few minutes. Serve garnished with green parsley.
Serve with boiled potatoes and salad.
Serves 4.

CARP WITH BEER
Karp z piwem

1 large onion, chopped
2 tablespoons butter
½ cup beer
1½ pounds carp, divided into serving pieces
Salt and pepper
½ teaspoon cloves
2 tablespoons vinegar
3 tablespoons yellow raisins
½ teaspoon grated lemon rind

Fry the onions in hot butter till golden. Add the beer, heat. Sprinkle fish pieces with salt, pepper, cloves, and vinegar. Place in the skillet with beer sauce. Cover and simmer 30 minutes. Remove the fish to a warmed dish. Add the raisins and lemon

rind to the sauce. Cook uncovered for 5 minutes on high heat.
Pour over the fish.
This is a gourmet dish.
Serves 4.

WHITE FISH IN WINE SAUCE
Ryba w winie

1 onion, chopped	*½ cup vinegar*
¼ head small savoy cabbage,	*1½ pounds fish fillets*
finely chopped	*½ cup boiling water*
1 large carrot, grated	*½ cup white table wine*
1 stalk celery, grated	*Salt and pepper*
1 parsley root, grated	*½ teaspoon paprika*
5 tablespoons butter	*½ cup sour cream*
4 tablespoons water	

Simmer the vegetables with butter and 4 tablespoons water for
10 minutes.
Pour boiling vinegar over the fish. Let stand for 10 minutes.
Transfer the vegetables into a casserole dish. Arrange fish fillets
on it. Pour over ½ cup boiling water, the wine, and some of the
vinegar. Season with salt, pepper, and paprika. Place covered in a
moderate 350° F. oven for 30 minutes.
Pour sour cream over and serve.
Serves 4.

PIKE GOULASH
Gulasz ze szczupaka

2 pounds pike fillets, cut up	*1 large onion, chopped*
Salt and pepper	*½ teaspoon paprika*
2 tablespoons flour	*1 cup boiling water*
2 tablespoons shortening	*½ cup sour cream*

Sprinkle the fish with salt, pepper, and some of the flour. Fry on
both sides in 1½ tablespoon shortening till golden. Fry the

onions in a separate skillet in the rest of the shortening till pale gold.

Transfer the onions into a kettle, place the fish on them. Season with salt and paprika, add 1 cup boiling water. Cover and simmer for 20 minutes.

Add the rest of the flour, bring to a boil. Remove from the heat, add sour cream.

Serves 6.

FLOUNDER WITH ASPARAGUS
Flądra ze szparagami

¼ pound mushrooms, sliced
3 tablespoons soft butter
2 pounds flounder fillets
Salt
1 cup boiling water
1½ tablespoons instant flour
1 cup Vegetable Fish Bouillon*
1 teaspoon lemon juice
2 egg yolks
1 tablespoon water
2 packages frozen asparagus, cooked
1 tablespoon chopped green parsley

Sauté the mushrooms in small amount of butter. Sprinkle fish with salt, place over the mushrooms. Add 1 cup boiling water, cover and simmer for 20 minutes.

Mix the flour with the rest of the butter. Add half of the boiling bouillon. Mix well, bring to a boil, add the rest of the bouillon.

Transfer the fish to a warmed dish. Add the sauce to the mushrooms, bring to boil. Remove from heat. Season with salt and lemon juice. Add the egg yolks mixed with 1 tablespoon water.

Place hot asparagus around the fish. Pour the sauce over; sprinkle with parsley.

Serve with cauliflower instead of asparagus for change.

Serves 6.

BAKED FISH
Ryba pieczona

2 pounds fish fillets	*2 hard-boiled eggs, chopped*
Salt	*A few green parsley sprigs*
2 tablespoons butter, melted	

Sprinkle fish fillets with salt. Place in a buttered baking dish.
Pour the butter over.
Bake in moderate 350° F. oven for 40 minutes. Baste often.
Sprinkle with eggs, garnish with parsley. Serve with horseradish
and boiled potatoes.
Serves 6.

FISH AU GRATIN WITH TOMATOES
Ryba zapiekana z pomidorami

1 carrot, sliced
1 celery stalk, sliced
1 parsley root, sliced
1 onion, sliced
4 tablespoons water
3 tablespoons butter
Salt
2 pounds sole or any white fish fillets
4 tomatoes, thickly sliced
2 tablespoons grated cheese

Simmer the vegetables with 4 tablespoons water and half of the
butter for 10 minutes. Season with salt.
Sprinkle fish fillets with salt, arrange on a buttered baking dish,
sprinkle with the rest of the butter. Cover with vegetables. Arrange tomato slices on the top, sprinkle with cheese. Bake in
moderate 375° F. oven for 20 minutes.
Serve with potatoes.
Serves 6.

FISH À LA NELSON
Ryba po nelsońsku

½ ounce dried mushrooms or ¼ pound fresh ones, sliced
4 tablespoons water (for dried mushrooms) or 2 tablespoons
    water (for fresh ones)
1½ pounds fish fillets
Salt
1 tablespoon flour
2 tablespoons shortening
2 onions, sliced
6 potatoes, half cooked, peeled, sliced
½ cup sour cream
1 tablespoon chopped green parsley

Wash dried mushrooms very well. Simmer with 4 tablespoons water
for 1 hour. Remove, slice. Simmer fresh sliced mushrooms in 2
tablespoons water for 10 minutes. Remove. Save the broth.
Sprinkle fish fillets with salt and flour. Fry on both sides in hot
shortening until golden. Remove from the skillet. Add the onions
to the skillet and fry till golden.
Place half of the potatoes in a buttered baking dish. Sprinkle with
salt. Arrange the fish on potatoes. Cover with onions, mushrooms,
and the rest of the potatoes. Sprinkle with salt. Pour sour cream,
salted and mixed with mushroom broth, over potatoes. Bake in
400° F. oven for ½ hour.
Sprinkle with parsley before serving. Serve with a salad.
Serves 6.

FISH AU GRATIN
Ryba zapiekana w sosie beszamelowym

2 pounds pike, sole, or any   *1 tablespoon butter, melted*
    white fish fillets   *1½ cups Béchamel Sauce**
Salt   *3 tablespoons grated cheese*
1 teaspoon lemon juice   *1 tablespoon bread crumbs*

Sprinkle the fish fillets with salt. Place in a buttered dish, sprinkle

with lemon juice and butter. Bake in a hot 400° F. oven for 10 minutes.
Pour the Béchamel Sauce over the fish. Sprinkle with cheese and bread crumbs. Bake in hot 425° F. oven for 10 minutes or until golden.
Serves 6.

FISH AU GRATIN WITH MUSHROOMS
Ryba zapiekana z grzybami

2 pounds carp, pike, or white fish fillets
Salt
2 tablespoons butter, melted
½ pound mushrooms, thinly sliced
2 onions, sliced
2 tablespoons water
Pepper
½ cup sour cream
5 tablespoons grated cheese
1 tablespoon bread crumbs

Sprinkle the fish fillets with salt. Place in a buttered dish, sprinkle with melted butter. Bake in a hot 400° F. oven for 10 minutes. Simmer the mushrooms with onions and 2 tablespoons water for 10 minutes. Season with salt and pepper. Place over the fish. Pour sour cream over. Sprinkle with cheese and bread crumbs.
Bake another 10 minutes.
Serve with mashed potatoes and red cabbage.
Serves 6.

FISH AU GRATIN WITH HORSERADISH
Ryba zapiekana w sosie chrzanowym

1½ pounds fish or fish fillets
Salt
1 teaspoon vinegar

2 tablespoons butter, melted
*1½ cups Horseradish Sauce**

Sprinkle the fish with salt and vinegar. Place in a buttered baking dish, sprinkle with melted butter.

Bake in a hot 400° F. oven for 10 minutes. Pour the Horseradish Sauce* over. Bake another 15 minutes.

Serve with boiled potatoes and Creamed Spinach*.

This is a dish for refined tastes.

Serves 4.

FISH WITH MACARONI
Ryba z makaronem

2 cups cooked elbow macaroni
1 tablespoon butter
1 onion, sliced
1 tablespoon shortening
1 pound white fish fillets
Salt and pepper
½ cup water
½ cup sour cream
1 egg yolk
1 bouillon cube
2 tablespoons boiling water
3 tablespoons grated cheese

Mix the macaroni with butter. Fry the onions in shortening till golden, add fish fillets to the skillet, sprinkle with salt and pepper. Add ½ cup water, cover and simmer for 20 minutes.

Place half of the macaroni in a buttered baking dish. Cover with fish and onions. Cover with the rest of the macaroni. Pour sour cream mixed with egg yolk and bouillon cube dissolved in 2 tablespoons boiling water over macaroni. Sprinkle with cheese. Bake in a hot 450° F. oven for 10–15 minutes.

Serve with a salad.

Serves 3.

MEATS

MEAT	POTRAWY MIESNE
Chicken Fricassee	*Potrawka z kury*
Cutlets de Volaille	*Kotleciki de volaille*
Chicken Balls	*Kotleciki z kury*
Chicken with Bacon and Rice	*Kura z boczkiem i ryżem*
Chicken with Vegetables	*Kura duszona z jarzynami*
Chicken in Dill Sauce	*Kurczęta w sosie koperkowym*
Chicken with Paprika	*Kurczę w papryce*
Chicken in Tomato Sauce	*Kurczę w tomacie*
Chicken with Mushrooms	*Kurczę z grzybami*
Chicken Polish Style	*Kurczęta po polsku*
Goose with Cabbage	*Gęś z kapustą*
Duck with Apples	*Kaczka z jabłkami*
Roast Turkey	*Pieczony indyk*
Roast Pheasant	*Pieczony bażant*
Wild Duck, Goose, or Partridge	*Dzika kaczka, gęś lub kuropatwy*

Veal Fricassee	*Potrawka cielęca*
Veal Fricassee with Dill	*Potrawka cielęca z koprem*
Veal Fricassee with Apples	*Potrawka cielęca z jabłkami*
Veal Chop Sauté	*Kotlety cielęce z kostką*
Veal Steak	*Stek cielęcy*
Vienna Schnitzels	*Sznycel po wiedeńsku*
Pozarski Cutlets	*Kotlety pożarskie*
Veal Chops with Tomatoes	*Kotlety cielęce z pomidorami*
Veal Chops with Wine	*Kotlety cielęce z winem*
Veal with Paprika	*Paprykarz cielęcy*
Veal with Vegetables	*Zraziki cielęce z jarzynami*
Veal with Mushrooms	*Zrazy cielęce z pieczarkami*
Veal with Ham	*Zraziki cielęce z szynką*
Veal Goulash	*Gulasz cielęcy*
Veal Pot Roast	*Pieczeń cielęca duszona*
Roast Veal	*Pieczeń cielęca*
Roast Veal in Béchamel	*Pieczeń cielęca w sosie beszamelowym*
Veal Balls with Dill	*Klopsiki cielęce z koperkiem*
Meatballs with Mushroom Sauce	*Klopsiki w grzybowym sosie*
Veal Balls Stuffed with Mushrooms	*Klopsiki cielęce z grzybami*
White Sausage Baked	*Kiełbasa biała pieczona*
Polish Sausage with Savoy Cabbage	*Kiełbasa z kapustą włoską*
Sausage in Tomato Sauce	*Kiełbasa w sosie pomidorowym*
Pork Chop Sauté	*Kotlety schabowe sauté*
Pork Steaks	*Stek wieprzowy*
Pork Cutlets	*Kotlety schabowe panierowane*
Ground Pork Cutlets	*Kotlety wieprzowe mielone*
Pork Goulash	*Gulasz wieprzowy*
Pork and Sauerkraut	*Wieprzowina z kapustą*
Pork with Sour Cream	*Zrazy wieprzowe ze śmietaną*
Pork with Tomatoes	*Wieprzowina z pomidorami*
Pork Ribs with Onions	*Żeberka wieprzowe z cebulą*
Ham Pot Roast	*Szynka duszona*
Pork Loin with Apples	*Schab z jabłkami*
Pork Roast with Potatoes	*Schab pieczony z kartoflami*

Pork Loin with Prunes	*Schab z suszonymi śliwkami*
Hamburgers Polish Style	*Kotlety siekane*
Meat Loaf	*Klops*
Meat Loaf with Eggs	*Klops z jajami*
Boiled Beef	*Sztuka mięsa*
Boiled Beef au Gratin	*Sztuka mięsa zapiekana*
Boiled Beef and Horseradish	*Sztuka mięsa z chrzanem*
Beef Steaks Polish Style	*Befsztyki po polsku*
Beef Steaks Country Style	*Befsztyki gospodarskie*
Minced Steaks	*Befsztyki mielone*
Boeuf Stroganov	*Boeuf Stroganow*
Beef Shashlik	*Szaszłyk wołowy*
Beef Goulash	*Gulasz wołowy*
Beef Rolls with Mustard	*Zrazy zawijane z musztardą*
Beef Rolls with Dill Pickles	*Zrazy zawijane z ogórkiem*
Beef Rolls Warsaw Style	*Zrazy zawijane po warszawsku*
Beef with Sour Cream	*Zrazy wołowe ze śmietaną*
Beef with Vegetables	*Zrazy wołowe z jarzynami*
Beef with Mushrooms	*Zrazy wołowe z grzybami*
Beef à la Nelson	*Zrazy po nelsońsku*
Beef Pot Roast	*Pieczeń wołowa duszona*
Beef Pot Roast with Mushrooms	*Pieczeń wołowa duszona z grzybami*
Pot Roast Marinated	*Pieczeń wołowa na dziko*
Roast Beef	*Rostbef*
Lamb Chop Sauté	*Kotlety baranie sauté*
Lamb Chops Broiled	*Kotlety baranie z rusztu*
Turkish Shashlik	*Szaszłyk turecki*
Lamb Stew	*Gulasz barani*
Lamb and Potato Casserole	*Baranina duszona z kartoflami*
Lamb Ragout	*Ragout z baraniny*
Lamb Pot Roast with Cabbage	*Baranina duszona z kapustą*
Leg of Lamb with Sour Cream	*Comber barani ze śmietaną*
Venison	*Sarnina*
Hare Polish Style	*Zając po polsku*
Brains au Gratin	*Móżdżek zapiekany*
Brains Polish Style	*Móżdżek po polsku*
Braised Liver	*Wątróbka duszona*

Liver in Bread Crumbs	*Wątróbka panierowana*
Calf's Liver Sauté	*Wątróbka cielęca smażona*
Liver and Tomatoes	*Wątróbka z pomidorami*
Chicken Liver Sauté	*Wątróbki kurze smażone*
Ham and Egg Noodle Casserole	*Łazanki zapiekane z szynką*
Risotto	*Rizotto*
Stuffed Kohlrabi	*Kalarepa faszerowana*
Stuffed Eggplant	*Bakłażany faszerowane*
Stuffed Tomatoes	*Pomidory faszerowane*

CHICKEN FRICASSEE
Potrawka z kury

1 chicken, quartered
1 onion, quartered, browned
2 carrots
1 parsley root
2 celery stalks
Salt to taste
2 tablespoons soft butter

3 tablespoons instant flour
2 egg yolks
2 tablespoons cold water
1 teaspoon lemon juice
1 tablespoon chopped
   green parsley

Place the chicken in a kettle, cover with water. Simmer for 1½ hours. Add the vegetables and salt. Simmer another ½ hour.
Mix the butter with the flour well. Add 5 tablespoons hot broth one by one, mixing. Add the mixture to a saucepan with 1¾ cups boiling broth. Remove from the heat. Season with salt. Add egg yolks mixed with 2 tablespoons cold water and lemon juice. Skin the chicken. Place on a warmed dish. Pour the sauce over the chicken, sprinkle with parsley.
Serve with rice or mashed potatoes.
Serves 4.

CUTLETS DE VOLAILLE
Kotleciki de volaille

Breasts from 2 chickens, skinned and boned carefully
Salt
¼ pound butter
2 eggs
1 cup fine bread crumbs
2 tablespoons butter
A few green parsley sprigs
1 lemon, sliced

Flatten the chicken breasts, sprinkle with salt. Put ¼ of the butter on the middle of each breast. Roll tightly.

Dip each roll in the eggs and bread crumbs twice. Fry in hot butter on both sides till golden.

Garnish with parsley and lemon slices. Serve with French fries and vegetables (peas, asparagus, Brussels sprouts, carrots).

Serves 4.

CHICKEN BALLS
Kotleciki z kury

1 large chicken, skinned, boned, and ground twice
3 slices white bread, soaked in milk and squeezed
Salt
1½ tablespoons butter, melted
2 egg yolks
½ cup fine bread crumbs
2 tablespoons shortening
A few green parsley sprigs
1 lemon, sliced

Mix the chicken meat with bread. Season with salt. Add butter and egg yolks, mix well. Form small balls, roll in bread crumbs. Heat the shortening. Fry chicken balls on both sides till golden. Arrange on a warmed dish. Garnish with parsley and lemon slices.

Serve with vegetable, salad, and potatoes.

Serves 6.

CHICKEN WITH BACON AND RICE
Kura z boczkiem i ryżem

6 slices bacon, cut up
2 cups coarsely chopped baked or boiled chicken
½ cup strong chicken bouillon
2 cups cooked rice
1 tablespoon chopped green parsley
Salt and pepper

Fry the bacon till golden. Sprinkle the chicken meat with bouillon.

Combine all the ingredients, season and heat.
Serve with peas and carrots.
Serves 3.

CHICKEN WITH VEGETABLES
Kura duszona z jarzynami

1 large chicken, cut up
Salt
1½ tablespoons shortening
1 onion, sliced
½ pound mushrooms, thinly sliced
2 carrots, sliced
1 parsley root, sliced
2 stalks celery, shredded
¼ small head savoy cabbage
1 tablespoon butter
2½ tablespoons instant flour
1 tablespoon chopped green parsley

Sprinkle the chicken with salt. Fry in hot shortening on both sides
till golden. Place in a kettle, add small amount of water, cover and
simmer for ½ hour.
Add the onions to the drippings in the skillet. Fry for few minutes.
Add the vegetables and fry some more. Add it all to the chicken.
Simmer 15 minutes. Remove the chicken to a warmed dish.
Heat the butter, add the flour. Fry for a few minutes, mixing.
Dilute with hot broth from the kettle, add to the vegetable sauce.
Bring to a boil. Pour over the chicken. Sprinkle with parsley.
Serves 5.

CHICKEN IN DILL SAUCE
Kurczęta w sosie koperkowym

2 chickens, quartered   *Salt*
1½ tablespoons flour   *1 cup water*
1½ tablespoons shortening   *1½ cups Dill Sauce**

Sprinkle the chickens with flour and fry in the shortening till golden.

Season with salt, add 1 cup water. Cover and simmer for 1 hour.

Pour the Dill Sauce* over. Simmer 10 minutes more.

Serve with rice.

Serves 8.

CHICKEN WITH PAPRIKA
Kurczę w papryce

1 chicken, quartered	*1 large tomato, peeled,*
Salt	*quartered*
2½ tablespoons shortening	*½ green pepper, chopped*
1 onion, chopped	*½ cup sour cream*
1 teaspoon paprika	*3 teaspoons flour*
½ cup water	

Sprinkle the chicken with salt. Fry in 2 tablespoons hot shortening on both sides till golden.

Fry the onions in the rest of shortening, add to the chicken. Sprinkle with paprika. Add ½ cup water, tomato, and green pepper. Cover and simmer 1 hour. Add sour cream mixed with flour. Bring to a boil and serve.

Serves 4.

CHICKEN IN TOMATO SAUCE
Kurczę w tomacie

1 chicken, quartered	*1 tablespoon dill leaves*
Salt	*2 tablespoons chopped*
½ cup catsup	*green onion*
½ cup water	

Sprinkle the chicken with salt. Place in a buttered baking dish. Bake in hot 450° F. oven for 45 minutes.

Remove from the oven. Pour out the melted chicken fat. Cover

with catsup mixed with ½ cup water, sprinkle with dill. Cover
and bake another 20 minutes in moderate 350° F. oven.
Before serving sprinkle with green onions.
Serves 4.

CHICKEN WITH MUSHROOMS
Kurczę z grzybami

2 chickens, quartered	*½ pound mushrooms, sliced*
Salt	*Pepper*
2½ tablespoons flour	*½ cup sour cream*
2½ tablespoons shortening	*1 teaspoon dill leaves*
1 onion, sliced	*1 teaspoon chopped*
1 cup water	*green parsley*

Sprinkle the chicken with salt and flour. Fry in 2 tablespoons hot
shortening on both sides till golden.
Fry the onions in the rest of the shortening, add to the chicken.
Add 1 cup water, cover and simmer for 1 hour. Add the mush-
rooms, simmer 10 minutes.
Remove from the heat, season with salt and pepper. Add sour
cream. Transfer to a warmed dish, sprinkle with dill and parsley.
Serve with boiled potatoes or groats.
Serves 8.

CHICKEN POLISH STYLE
Kurczęta po polsku

2 small chickens, fryers	*2 eggs*
or broilers	*4 tablespoons butter, melted*
Salt	*Pepper*
2 chicken livers	*1 teaspoon dill leaves*
1 cup bread crumbs	*⅔ cup milk*

Sprinkle the chickens with salt.
Chop the livers finely. Combine with bread crumbs. Add the eggs,
3 tablespoons melted butter, salt, pepper, dill, and as much milk
as needed for a loose, sour-creamlike consistency.

Stuff the birds, and roast in a hot 400° F. oven for 2 hours, basting with the rest of the butter.

Cut into halves or quarters. Serve with young potatoes, cucumbers, or lettuce in sour cream.

Serves 4.

GOOSE WITH CABBAGE
Gęś z kapustą

1 (8-pound) goose
Salt to taste
2 cups water
1 head (2 pounds) red cabbage, finely sliced
1 onion, sliced
1 teaspoon caraway seeds
4 slices bacon
1½ tablespoons instant flour
4 tablespoons water
½ teaspoon sugar
1 teaspoon lemon juice
½ cup red table wine

Sprinkle the goose with salt. Pour 1 cup water into a roasting pan, put in the goose, breast down. Cover and roast in moderate 375° F. oven for 1½ hours. Turn the goose over and roast uncovered for 1 hour longer. During the roasting pierce the skin several times. Skim off the excess fat and sprinkle with cold water several times, using the second cup.

Cook the cabbage with onions and caraway seeds in a small amount of water for 10 minutes.

Cut up the goose, place over the cabbage, cover and simmer for 15 minutes. Remove the goose to a warmed plate.

Fry the bacon till golden, remove half of the fat. Add the flour, fry for few minutes mixing, dilute with 4 tablespoons of water. Add to cabbage, bring to boil. Season with salt, sugar, lemon juice. Add wine and serve.

Serves 8.

DUCK WITH APPLES
Kaczka z jabłkami

1 young duck
Salt
1 teaspoon marjoram
5 apples, peeled, quartered, cored
1 cup water

Rub the duck with salt and marjoram. Leave for 1 hour.
Stuff with apples. Pour 1 cup water into a roasting pan, put in
the duck. Roast in moderate 350° F. oven for 2 hours, basting
with drippings and water. Remove the excess fat 3 times during
the roasting.
Serve with cabbage or beets.
Serves 4.

ROAST TURKEY
Pieczony indyk

1 (14–16-pound) turkey
Salt
½ cup butter
Turkey liver

STUFFING: 1

8 slices white bread, soaked in milk and squeezed
2 tablespoons butter, melted
3 eggs, separated
Chopped turkey liver
¼ teaspoon nutmeg
Salt and pepper
½ cup bread crumbs
Milk, if needed

SWEET STUFFING: 2

6 slices white bread, soaked in milk and squeezed
Chopped turkey liver
2 tablespoons butter, metled
3 eggs, separated
½ cup raisins
3 tablespoons almonds, peeled, finely sliced
Dash nutmeg
¼ teaspoon cloves
¼ teaspoon sugar
Salt to taste
1 cup bread crumbs
Milk, if needed

Sprinkle the turkey with salt, rub with butter. Chop the liver very finely.

STUFFING 1: Mix the bread with butter, egg yolks, liver, and seasonings. Beat the egg whites until stiff. Add to the stuffing alternately with bread crumbs. If too stiff, add milk. Mix lightly.

STUFFING 2: Mix the bread with liver, butter, egg yolks, raisins, almonds, and spices. Beat the egg whites until stiff. Add to the stuffing alternately with bread crumbs. Add milk if needed. Mix lightly. The stuffing must have sour cream consistency.

Stuff the neck and body cavities, and close with skewers. Place the bird in oven preheated to 450° F. Reduce the heat to 350° F. Roast 25 minutes per pound.
Baste frequently with pan drippings.
Cut up the turkey in the kitchen. Arrange on a warmed dish. Sprinkle with pan drippings. Place in a slow oven for few minutes to reheat. Serve with vegetable salad, cranberries, fruit salad. Serves 12.

ROAST PHEASANT
Pieczony bażant

1 pheasant
Salt
¼ pound bacon cut up into ½-inch strips

Rub the pheasant with salt and lard with half the bacon. Melt the remaining bacon in the roasting pan. Place the bird on it and roast in moderate 375° F. oven for 2 hours. Add water as needed. Serve with French fries, cranberries, lettuce.
Serves 3–4.

WILD DUCK, GOOSE, OR PARTRIDGE
Dzika kaczka, gęś lub kuropatwy

2 partridge, 1 duck, or 1 goose
Salt
Juniper seeds, ground
2½ tablespoons bacon drippings
½ cup water
1 small head red cabbage, sliced
1 large onion, sliced
½ cup water
1¾ tablespoons instant flour
½ teaspoon sugar
1 teaspoon vinegar
¾ cup red table wine

Refrigerate the bird for 3 days. Sprinkle with salt and juniper. Let stand for 1 hour.
Brown in half of the drippings on all sides. Divide into serving portions. Place in a saucepan, add ½ cup water. Cover and simmer for 1 hour.

Add the cabbage, onions, and another ½ cup water. Cover and simmer ½ hour. Remove the meat to a warmed platter.

Mix the flour with the rest of the drippings, dilute with 1 tablespoon liquid from the saucepan. Add to the cabbage. Add sugar and vinegar, bring to a boil. Add wine before serving.

Serve with potatoes.

Serves 4–5.

VEAL FRICASSEE
Potrawka cielęca

1½ pounds shoulder veal	*3 tablespoons instant flour*
2 carrots	*2 tablespoons soft butter*
1 parsley root	*1 egg yolk*
2 celery stalks	*1 tablespoon cold water*
1 onion	*1 tablespoon chopped green*
Salt	*parsley*

Place the meat in salted, boiling water. Simmer for 1 hour. Add the vegetables and salt, simmer another ½ hour. Slice the meat and the vegetables.

Mix the flour with butter and few tablespoons hot broth. Add to a saucepan with 2 cups broth, bring to a boil. Add the egg yolk mixed with 1 tablespoon cold water. Add the meat and the vegetables; heat but do not boil. Sprinkle with parsley before serving.

Serve with noodles, rice, or groats and Brussels sprouts or cauliflower.

Serves 5.

VEAL FRICASSEE WITH DILL
Potrawka cielęca z koprem

1½ pounds shoulder veal
Salt
1 cup Dill Sauce*

Place the meat in salted, boiling water. Simmer for 1½ hours.

Slice, place in a dish. Pour Dill Sauce* over the meat.
Serve with rice, or noodles and carrots, cauliflower or savoy cabbage.
Serves 4.

VEAL FRICASSEE WITH APPLES
Potrawka cielęca z jabłkami

1½ pounds shoulder veal
Salt
3 cooking apples, peeled, shredded
1 tablespoon soft butter
2½ tablespoons instant flour
½ cup sour cream

Place the meat in salted, boiling water. Simmer for 1½ hours.
Slice.
Stew the apples with a little water. Add 1 cup veal broth. Add
butter mixed with the flour and few tablespoons hot broth. Bring
to a boil. Remove from the heat, season with salt, add sour cream.
Pour over the meat. Serve with rice and young carrots.
Serves 4.

VEAL CHOP SAUTÉ
Kotlety cielęce z kostką

2 pounds veal chops   *1½ tablespoons shortening*
Salt   *1 tablespoon butter*
2 tablespoons flour

Separate the meat half the length of the bone. Pound well. Sprinkle
the chops with salt and flour.
Heat the shortening. Fry the chops on both sides till golden. Reduce
heat. Put a piece of butter on each chop. Fry 5 more minutes.
Place the chops on a warmed dish. Sprinkle with pan drippings
mixed with few tablespoons water.
Serve with potatoes and salad.
Serves 4–5.

VEAL STEAK
Stek cielęcy

1½ pounds white veal   *1½ tablespoons shortening*
Salt   *1 tablespoon butter*
2 tablespoons flour

Pound the meat well and form small steaks. Sprinkle with salt and flour.
Heat the shortening. Fry the steaks on both sides till golden. Reduce heat. Put a piece of butter on each steak. Fry 5 more minutes.
Place on a warmed dish. Sprinkle with pan drippings. Serve with potatoes, cauliflower, Brussels sprouts, or spinach and a salad. Serves 4.

VIENNA SCHNITZELS
Sznycel po wiedeńsku

1 (½ inch thick) slice veal from the round
Salt
3 tablespoons flour
1 egg, beaten
¾ cup bread crumbs
2 tablespoons shortening
2 tablespoons butter
4 eggs, fried in butter sunny side up
1 teaspoon chopped green onion
4 slices lemon

Trim the edges and remove the bone from the meat. Pound well. Form 4 cutlets. Sprinkle with salt and flour. Dip in the egg, roll in bread crumbs, and press them with a hand to the surface.
Heat the shortening in a skillet. Fry the cutlets on high heat on both sides till golden. Reduce the heat. Put on each ½ tablespoon butter. Cook 4 more minutes.

Transfer the schnitzels to a warmed dish. Place over each an egg sprinkled with green onions. Garnish with lemon.
Serve with mashed potatoes, peas and carrots.
Serves 4.

POZARSKI CUTLETS
Kotlety pożarskie

3 slices white bread
½ cup milk
1 pound ground veal
2 tablespoons butter, melted
2 egg whites, beaten until
  stiff

1 teaspoon dill leaves
Salt
3 tablespoons flour
1 egg
¼ cup bread crumbs
1 tablespoon shortening

Soak bread in milk. Mix with veal. Add half of the butter, egg whites, dill, and salt. Mix very well.
Form 8 cutlets, sprinkle with flour, dip in the egg, roll in bread crumbs. Fry in hot shortening on both sides on moderate heat till golden. Reduce the heat. Sprinkle each one with the rest of the butter. Fry for 10 more minutes.
Serve with mashed potatoes, cauliflower, carrots, or asparagus.
Serves 4.

VEAL CHOPS WITH TOMATOES
Kotlety cielęce z pomidorami

1½ pounds veal chops
Salt
4 ounces grated cheese
3 tablespoons milk
1 egg
½ cup bread crumbs
2 tablespoons shortening
2 cups cooked elbow macaroni
1 tablespoon butter
1 cup Tomato Sauce*
1 tablespoon chopped green parsley

Separate the meat half the length of the bone. Pound well. Sprinkle with salt.

Mix the cheese with milk and egg. Season with salt. Dip the chops in the mixture, roll in the bread crumbs.

Heat the shortening in a large skillet. Fry the chops on both sides till golden. Reduce heat. Fry 5 more minutes.

Mix the macaroni with butter. Place in a dish. Arrange the chops on it, pour the sauce over. Sprinkle with parsley.
Serves 3.

VEAL CHOPS WITH WINE
Kotlety cielęce z winem

1 medium onion, chopped
1½ tablespoons shortening
4 loin veal chops, well trimmed
Salt
1 tablespoon flour
1 (8-ounce) can tomato sauce
1 bouillon cube
½ cup boiling water
½ cup sour cream
2 tablespoons white table wine
1 tablespoon chopped green parsley

Fry the onions in 1 teaspoon shortening till golden.

Sprinkle the chops with salt and flour. Add the rest of the shortening and the chops to the onions. Brown on both sides.

Stir in the tomato sauce and bouillon cube dissolved in ½ cup boiling water. Simmer covered, about ½ hour. Arrange the chops on warmed serving platter.

Stir sour cream and wine into the gravy. Heat, but do not boil, then pour over the meat. Sprinkle with parsley.
Serves 4.

VEAL WITH PAPRIKA
Paprykarz cielęcy

1½-pound veal breast	*1 onion, diced*
or shoulder	*Dash garlic powder*
Salt	*1 cup water*
2½ tablespoons flour	*½ teaspoon paprika*
1½ tablespoons shortening	*½ cup sour cream*

Cut the meat into small pieces, counting 6 per person. Sprinkle with salt, roll in flour. Fry in hot shortening on both sides until golden.

Add the onions, garlic, and 1 cup water. Simmer 1 hour. Add the leftover flour, season with salt and paprika. Bring to a boil. Remove from the heat.

Add sour cream before serving. Serve with noodles, rice, or groats and vegetables.

Serves 4.

VEAL WITH VEGETABLES
Zraziki cielęce z jarzynami

1½ pounds veal, sliced	*1 parsley root, sliced*
Salt	*1 celery stalk, sliced*
1¾ tablespoons flour	*1 cup water*
1½ tablespoons shortening	*½ cup sour cream*
1 onion, sliced	*1 tablespoon dill leaves*
2 carrots, sliced	

Pound veal slices well. Sprinkle with salt and flour. Fry in hot shortening until golden.

Add the vegetables and 1 cup water. Simmer for 1 hour. Season with salt, add the leftover flour. Bring to a boil. Remove from the heat.

Add sour cream. Sprinkle with dill before serving.

Serve with boiled potatoes, groats, or noodles.

Serves 4.

VEAL WITH MUSHROOMS
Zrazy cielęce z pieczarkami

1½ pounds shoulder veal
Salt
1¾ tablespoons flour
1½ tablespoons bacon drippings
¼ pound mushrooms, sliced
1 cup water
1 tablespoon cornstarch
1 tablespoon cold water
½ cup red table wine
4 pieces toast
1 tablespoon chopped green parsley

Cut the veal into 4 slices. Pound well. Sprinkle with salt and flour. Fry in hot drippings on both sides till golden. Add the mushrooms and 1 cup water. Bring to a boil. Simmer for 30 minutes. Remove the meat. Add the cornstarch mixed with 1 tablespoon cold water; add the wine. Bring to a boil.
Place the toast on a warmed serving platter. Place a slice of meat on each piece of toast. Pour the mushroom sauce over the meat. Sprinkle with parsley.
Serve with peas and tomatoes.
Serves 4.

VEAL WITH HAM
Zraziki cielęce z szynką

1½ pounds shoulder veal
Salt and pepper
6 slices ham
1½ tablespoons bacon drippings

Cut the veal into 6 slices. Pound well. Sprinkle with salt and pepper. Place a slice of ham on each slice of veal. Roll ham inside. Seal with wooden toothpicks.

Fry in hot fat on both sides until golden. Sprinkle with boiling water. Cover and simmer for ½ hour.
Serve with potatoes or rice and lettuce.
Serves 6.

VEAL GOULASH
Gulasz cielęcy

1½ pounds shoulder veal	*1 cup water*
Salt and pepper	*1 cup tomato purée, canned*
2½ tablespoons flour	*½ teaspoon paprika*
1½ tablespoons bacon	*Dumplings**
drippings	*½ cup sour cream*
1 onion, chopped	*1 tablespoon dill leaves*

Cut the meat into 8 slices. Pound well. Sprinkle with salt, pepper, and flour. Brown in hot drippings. Add the onions, fry few more minutes. Add 1 cup water, cover and simmer for ½ hour. Add tomato purée, season with salt and paprika. Bring to a boil. Remove the meat to a warmed serving platter.
Add the Dumplings* to the gravy. Mix with sour cream. Pour over the meat. Sprinkle with dill.
Serve with a salad.
Serves 4.

VEAL POT ROAST
Pieczeń cielęca duszona

1½-pound veal roast	*1 cup water*
Salt	*1 onion, sliced*
⅛ teaspoon garlic powder	*A few green parsley sprigs*
1¾ tablespoons flour	
1½ tablespoons bacon	
drippings	

Sprinkle the roast with salt, garlic, and flour. Fry in hot fat on all sides till golden. Place in a kettle. Add 1 cup water, pan drippings, and the onions. Simmer until tender, about 1½ hours, turning 3 times.

Take the roast out, slice with a sharp knife. Arrange on a warmed platter. Season the gravy with salt. Pour over the meat. Garnish with parsley.

Serve with potatoes and vegetables.

Serves 4.

ROAST VEAL
Pieczeń cielęca

6-pound veal roast	*¼ teaspoon garlic powder*
Salt	*3 tablespoons boiling water*
6 tablespoons bacon	
drippings	

Sprinkle the roast with salt. Brown on all sides in hot fat. Place in a roasting pan, pour the drippings over. Sprinkle with water. Bake in moderate 350° F. oven for 2½ hours, basting often. After the last basting sprinkle with garlic.

Place the roast on a cutting board. Slice. Arrange on a warmed platter. Pour the gravy mixed with 3 tablespoons boiling water over the meat.

Serve with potatoes and green vegetables.

Serves 12.

ROAST VEAL IN BÉCHAMEL
Pieczeń cielęca w sosie beszamelowym

1½-pound veal roast, sliced	*1 tablespoon butter, melted*
1½ cups Béchamel Sauce*	*Macaroni*
2 tablespoons grated cheese	

Place the meat in a buttered baking dish. Pour the sauce over. Sprinkle with cheese and butter. Bake in a hot 450° F. oven for 20 minutes until golden.

Serve with macaroni and salad.

Serves 4.

VEAL BALLS WITH DILL
Klopsiki cielęce z koperkiem

2 slices white bread, soaked in milk and squeezed
½ onion, chopped very finely
1 egg
1 pound ground veal
Salt and pepper
2¾ tablespoons flour
1½ tablespoons shortening
1 bouillon cube dissolved in 1 cup water
½ cup sour cream
1 tablespoon dill leaves

Mix the bread with the onions, egg, and meat very well. Season with salt and pepper. Form small balls, roll in the flour. Brown in the hot shortening on all sides.

Place the veal balls in a saucepan. Pour over the cube bouillon, cover and simmer for 20 minutes. Remove to a warmed serving platter.

Add the leftover flour to the gravy, bring to a boil. Remove from the heat. Season with salt, add sour cream and dill. Pour over meat.

Serve with rice or mashed potatoes and carrots.
Serves 4.

MEATBALLS WITH MUSHROOM SAUCE
Klopsiki w grzybowym sosie

Prepare meatballs as for Veal Balls with Dill* from veal, beef, or pork
½ cup water
1½ cups Mushroom Sauce*

Place the browned meatballs in a saucepan, add ½ cup water. Cover and simmer for 15 minutes.

Add the Mushroom Sauce*. Simmer another 5 minutes.
Serves 4.

VEAL BALLS STUFFED WITH MUSHROOMS
Klopsiki cielęce z grzybami

4 slices white bread, soaked in milk and squeezed
1 egg
1 pound ground veal
Salt and pepper
¼ pound mushrooms, finely chopped
1 onion, finely chopped
1 tablespoon butter
2¾ tablespoons instant flour
1½ tablespoons bacon drippings
½ cup water
½ cup sour cream
1 teaspoon dill leaves
1 teaspoon chopped green parsley

Mix half of the bread with the egg and the meat. Season and mix very well. Form 8 steaks.

Simmer the mushrooms with the onions and the butter, covered, for 10 minutes. Strain. Save the liquid.

Mix the mushrooms with the rest of the bread well. Season with salt and pepper. Spoon the stuffing on the steaks. Fold each steak. Seal the edges. Shape into balls. Roll in flour. Brown in hot drippings on all sides.

Place the veal balls in a saucepan, add the mushroom broth mixed with ½ cup water. Cover and simmer for 20 minutes. Remove the meat to a warmed serving platter.

Add the leftover flour to the gravy, bring to a boil. Remove from the heat. Season with salt, add sour cream. Pour over the meatballs. Sprinkle with dill and parsley.

Serve with potatoes, groats, or noodles and tomato salad.

This is a gourmet dish.

Serves 4.

WHITE SAUSAGE BAKED
Kiełbasa biała pieczona

1½ pounds white sausage
1 cup water
2 tablespoons bacon drippings, melted
2 onions, sliced

Place the sausage in a roasting pan. Pour over 1 cup water and the drippings. Bake in a moderate 350° F. oven for ½ hour. Add the onions, prick the sausage in a few places. Bake for another ½ hour. Cut the sausage into 4 pieces. Pour the onions over. Serve with potatoes and cabbage.
Serves 4.

POLISH SAUSAGE WITH SAVOY CABBAGE
Kiełbasa z kapustą włoską

1 small head (2 pounds) savoy cabbage, coarsely sliced
1 teaspoon caraway seeds
1 large onion, sliced
2 tablespoons bacon drippings
10 ounces Polish sausage, sliced
2½ tablespoons instant flour
Salt to taste
½ teaspoon sugar
1 tablespoon lemon juice

Place the cabbage in a saucepan with a small amount of boiling water. Bring to a boil. Add caraway seeds, cook for a few minutes. Cover and simmer for 15 minutes.
Fry the onions in half of the drippings till golden. Add the rest of the drippings and the sausage, fry for a few more minutes. Add the sausage, leaving drippings in the pan, to the cabbage, simmer for 10 more minutes.

Add the flour to the drippings. Fry for a few minutes. Dilute with some liquid from the cabbage; add to the cabbage. Bring to a boil.
Add salt, sugar, and lemon juice.
Serve with boiled potatoes.
Serves 3.

SAUSAGE IN TOMATO SAUCE
Kiełbasa w sosie pomidorowym

*1½ cups Tomato Sauce**
1 pound sausage, skinned and sliced

Heat the sauce, add the sausage, simmer for 5 minutes.
Serve with boiled potatoes or rice.
Serves 3.

PORK CHOP SAUTÉ
Kotlety schabowe sauté

1½ pounds pork loin chops
Salt
1¾ tablespoons flour
1½ tablespoons bacon drippings
¾ tablespoon butter

Separate the meat half the length of the bones. Pound well. Cut the edges in few places. Sprinkle with salt and flour. Fry in hot drippings on both sides until golden. Reduce the heat. Place some butter on each chop. Fry 10 more minutes. Place on a warmed platter, pour the drippings over the chops.
Serve with mashed potatoes and lettuce.
Serves 4.

PORK STEAKS
Stek wieprzowy

1½ pounds pork loin, boneless, sliced
Salt and pepper
1¾ tablespoons flour
1½ tablespoons bacon drippings
¾ tablespoon butter
A few green parsley sprigs

Sprinkle the meat with salt, pepper, and flour. Fry in hot drippings on both sides till golden. Reduce the heat. Place some butter on each steak, fry 5 more minutes.

Place on a warmed platter. Pour the drippings over the meat, garnish with parsley. Serve with potatoes and salad.

Serves 4.

PORK CUTLETS
Kotlety schabowe panierowane

1½ pounds pork loin, sliced
Salt
2½ tablespoons flour
1 egg
½ cup bread crumbs
2½ tablespoons bacon drippings

Trim the edges and pound the meat well. Sprinkle with salt and roll in flour. Dip in the egg, roll in bread crumbs, and press them to the surface.

Fry in hot drippings on both sides till golden. Place in a moderate 350° F. oven for 20 minutes.

Serve with potatoes and sauerkraut.

Serves 4.

GROUND PORK CUTLETS
Kotlety wieprzowe mielone

1 onion, diced
2 tablespoons bacon drippings
2 slices white bread, soaked in milk
1 egg
1 pound ground pork
Salt and pepper
¼ cup bread crumbs

Fry the onions in 1 teaspoon drippings. Add the bread and the egg. Mix well. Add to the pork, season with salt and pepper, mix very well. Form 8 cutlets. Roll in bread crumbs.
Fry on medium heat in remaining drippings on both sides till golden. Place in a medium 350° F. oven for 20 minutes.
Serve with potatoes and green vegetables.
Serves 4.

PORK GOULASH
Gulasz wieprzowy

1½ pounds pork, cut up
Salt
1¾ tablespoons instant flour
1½ tablespoons bacon drippings
1 onion, sliced
1 cup water
½ bay leaf
4 peppercorns

Sprinkle the meat with salt and flour. Fry in hot drippings till golden. Add the onions, fry some more. Add 1 cup water, the bay leaf, and the peppercorns. Cover and simmer 1 hour. Add the leftover flour, bring to boil.
Serve with groats, potatoes, or macaroni and salad.
Serves 4.

PORK AND SAUERKRAUT
Wieprzowina z kapustą

2 cups sauerkraut
1½ pounds pork shoulder, cut up
Salt
2½ tablespoons flour
1½ tablespoons bacon drippings
1 onion, sliced
Dash garlic powder
½ teaspoon paprika

Wash sauerkraut and squeeze. Cook in small amount of water for 1 hour.
Sprinkle the meat with salt and flour. Fry in hot drippings until golden. Add the onions, fry some more. Add to the sauerkraut. Simmer for ½ hour. Add the leftover flour, bring to a boil. Season with garlic and paprika.
Serve with rye bread or potatoes.
Serves 4.

PORK WITH SOUR CREAM
Zrazy wieprzowe ze śmietaną

1½ pounds pork shoulder or ham, sliced
Salt
2½ tablespoons flour
1½ tablespoons bacon drippings
½ cup water
2 tablespoons prepared mustard
½ cup sour cream
½ teaspoon chopped green parsley

Sprinkle the meat with salt and flour. Fry in hot drippings till golden. Add ½ cup water, cover and simmer for ½ hour.
Add the leftover flour, and the mustard, bring to a boil. Remove from the heat. Season with salt. Add sour cream.
Sprinkle with green parsley before serving. Serve with potatoes or macaroni and salad.
Serves 4.

PORK WITH TOMATOES
Wieprzowina z pomidorami

Prepare as for Pork with Sour Cream*, add tomato paste instead of the mustard.
Serves 4.

PORK RIBS WITH ONIONS
Żeberka wieprzowe z cebulą

1½ pounds pork ribs	*2 onions, sliced*
Salt	*1 tablespoon caraway seeds*
1 tablespoon flour	*½ cup water*
1 tablespoon bacon drippings	

Sprinkle the ribs with salt and flour. Fry in hot drippings till golden. Add the onions, fry a few more minutes. Add caraway seeds, ½ cup water, cover and simmer for 1 hour.
Divide the ribs. Place on a warmed platter, pour the gravy over the ribs. Serve with potatoes and cabbage.
Serves 3.

HAM POT ROAST
Szynka duszona

1½ pounds fresh ham	*3 tablespoons water*
Salt	*2 onions, sliced*
1 tablespoon flour	*1 tablespoon caraway seeds*
1¾ tablespoons bacon drippings	

Sprinkle the ham with salt and flour. Brown in hot drippings.

Transfer to a saucepan, add 3 tablespoons water, cover and simmer for ½ hour.

Fry the onions in the drippings. Add to the ham, add the caraway seeds. Simmer 1 hour.

Slice the meat and place on a warmed platter. Pour the gravy over the ham. Serve with potatoes and red cabbage.

Serves 4.

PORK LOIN WITH APPLES
Schab z jabłkami

1½ pounds pork loin, boneless
Salt
1¾ tablespoons flour
1 tablespoon bacon drippings
1 tablespoon caraway seeds
3 tablespoons water
1 large onion, sliced
4 cooking apples, peeled, cored

Sprinkle the meat with salt and flour. Brown in hot drippings. Place in a kettle, pour the drippings over, sprinkle with caraway seeds. Add 3 tablespoons water, cover and simmer for 1 hour. Add the onions and the apples, simmer ½ hour more.

Remove the meat, slice, place on a warmed platter. Rub the sauce through a sieve, add the leftover flour, bring to a boil. Pour over the meat.

Serve with potatoes, cabbage, and dill pickles.

Serves 4.

PORK ROAST WITH POTATOES
Schab pieczony z kartoflami

1½ pounds boneless pork
Salt
1 tablespoon flour
1¾ tablespoons bacon drippings
2 onions, sliced
4 tablespoons water
1 tablespoon caraway seeds
12 small potatoes, peeled

Sprinkle the loin with salt and flour. Brown in hot drippings. Place in a roasting pan, pour the drippings over. Add the onions and 4 tablespoons water, sprinkle with caraway seeds. Put in a moderate 350° F. oven for 1 hour. Add the potatoes to the pan, sprinkle with salt, baste with the gravy. Return to the oven for another hour. Baste often.
Serve with boiled cabbage, stewed sauerkraut, or red cabbage salad. Serves 4.

PORK LOIN WITH PRUNES
Schab z suszonymi śliwkami

1½ pounds boneless pork loin
Salt
1 tablespoon flour
1½ tablespoons bacon drippings
4 tablespoons boiling water
6 ounces pitted prunes

Sprinkle the loin with salt and flour. Brown in hot drippings. Place in a roasting pan, pour drippings mixed with 4 tablespoons boiling water over the meat. Bake in a moderate 350° F. oven for 1 hour. Add the prunes. Bake another hour basting often. Slice the loin and place on a warmed platter. Garnish with prunes, pour the gravy over.
Serve with potatoes and red cabbage.
Serves 4.

HAMBURGERS POLISH STYLE
Kotlety siekane

1 onion, chopped
2 tablespoons bacon drippings
3 slices white bread
½ cup milk
1 egg

1 pound ground beef chuck
½ pound ground pork
Salt and pepper
⅓ cup bread crumbs

Fry the onions in 1 teaspoon drippings till golden. Soak the bread in milk. Combine the onions, bread, milk, egg, beef, and pork. Season and mix very well.
Form 8 cutlets, roll in bread crumbs. Brown in remaining hot drippings. Place in a moderate 350° F. oven for 20 minutes.
Serve with mashed potatoes, peas and carrots.
Serves 8.

MEAT LOAF
Klops

3 slices white bread
½ cup milk
1 onion, chopped
2 tablespoons bacon
    drippings
1 egg

1 pound ground beef chuck
1 pound ground pork
    shoulder
Salt and pepper
⅓ cup bread crumbs
3 tablespoons water

Soak the bread in milk. Fry the onions in 1 teaspoon drippings till golden. Mix the bread with the onions and the egg. Add the meat, season, and mix very well.
Form a long loaf. Roll in bread crumbs. Place in a roasting pan with melted drippings. Bake in a hot 450° F. oven for 45 minutes basting often.
Cut into thick slices. Place on a warmed platter. Pour over the drippings mixed with 3 tablespoons water.
Serve with boiled potatoes and cauliflower.
Serves 8.

MEAT LOAF WITH EGGS
Klops z jajami

2 *slices white bread*
⅓ *cup milk*
1 *onion, chopped*
2 *tablespoons bacon drippings*
1 *egg, raw*
1 *pound ground chuck*
½ *pound ground pork*
Salt and pepper
2 *hard-boiled eggs, quartered*
½ *cup sour cream*
2½ *tablespoons instant flour*
1 *teaspoon chopped green parsley*

Soak the bread in milk. Fry the onions in 1 teaspoon drippings till golden. Mix the bread with onions and egg. Add the meat, season, and mix very well.

Form a rectangle. Arrange the eggs in a row on one side. Fold forming a loaf, seal the edges. Place in a roasting pan with melted drippings. Bake in a hot 450° F. oven for 45 minutes basting often.

Mix sour cream with flour, add salt. Pour over the meat loaf. Put under the broiler for a few minutes or until golden. Sprinkle with parsley before serving.

Serve with potatoes or macaroni and salad.

Serves 6.

BOILED BEEF
Sztuka mięsa

1½ pounds beef chuck or shank
2 onions, quartered, browned
2 carrots
1 parsley root
2 celery stalks
⅛ head savoy cabbage
3 peppercorns
½ bay leaf
Salt to taste
Tomato*, Onion*, Horseradish*, or Dill Sauce*

Place the meat in a kettle with boiling water. Cover and simmer
for 1½ hours.
Add the vegetables, peppercorns, bay leaf, and salt. Simmer another hour.
Serve with Tomato*, Onion*, Horseradish*, or Dill Sauce* and
boiled potatoes.
Serves 4.

BOILED BEEF AU GRATIN
Sztuka mięsa zapiekana

2 pounds boiled beef, sliced
1½ cups Béchamel* or Horseradish Sauce*
3 tablespoons grated cheese for the Béchamel
2 tablespoons bread crumbs
2½ tablespoons butter, melted
1 teaspoon chopped green parsley for the Horseradish Sauce*

Place the meat in a baking dish. Pour the sauce over. Sprinkle
the Béchamel with grated cheese. Sprinkle with bread crumbs and
butter.

Bake in a hot 450° F. oven for 15–20 minutes. Sprinkle the Horseradish Sauce* with parsley before serving.
Serve with boiled potatoes and dill pickles.
Serves 6.

BOILED BEEF AND HORSERADISH
Sztuka mięsa z chrzanem

1½ pounds boiled beef, sliced
6 ounces prepared horseradish
1 tablespoon instant flour
1 tablespoon butter
1 cup beef broth
Salt
⅛ teaspoon sugar
3 tablespoons grated cheese

Spread each slice of beef with horseradish and arrange in a buttered baking dish.
Fry the flour in the butter for a few minutes. Add the broth, bring to a boil, pour over the meat. Season with salt and sugar. Sprinkle with cheese. Bake in a hot 450° F. oven for ½ hour.
Serves 4.

BEEF STEAKS POLISH STYLE
Befsztyki po polsku

1½ pounds beef tenderloin, cut into 4 slices
1 tablespoon salad oil
1½ tablespoons shortening
1½ tablespoons butter
Salt and pepper
1 horseradish root, shredded

Spread the steaks with oil, cover and leave for 3 hours. Heat the shortening in a large pan. Fry the steaks on high heat 3 minutes, turn. Add the butter, sprinkle with salt and pepper. Fry another 3 minutes. Sprinkle with horseradish, serve immediately.
Serves 4.

BEEF STEAKS COUNTRY STYLE
Befsztyki gospodarskie

1½ pounds sirloin steak, well trimmed
1¾ tablespoons flour
Salt
2 onions, sliced
2 tablespoons shortening
4 eggs, fried in butter, sunny side up

Cut the sirloin into 4 steaks, pound very well. Sprinkle with flour and salt.
Fry the onions in 1 teaspoon shortening till golden. Heat the rest of the shortening in a large pan. Fry the steaks on high heat for 3 minutes. The steaks should not touch one another. Turn, add the onions, and fry another 3 minutes.
Place an egg on each steak. Serve with potatoes and green beans or Brussels sprouts.
Serves 4.

MINCED STEAKS
Befsztyki mielone

1½ pounds ground round steak
1 egg
4 tablespoons water
Salt and pepper
2½ tablespoons flour
2 onions, sliced
1½ tablespoons shortening
¾ tablespoon butter

Mix the meat with the egg and 4 tablespoons water. Season with salt and pepper. Form 4 steaks, 1 inch thick. Sprinkle with flour. Fry the onions in 1 teaspoon shortening.

Heat the rest of the shortening in a large pan. Fry the steaks on high heat 4 minutes on each side. Place some butter on each steak, cover with onions, reduce heat, fry another 5 minutes. Serve with potatoes and green beans or cauliflower.
Serves 4.

BOEUF STROGANOV
Boeuf Stroganow

1½ pounds sirloin steak, well trimmed
1 onion, sliced
2 tablespoons bacon drippings
1¾ tablespoons flour
1 cup canned tomato purée
Salt and pepper
½ teaspoon paprika
1 cup sour cream
1 teaspoon chopped green parsley

Cut the meat into long strips ¼ inch thick and ¼ inch wide.
Fry the onions in 1 teaspoon bacon drippings till golden.
Heat the rest of the drippings in a large pan. Fry the meat in 2–3 parts, cooking each part 2 minutes on high heat, stirring constantly. Sprinkle with the flour during frying.
Place the onions in a saucepan, add the meat and the tomato purée. Sprinkle with salt, pepper, and paprika, bring to a boil. Add sour cream, heat, but do not boil.
Sprinkle with parsley before serving. Serve with potatoes and vegetables.
Serves 4.

BEEF SHASHLIK
Szaszłyk wołowy

1½ pounds sirloin or round steak, well trimmed
1 onion, chopped
Salt and pepper
1 tablespoon vinegar
1 tablespoon flour
2½ tablespoons bacon drippings
2 tablespoons chopped green onions

Cut the meat into 30 pieces. Pound it into small disks. Place the meat in a bowl, sprinkle with onions, salt, pepper, and vinegar. Cover and let stand 3 hours at room temperature.

Thread the meat on 4 skewers. Sprinkle with flour. Heat the drippings, fry the shashliks on high heat on all sides for a few minutes. Sprinkle with green onions. Serve immediately with sliced tomatoes and French fries.

Serves 4.

BEEF GOULASH
Gulasz wołowy

1½ pounds round steak, cut up into 30 pieces
Salt
2½ tablespoons flour
2 tablespoons bacon drippings
¼ cup water
2 onions, sliced
⅓ cup canned tomato purée
½ teaspoon paprika

Sprinkle the meat with salt and flour. Brown in hot drippings, transfer to a saucepan, add ¼ cup water.

Fry the onions in the drippings till golden. Add to the meat, cover and simmer for 1 hour.

Add the tomato purée and the paprika to the frying pan with the

drippings. Fry for 5 minutes, stirring. Add to the meat, simmer together a few more minutes.
Serve with noodles, macaroni, or potatoes and salad.
Serves 4.

BEEF ROLLS WITH MUSTARD
Zrazy zawijane z musztardą

1½ pounds flank steak
2 tablespoons prepared mustard
2 onions, chopped
6 strips bacon, finely diced
Salt and pepper
3 tablespoons bread crumbs
2½ tablespoons flour
1½ tablespoons bacon drippings
½ cup water

Cut each flank steak into 3 strips widthwise. Pound well. Spread each piece with mustard, sprinkle with the onions, bacon, salt, pepper, and bread crumbs. Roll and fasten with a toothpick. Sprinkle with flour.
Brown in the drippings, transfer to a baking dish, add ½ cup water. Cover and bake in moderate 350° F. oven for 1½ hours.
Serve with groats or potatoes and dill pickles.
Serves 4.

BEEF ROLLS WITH DILL PICKLES
Zrazy zawijane z ogórkiem

1½ pounds flank steak
6 strips bacon, sliced
3 dill pickles, peeled, cut out lengthwise into sticks
Salt and pepper
2½ tablespoons flour
1½ tablespoons bacon drippings
½ cup water
½ cup sour cream

Cut each flank steak into 3 strips widthwise. Pound well. Arrange the bacon and the pickles on each piece. Roll and fasten with toothpicks. Sprinkle with salt, pepper, and flour.

Brown in the hot drippings. Transfer to a baking dish, add ½ cup water, cover. Bake in a moderate 350° F. oven for 1½ hours. Remove to a warmed platter.

Add the leftover flour to the gravy, bring to a boil. Remove from the heat, add sour cream. Pour over the meat.

Serve with rice or groats and cauliflower.

Serves 4.

BEEF ROLLS WARSAW STYLE
Zrazy zawijane po warszawsku

1½ pounds flank steak
6 strips bacon, cut up coarsely
1 onion, chopped
½ cup bread crumbs
Salt and pepper
2½ tablespoons flour
½ cup water

Cut each flank steak into 3 strips widthwise. Pound well.

Fry the bacon till golden, remove from the drippings. Mix the bacon, onions, and bread crumbs. Add 2 tablespoons bacon drippings and as much water as needed to get a sour cream consistency. Season with salt and pepper.

Spread the stuffing on each strip of meat. Roll and fasten with toothpicks. Sprinkle with flour.

Brown in hot drippings, transfer to a baking dish. Add ½ cup water, cover and bake in moderate 350° F. oven for 1½ hours.

Serve with groats, noodles, or rice and salad.

Serves 4.

BEEF WITH SOUR CREAM
Zrazy wołowe ze śmietaną

1½ pounds beef brisket, sliced
Salt
1¾ tablespoons flour
1½ tablespoons bacon drippings
½ cup water
2 onions, sliced
½ cup sour cream
1 teaspoon chopped green parsley

Sprinkle the meat with salt and flour. Brown in hot drippings. Transfer to a saucepan, add ½ cup water.
Fry the onions in the drippings till golden, add to the meat. Simmer for 1½ hours. Add the leftover flour, bring to a boil. Remove from the heat, season with salt. Add sour cream.
Sprinkle with parsley before serving. Serve with groats or rice and salad.
Serves 4.

BEEF WITH VEGETABLES
Zrazy wołowe z jarzynami

1 pound beef brisket, sliced
1¾ tablespoons flour
1½ tablespoons bacon drippings
½ cup water
Salt
2 onions, diced
3 carrots, sliced
1 parsley root, diced
2 celery stalks, diced
½ cup sour cream
1 tablespoon dill leaves or chopped green parsley

Sprinkle the meat with the flour. Brown in hot drippings, add ½ cup water, cover and simmer for 1 hour. Add salt.

Add the vegetables, simmer another ½ hour. Add the leftover flour, bring to a boil. Remove from the heat, season with salt, add sour cream and dill or parsley.

Serve with groats, rice, or noodles.

Serves 3.

BEEF WITH MUSHROOMS
Zrazy wołowe z grzybami

1½ pounds beef brisket, sliced	2 tablespoons shortening
Salt	½ cup water
1¾ tablespoons flour	2 onions, sliced
	6 ounces mushrooms, sliced

Pound the meat well. Sprinkle with salt and flour. Brown in hot shortening. Transfer to a saucepan, add ½ cup water.

Fry the onions in the drippings. Add to the meat. Simmer for 1 hour. Add the mushrooms, simmer another 15 minutes. Add the leftover flour, bring to a boil, season with salt.

Serve with groats, macaroni, or potatoes and salad.

Serves 4.

BEEF À LA NELSON
Zrazy po nelsońsku

½ ounce dried mushrooms or 4 ounces fresh ones, sliced
½ cup water
6 medium potatoes, thickly sliced
1½ pounds round steak, well trimmed
Salt
1¾ tablespoons flour
1½ tablespoons bacon drippings
2 onions, sliced
Pepper
½ cup sour cream

Stew the dried mushrooms in ½ cup water for 1 hour or fresh mushrooms for 10 minutes.

Pour boiling water over the potatoes and cook 10 minutes. Drain. Cut the round steak into 8 pieces. Pound very well. Sprinkle with salt and flour, brown in hot fat on both sides. Remove from the pan. Fry the onions in the drippings.

Arrange in layers in a baking dish: potatoes, meat, sliced mushrooms, and onions. Sprinkle each layer with salt and pepper. Top with potatoes.

Mix sour cream with the liquid from the mushrooms and leftover flour. Pour over the potatoes. Cover. Bake in a hot 450° F. oven for 20 minutes.

Serve with lettuce and dill pickles.

Serves 4.

BEEF POT ROAST
Pieczeń wołowa duszona

1½ pounds chuck or rump roast, well trimmed
Salt
1¾ tablespoons flour
2 tablespoons bacon drippings
2 onions, sliced
2 tablespoons water

Pound the roast, sprinkle with salt and flour. Brown in hot drippings, transfer to a baking dish.

Fry the onions in the drippings till golden. Add 2 tablespoons water, pour over the meat. Cover, bake in a moderate 375° F. oven for 2 hours. Add the leftover flour, bake another 10 minutes. Slice meat, place on a warmed platter; pour the sauce over the meat. Serve with boiled potatoes or macaroni and vegetables. Serves 4.

BEEF POT ROAST WITH MUSHROOMS
Pieczeń wołowa duszona z grzybami

Prepare as for Pot Roast*. Add ¼ pound sliced mushrooms after 1½ hours baking.

Serves 4.

POT ROAST MARINATED
Pieczeń wołowa na dziko

1 cup water	Salt
1 bay leaf	1¾ tablespoons flour
1 onion, sliced	2½ tablespoons bacon
5 peppercorns	drippings
½ cup vinegar	1 small dried mushroom
1½ pounds rump roast	½ cup sour cream

Bring to a boil 1 cup water with bay leaf, onions, and peppercorns. Cool, add vinegar. Pour over the roast. Refrigerate for 3 days. Remove the meat, reserving marinade. Sprinkle with salt and flour. Brown in hot drippings on all sides. Transfer to a saucepan. Pour the drippings mixed with 4 tablespoons liquid and the onions from the marinade over the meat. Add the mushrooms. Simmer for 2 hours.

Slice the meat and put on a warmed platter. Add the leftover flour to the gravy, bring to a boil. Remove from the heat. Season with salt, add sour cream. Pour over the meat.

Serves 4.

ROAST BEEF
Rostbef

1 onion, diced	5 peppercorns
1 celery stalk, diced	2 pounds good boneless roast
1 parsley root, diced	Salt
1 small carrot, diced	1 tablespoon flour
1 tablespoon salad oil	1½ tablespoons shortening
1 tablespoon sugar	1 tablespoon butter
½ bay leaf	

Mix the vegetables with the oil and sugar, bay leaf, and peppercorns. Squash them and pour over the meat. Cover and refrigerate for 24 hours.

Remove the vegetables, sprinkle the meat with salt and flour.

Brown in hot shortening on all sides. Bake in a hot 450° F. oven for 15–20 minutes, basting with butter.
Serves 6.

LAMB CHOP SAUTÉ
Kotlety baranie sauté

1½ pounds lamb chops
Salt and pepper
Dash garlic powder
1¾ tablespoons flour
2½ tablespoons bacon drippings

Pound the chops well. Let stand at room temperature for 2 hours. Sprinkle with salt, pepper, and garlic. Roll in the flour. Brown in hot drippings on both sides, no more than 2 chops at a time. Serve with French fries and Vegetable Bouquet*.
Serves 4.

LAMB CHOPS BROILED
Kotlety baranie z rusztu

1½ pounds lamb chops
Salt and pepper
1 tablespoon salad oil

Pound the chops slightly. Sprinkle with salt and pepper. Spread with oil. Broil for 2–3 minutes on each side.
Serve with mashed potatoes and spinach.
Serves 4.

TURKISH SHASHLIK
Szaszłyk turecki

1½ pounds lamb, well trimmed
Salt and pepper
¼ teaspoon garlic powder
1 tablespoon vinegar
3 onions, sliced
6 slices bacon, diced
2 cups cooked rice
½ cup canned tomato purée
3 small tomatoes, sliced
1 tablespoon bacon drippings
2 teaspoons coarsely chopped green parsley

Cut up the lamb into 30 pieces. Sprinkle with salt, pepper, garlic, and vinegar. Mix with half of the onions. Cover and let stand at room temperature for 3 hours.

Fry the rest of the onions with ⅓ of the bacon. Add to the rice; mix with tomato purée. Put in a moderate 325° F. oven for 15 minutes.

Thread the meat alternately with remaining bacon, tomato, and onion slices on 4 skewers. Brown in hot drippings. Sprinkle with green parsley before serving.

Place the shashliks on the rice. Serve with lettuce.
Serves 4.

LAMB STEW
Gulasz barani

1½ pounds lamb
Salt
2½ tablespoons flour
1½ tablespoons bacon drippings
2 onions, sliced
1 cup water
1 cup canned tomato purée
¼ teaspoon paprika
1 teaspoon chopped green parsley

Cut up the meat into 24 pieces. Sprinkle with salt and flour. Brown in hot drippings. Add the onions, reduce the heat, fry 5 more minutes.

Add 1 cup water, cover and simmer for ½ hour. Add the tomato purée and paprika. Simmer another 15 minutes. Add the leftover flour, bring to a boil. Sprinkle with parsley before serving. Serve with boiled potatoes or noodles and salad.

Serves 4.

LAMB AND POTATO CASSEROLE
Baranina duszona z kartoflami

1½ pounds lamb, cut in 8 slices
Salt and pepper
1¾ tablespoons flour
1½ tablespoons bacon drippings
1 onion, sliced
6 potatoes, peeled, sliced
1 bouillon cube
1 teaspoon chopped green parsley

Pound the meat well. Sprinkle with salt, pepper, and flour. Brown meat in hot drippings on both sides. Add the onions, reduce the heat, fry 5 more minutes.

Place in a baking dish alternately: potatoes, meat, and onions. Top with potatoes. Sprinkle with salt and pepper. Pour over 1 bouillon cube dissolved in 1 cup water. Cover and bake in a moderate 350° F. oven for 1 hour. Sprinkle with parsley before serving.

Serves 4.

LAMB RAGOUT
Ragout z baraniny

1½ pounds lamb	1 carrot, coarsely sliced
Salt	1¾ tablespoons instant flour
Dash garlic powder	2 tablespoons cold water
1½ tablespoons bacon	½ teaspoon paprika
drippings	½ cup canned tomato purée
1 onion, sliced	½ cup sour cream
1 celery stalk, sliced	1 teaspoon chopped green
1 parsley root, sliced	parsley

Cut the meat into 24 pieces. Sprinkle with salt and garlic. Brown in hot drippings on all sides. Add the onions, fry 5 more minutes. Add water just to cover it. Simmer for 45 minutes.

Add the vegetables, simmer 20 minutes more. Add the flour mixed with 2 tablespoons cold water. Mix with paprika and tomato purée. Bring to a boil. Remove from the heat. Season with salt, add sour cream.

Place on a serving platter and sprinkle with green parsley. Serve with rice and salad.

Serves 4.

LAMB POT ROAST WITH CABBAGE
Baranina duszona z kapustą

1½ pounds lamb, well trimmed
Salt
¼ teaspoon garlic powder
3 tablespoons instant flour
2 tablespoons bacon drippings
½ cup water
1 small head savoy cabbage, thickly sliced
½ cup water
1 teaspoon caraway seeds
3 tablespoons water
½ teaspoon sugar
1 teaspoon vinegar

Pound the meat, sprinkle with salt, garlic, and some flour. Brown in hot drippings on all sides. Transfer meat to a saucepan, add ½ cup water, cover, and simmer for 1 hour.

Slice the meat. Return the meat to the saucepan, place cabbage between meat slices, add ½ cup water, and caraway seeds. Cover and simmer for 20 minutes.

Fry the leftover flour in the drippings, mix with 3 tablespoons water. Season with salt, sugar, and vinegar. Add to the meat. Bring to a boil. Serve with potatoes.

Serves 4.

LEG OF LAMB WITH SOUR CREAM
Comber barani ze śmietaną

1 large onion, sliced	*½ teaspoon garlic powder*
3 cups boiling water	*Salt*
1 tablespoon salt	*2¾ tablespoons instant flour*
3 bay leaves	*1¾ tablespoons bacon*
5 peppercorns	*drippings*
1 cup vinegar	*½ cup sour cream*
3-pound leg of lamb	

Cook the onions in 3 cups boiling water with salt, bay leaves, and peppercorns for 5 minutes. Cool, add vinegar. Pour over the meat, cover and refrigerate for 3 days. Turn each day.

Sprinkle the meat with garlic, salt, and some flour. Brown on both sides in hot drippings. Place in a moderate 375° F. oven for 1½ hours. Baste with pan drippings and the marinade.

Mix sour cream with leftover flour. Pour over the meat. Place under the broiler until golden.

Slice the lamb, place on a warmed platter. Pour the gravy over the meat.

Serve with potatoes or macaroni, and red beets.

Serves 5.

VENISON
Sarnina

Marinade as for Leg of Lamb with Sour Cream*
3-pound venison roast
6 slices bacon, cut up
Salt
2¾ tablespoons instant flour
2 tablespoons bacon drippings
¾ cup sour cream

Pour the marinade over the meat, cover and refrigerate for 4 days. Turn each day. Remove, rinse. Thread strips of bacon through the meat.

Sprinkle the meat with salt and some flour. Brown and bake as in Leg of Lamb with Sour Cream*.

Serve with baked potatoes, red beets, and lettuce.
Serves 8.

HARE POLISH STYLE
Zając po polsku

2 onions, sliced
1 bay leaf
5 peppercorns
2 cups water
1 cup vinegar
Saddle and thighs of hare
4 ounces bacon, cut up
  in strips

Salt
2 tablespoons bacon
  drippings
½ cup water
2 tablespoons instant flour
2 tablespoons cold water
¾ cup sour cream

Cook the onions, bay leaf, and peppercorns in 2 cups water for 5 minutes. Cool and add the vinegar.

Pour the marinade over the hare. Cover and refrigerate for 4 days. Turn each day.

Rinse the hare, trim, and thread strips of bacon through the meat. Sprinkle with salt.

Place in a roasting pan with melted drippings. Bake in a 375° F. oven for 2 hours. Baste often with the drippings and water, using ½ cup. Cut into serving portions. Place on a warmed platter. Mix the flour with 2 tablespoons cold water. Stir into the drippings. Bring to a boil stirring. Remove from the heat, add sour cream. Pour over the meat.
Serve with potatoes and red beets.
Serves 5.

BRAINS AU GRATIN
Móżdżek zapiekany

1½ pounds brains
4 cups water
Salt
1 tablespoon vinegar
1½ cups Béchamel Sauce*
1 tablespoon lemon juice
3 tablespoons grated cheese
1½ tablespoons butter, melted
2 tablespoons bread crumbs
1 lemon, sliced
A few green parsley sprigs

Clean the brains, place in a saucepan. Pour 4 cups salted water with vinegar over brains. Cook 4 minutes. Remove brains with a colander spoon. Dice coarsely. Add ½ cup Béchamel Sauce*, mix slightly.
Place the brains in a baking dish. Pour the rest of the sauce over the brains. Sprinkle with 1 tablespoon lemon juice, cheese, butter, and bread crumbs. Place in a hot 400° F. oven for 20 minutes. Garnish with lemon slices and parsley. Serve with macaroni and tomato salad.
Serves 4.

BRAINS POLISH STYLE
Móżdżek po polsku

1½ pounds brains
4 cups water
Salt
1 tablespoon vinegar
1 large onion, diced
2 tablespoons butter
2 egg yolks
Pepper
1 tablespoon chopped green parsley

Cook the brains as in Brains au Gratin*.
Fry the onions in the butter till golden. Add to the brains. Mix slightly with egg yolks, season with salt and pepper. Sprinkle with parsley before serving.
Serve with French fries and tomato salad.
Serves 4.

BRAISED LIVER
Wątróbka duszona

1½ pounds liver, sliced
2½ tablespoons instant flour
Salt and pepper
6 slices bacon, diced
½ cup water
½ cup sour cream
1 tablespoon chopped green parsley

Sprinkle the liver with some flour, salt, and pepper.
Fry the bacon till golden, remove to a saucepan. Fry the liver in the drippings.
Add the liver to the bacon, add ½ cup water. Cover and simmer 15 minutes. Stir in the leftover flour, bring to a boil.

Remove from the heat, season with salt and pepper, add sour cream. Sprinkle with parsley before serving.
Serve with potatoes and green beans.
Serves 4.

LIVER IN BREAD CRUMBS
Wątróbka panierowana

1½ pounds liver, sliced	*1½ tablespoons bacon*
2½ tablespoons flour	*drippings*
1 egg	*Salt*
½ cup bread crumbs	*½ tablespoon butter*

Roll the liver in the flour. Dip in the egg, roll in the bread crumbs. Press them to the surface.
Fry in hot drippings on high heat for a few minutes on both sides. Sprinkle with salt, add butter.
Serve immediately with potatoes, carrots, and lettuce.
Serves 4.

CALF'S LIVER SAUTÉ
Wątróbka cielęca smażona

1½ pounds liver, sliced	*1 tablespoon shortening*
Pepper	*1 tablespoon butter*
1¾ tablespoons flour	*Salt*
1 large onion, sliced	

Sprinkle the liver with pepper and flour. Fry the onions in ½ tablespoon shortening. Fry the liver in remaining shortening and butter on high heat for a few minutes on each side. Sprinkle with salt. Cover with the onions. Place in a moderate 350° F. oven for 5 minutes. Serve immediately.
Serve with potatoes, lettuce or sauerkraut salad.
Serves 4.

LIVER AND TOMATOES
Wątróbka z pomidorami

2 onions, sliced
1½ tablespoons shortening
1½ pounds liver, cut up into small pieces
Salt and pepper
½ cup sour cream
1 tablespoon tomato paste

Fry the onions in ½ tablespoon shortening till golden.
Fry the liver in the rest of the shortening on high heat for a few minutes. Sprinkle with salt and pepper, add sour cream mixed with tomato paste. Heat, but do not boil.
Serve with potatoes or noodles and cucumbers.
Serves 4.

CHICKEN LIVER SAUTÉ
Wątróbki kurze smażone

1 large onion, sliced	Salt
1½ tablespoons shortening	¾ tablespoon butter
1 cup chicken livers, sliced	3 tablespoons water
1¾ tablespoons flour	

Fry the onions in ½ tablespoon shortening till golden.
Sprinkle the livers with the flour. Fry in remaining hot shortening on high heat on both sides. Sprinkle with salt, add the onions. Add the butter and 3 tablespoons water. Bring to a boil. Serve immediately.
Serve with mashed potatoes and red cabbage.
Serves 3.

HAM AND EGG NOODLE CASSEROLE
Łazanki zapiekane z szynką

3 cups cooked egg noodles
2 cups finely chopped ham
1 tablespoon bacon drippings
2 tablespoons chopped green onion
½ tablespoon dill leaves
2 tablespoons bread crumbs

Mix the noodles with ham, drippings, onions, and dill. Place in a baking dish. Sprinkle with bread crumbs.
Bake in a hot 400° F. oven for 35 minutes.
Use chopped sausage instead of ham for a change.
Serve with Tomato juice or Tomato Sauce* and salad.
Serves 4.

RISOTTO
Rizotto

1 onion, chopped
1½ tablespoons bacon drippings
6 ounces mushrooms, sliced
2 cups any chopped leftover meat
3 cups rice cooked in bouillon instead of water
Salt and pepper
½ cup sour cream
1 egg yolk
3 tablespoons grated cheese

Sauté the onions in half of the drippings till pale gold. Add the rest of the drippings and the mushrooms. Sauté till pale gold. Add the meat, fry for 5 minutes stirring. Add the rice, mix well, season. Place in a baking dish. Pour sour cream mixed with the egg yolk over the meat-rice mixture. Sprinkle with cheese. Bake in a hot 450° F. oven for 20 minutes.
Serve with green beans and tomato salad.
Serves 5.

STUFFED KOHLRABI
Kalarepa faszerowana

STUFFING

2 cups ground leftover meat
2 slices white bread, soaked in water and squeezed
1 onion, grated
1 egg
Salt and pepper
12 kohlrabies, peeled
½ cup water

SAUCE

1 tablespoon butter
1½ tablespoons instant flour
Dash sugar
1 teaspoon lemon juice
1 tablespoon chopped green parsley

Mix the meat well with bread, onions, and egg. Season with salt and pepper.
Cut the tops of the kohlrabies off. Scoop out the middle. Stuff and cover with the tops. Place in a large skillet. Add ½ cup water. Cover and simmer for ½ hour.
Transfer the kohlrabies to a warmed serving platter.
Mix the butter with the flour, add some hot kohlrabi sauce. Stir into the rest of the sauce. Bring to a boil, add sugar and lemon juice and pour over the kohlrabies. Sprinkle with parsley.
Serve with mashed potatoes.
Serves 4.

STUFFED EGGPLANT
Bakłażany faszerowane

STUFFING

2 cups finely chopped leftover meat
1 cup cooked rice
1 onion, chopped
1 teaspoon dill leaves
1 egg
Salt and pepper

3 small eggplants
1 cup water

SAUCE

1 tablespoon butter
1½ tablespoons instant flour
½ cup bouillon
2 tablespoons tomato paste
Salt
½ teaspoon sugar
1 tablespoon chopped green parsley

Mix the meat with rice, onions, dill, and egg. Season with salt and pepper.
Cut the eggplants lengthwise. Scoop out the seedy section. Stuff. Place in a large baking dish, add 1 cup water. Bake uncovered for ½ hour in hot 450° F. oven.
Mix the butter with the flour. Stir in hot bouillon and tomato paste. Season with salt and sugar. Pour over the eggplants.
Place under a broiler till golden. Sprinkle with parsley before serving.
Excellent late supper dish.
Serves 6.

STUFFED TOMATOES
Pomidory faszerowane

12 small tomatoes (2 pounds)
Prepare stuffing as for Stuffed Eggplant*
½ cup sour cream
Salt
1 tablespoon dill leaves

Cut off the tops of the tomatoes. Scoop out the middle. Stuff. Cover with the tops. Place in a baking dish. Pour over sour cream, sprinkle with salt.
Place in hot 450° F. oven for 15 minutes. Sprinkle with dill before serving.
Serves 4.

EGG, MUSHROOM, CHEESE, AND FLOUR DISHES

EGG, MUSHROOM, CHEESE, AND FLOUR DISHES	POTRAWY Z JAJ, GRZYBÓW, SERA I MĄKI
Eggs Fried with Potatoes	*Jaja smażone z kartoflami*
Eggs, Mushrooms, and Potatoes au Gratin	*Jaja zapiekane z grzybami i kartoflami*
Eggs au Gratin with Tomatoes and Potatoes	*Jaja zapiekane z pomidorami i kartoflami*
Eggs and Macaroni au Gratin	*Jaja zapiekane z makaronem*
Mushroom Pie	*Grzybowy tort*
Mushroom Sauté	*Grzyby smażone*
Braised Mushrooms	*Grzyby duszone*
Mushrooms à la Nelson	*Grzyby po nelsońsku*
Stuffed Mushrooms	*Pieczarki nadziewane*

Mushroom and Noodle Casserole	*Zapiekanka z grzybów z łazankami*
Cheese Dumplings	*Kluski z sera*
Cheese Pancakes	*Racuszki z sera*
Cottage Cheese Casserole	*Zapiekanka z twarogiem*
Pierogi with Cabbage	*Pierożki z kapustą*
Pierogi with Meat	*Pierożki z mięsem*
Pierogi with Cheese	*Pierożki z serem*
Dumplings	*Kluski kładzione*
Buckwheat Groats	*Kasza gryczana*

EGGS FRIED WITH POTATOES
Jaja smażone z kartoflami

4 *large boiled potatoes, sliced*
2 *tablespoons bacon drippings*
4 *eggs*
4 *tablespoons sour cream*
Salt
2 *tablespoons chopped green onions*

Fry the potatoes in the drippings in a large skillet till golden. Add eggs mixed with sour cream. Fry till lightly set. Sprinkle with salt and green onions.
Serves 4.

EGGS, MUSHROOMS, AND POTATOES AU GRATIN
Jaja zapiekane z grzybami i kartoflami

½ *pound mushrooms, sliced*
1 *onion, diced*
1½ *tablespoons butter*
4 *large potatoes, boiled and sliced*
4 *hard-boiled eggs, sliced*
Salt and pepper
⅓ *cup sour cream*
1 *teaspoon instant flour*
¼ *cup bouillon (from a cube)*

Sauté the mushrooms with the onions in the butter till golden. Arrange in a baking dish alternately: potatoes, mushrooms, and eggs, top with potatoes. Sprinkle each layer with salt and pepper. Pour sour cream mixed with flour and bouillon over potatoes. Bake in a hot 450° F. oven for 10 minutes, or until golden. Serve with lettuce or tomato salad.
Serves 4.

EGGS AU GRATIN WITH TOMATOES AND POTATOES
Jaja zapiekane z pomidorami i kartoflami

2 large onions, thickly sliced
1½ tablespoons butter
4 large boiled potatoes, sliced
4 hard-boiled eggs, sliced
4 large tomatoes, thickly sliced
Salt and pepper
½ cup sour cream
1 teaspoon dill leaves
1 teaspoon chopped green parsley

Sauté the onions in the butter till golden.
Arrange in a baking dish alternately: potatoes, eggs, onions, and tomatoes. Top with potatoes. Sprinkle each layer with salt and pepper.
Pour salted sour cream over the top. Bake in a hot 450° F. oven for 10 minutes, or until golden. Sprinkle with dill leaves and chopped green parsley before serving.
Serve with lettuce.
Serves 4.

EGGS AND MACARONI AU GRATIN
Jaja zapiekane z makaronem

2 cups cooked elbow macaroni
4 hard-boiled eggs, coarsely chopped
¾ tablespoon butter, melted
¾ cup sour cream
1 egg yolk
Salt
2 tablespoons grated cheese

Combine the macaroni with eggs and butter. Place in a baking dish. Pour sour cream mixed with egg yolk and some salt over top. Sprinkle with cheese. Put under broiler for few minutes until golden.

Serve with tomato salad.

Serves 2.

MUSHROOM PIE
Grzybowy tort

½ pound mushrooms, sliced	*1 tablespoon instant flour*
½ onion, diced	*Salt and pepper*
2 tablespoons butter	*2 tablespoons grated cheese*
4 eggs	

Sauté the mushrooms with the onions in 1 tablespoon butter till golden.

Beat the eggs till fluffy, add the flour and salt, beat some more.

Heat the remaining butter in two small skillets. Pour half of the eggs into each. Fry on low heat without mixing till set.

Transfer 1 omelet onto a warmed serving platter. Cover with mushrooms. Sprinkle with salt and pepper. Cover with the second omelet. Sprinkle with cheese.

Serve with fried potatoes and tomatoes.

Serves 3.

MUSHROOM SAUTÉ
Grzyby smażone

1 pound mushrooms
2½ tablespoons butter
Salt and pepper

Wash the mushrooms, remove the stems. Fry the heads in hot butter in small portions. Fry on both sides till golden.

Sprinkle with salt and pepper, and serve immediately with steaks, vegetables, or fish.

Serves 4.

BRAISED MUSHROOMS
Grzyby duszone

1 large onion, diced	*Salt and pepper*
1 tablespoon butter	*½ cup sour cream*
1 pound mushrooms, sliced	*1 egg yolk*
3 tablespoons water	*1 tablespoon dill leaves*

Sauté the onions in hot butter. Add the mushrooms and 3 table-spoons water. Cover and simmer 10 minutes. Season with salt and pepper.

Mix sour cream with egg yolk. Combine with the mushrooms. Sprinkle with dill before serving.

Serve with boiled potatoes or rice and green beans.

Serves 3.

MUSHROOMS À LA NELSON
Grzyby po nelsońsku

1 ounce dried mushrooms or ½ pound fresh ones
½ cup milk
6 medium half boiled potatoes, sliced
2 onions, thickly sliced
2 tablespoons butter
Salt and pepper
½ cup sour cream

Wash the dried mushrooms and soak in milk for 1 hour. Bring to boil, simmer also for 1 hour. Cook the fresh mushrooms for 10 minutes in milk.

Arrange half of the potatoes in a baking dish. Add the onions, which have been sautéed in butter, and the mushrooms (reserve milk). Sprinkle with salt and pepper. Top with potatoes. Pour sour cream mixed with the mushroom milk over top.

Bake in hot 450° F. oven for 20 minutes.

Serves 4.

STUFFED MUSHROOMS
Pieczarki nadziewane

20 large mushrooms
1 onion, finely diced
1 tablespoon butter
1 egg
1 tablespoon chopped green parsley
Salt and pepper
2 tablespoons grated cheese
1 tablespoon bread crumbs
2 tablespoons butter, melted

Cut off the mushroom stems and chop finely. Combine with the onions which have been sautéed in butter, egg, parsley, salt, and pepper.
Stuff each mushroom head forming a rounded heap. Sprinkle with cheese and the bread crumbs.
Place the mushrooms in a shallow, buttered baking dish. Sprinkle with butter. Bake in a hot 450° F. oven for 10 minutes or until golden.
Serve with mashed potatoes and salad.
This is a gourmet dish.
Serves 4.

MUSHROOM AND NOODLE CASSEROLE
Zapiekanka z grzybów z łazankami

1 pound mushrooms, sliced
3 tablespoons water
2 onions, sliced
1 tablespoon butter
Salt and pepper

2 cups cooked egg noodles
¾ cup sour cream
1 egg yolk
2 tablespoons grated cheese

Cook the mushrooms with 3 tablespoons water for 10 minutes. Add the onions which have been sautéed in butter. Season and

combine with noodles. Place in a baking dish. Pour sour cream mixed with the egg yolk over the top. Sprinkle with cheese. Put under broiler for a few minutes until golden.
Serve with salad.
Serves 4.

CHEESE DUMPLINGS
Kluski z sera

1 *pound farmer cheese, ground*
    OR
1 *pound dry cottage cheese ground and 1 tablespoon butter*
4 *boiled potatoes, ground*
4 *eggs, separated*
1½ *cups flour*
Salt
2 *tablespoons butter*

Combine the cheese with potatoes and egg yolks.
Beat the egg whites till stiff. Add to the cheese mixture alternately with the flour. Mix slightly.
Drop the dough from a spoon in small portions into a kettle with boiling salted water. Bring to a boil. Cover and cook on low heat for 2 minutes. Remove with a colander spoon to a warmed serving platter. Dot with butter.
Serve with salad.
Serves 4.

CHEESE PANCAKES
Racuszki z sera

3 *eggs, separated*
¾ *tablespoon soft butter*
1 *pound farmer cheese, ground*
    OR
1 *pound dry cottage cheese ground and 1 tablespoon butter*
¼ *cup cornstarch*
Salt
2½ *tablespoons shortening*

Mix the egg yolks with the butter. Combine with the ground cheese.
Beat the egg whites until stiff. Fold into the cheese alternately
with the cornstarch. Sprinkle with salt. Mix slightly.
Fry small pancakes in the shortening on both sides on medium
heat.
Serve with sour cream and cranberries.
Serves 3.

COTTAGE CHEESE CASSEROLE
Zapiekanka z twarogiem

2 cups cooked egg noodles	*3 tablespoons bread crumbs*
1 pound cottage cheese	*1 tablespoon butter, melted*

Combine the noodles with cottage cheese. Place in a baking dish.
Sprinkle with bread crumbs and butter.
Bake in a hot 450° F. oven for 15 minutes.
Serve with tomato salad.
Serves 3.

PIEROGI WITH CABBAGE
Pierożki z kapustą

STUFFING

1½ pounds cabbage, boiled
½ pound dry cottage cheese
1 onion, chopped
1½ tablespoons butter
Salt and pepper

DOUGH

1 egg
3¼ cups flour
Salt
½ cup water

1½ tablespoons butter, melted
1½ tablespoons bread crumbs

Drain the cabbage well. Grind the cabbage with the cheese. Add
the onions which have been sautéed in butter, salt, and pepper.

Mix the egg with the flour, add a dash of salt and as much water as needed to knead a smooth loose dough.

Roll out as thinly as you can. Cut out into 2½–3-inch squares. Put a little of the stuffing on each square. Fold to form a triangle, pinch the edges together.

Cook in a large kettle with boiling salted water on high heat for 5 minutes. Remove with a colander spoon to a warmed serving platter.

Add the bread crumbs to the butter and fry for few minutes on low heat. Pour over the pierogi.

Serves 6.

PIEROGI WITH MEAT
Pierożki z mięsem

STUFFING

2 cups leftover meat pieces
2 slices white bread, soaked in water and squeezed
1 onion, chopped
1 tablespoon bacon drippings
Salt and pepper
Dough as for Pierogi with Cabbage*
3 slices bacon, diced

Grind the meat with bread. Add the onions which have been sautéed in the drippings. Season with salt and pepper.

Prepare the dough, roll, stuff, and boil as in Pierogi with Cabbage*. Fry the bacon, pour with the drippings over pierogi.

Serves 6.

PIEROGI WITH CHEESE
Pierożki z serem

STUFFING

1 pound farmer cheese, ground
  OR
1 pound dry cottage cheese ground and 1 tablespoon butter
1 egg yolk
Salt
Dough as for Pierogi with Cabbage*
1½ tablespoons butter, melted

Combine the cheese with the egg yolk, add some salt.
Prepare the dough, roll, stuff, and boil as in Pierogi with Cabbage*. Pour the melted butter over the pierogi.
Serve with salad.
Serves 6.

DUMPLINGS
Kluski kładzione

3 eggs
1 tablespoon butter, melted
Salt
3¾ cups flour
⅓ teaspoon baking powder
3 slices bacon, diced
6 ounces grated cheese

Beat the eggs, add butter and salt, beat some more.
Add the flour and as much water as needed to stir easily with a spoon. Stir for 5 minutes. Add baking powder.
Drop the dough from a spoon into a kettle with boiling, salted water. Cover and cook 5 minutes. Transfer with a colander spoon to a warmed serving platter.

Fry the bacon till golden, pour with the drippings over the dumplings. Sprinkle with cheese.

Serve with braised meats. Instead of bacon and cheese serve for a change with Tomato* or Mushroom Sauce*.

Serves 6.

BUCKWHEAT GROATS
Kasza gryczana

1 cup buckwheat groats
1 egg
1 tablespoon bacon drippings, melted
1 teaspoon salt
2 cups water

Combine the groats with the egg and the drippings in a saucepan. Add salt and cold water.

Cover and simmer for 15 minutes. Stir, cover, and place in a moderate 350° F. oven for 10 minutes.

Serve with braised meats.

Serves 4.

VEGETABLES

We often hear mothers complain: "I'm so tired of repeating to my children every day—eat your vegetables!—I certainly wish that the stuff could be made more appealing!"

But it can! Just try.

Vegetables served each day the same monotonous way are not tempting to our youngsters or husbands. But with a little thought and a little care the problem disappears quickly.

Think about a vegetable not as a necessary addition to a meal, but as a dish in itself, which needs its own seasoning.

Vegetables have an important part in a Polish dinner. In the times when refrigeration was difficult, and not many fresh greens could be obtained during the winter, especially in small villages, Polish people developed various ways of serving cabbage and sauerkraut.

During my childhood in Warsaw, though we still could not eat lettuce or tomatoes in January—carrots, beets, kohlrabi, peas, and beans were plentiful, and served in many delightful ways. And as soon as the lilacs were in bloom, we had radishes with cottage cheese for breakfast, Vegetable Bouquet* for lunch, young chicken with tiny potatoes and creamed spinach for dinner.

Having all these things year round makes them a bit less attractive. The constant remindings of their dietary values do not help. They will become more desirable if we try to forget how good vegetables are for us, but remember what a delectable meal they can make.

VEGETABLES / JARZYNY

VEGETABLES	JARZYNY
Brussels Sprouts Polonaise	*Brukselka po polsku*
Savoy Cabbage Polonaise	*Kapusta włoska po polsku*
Young Carrots Polonaise	*Karotka*
Green or Yellow String Beans Polonaise	*Fasolka szparagowa po polsku*
Cauliflower Polonaise	*Kalafior po polsku*
Leek Polonaise	*Pory z wody*
Asparagus Polonaise	*Szparagi po polsku*
Vegetable Bouquet	*Bukiet z jarzyn*
Carrots and Peas	*Marchewka z groszkiem*
Dill Pickles	*Kiszenie ogórków*
Red Beets with Horseradish	*Ćwikła*
Red Beets with Apples	*Buraki z jabłkami*
Red Beets with Sour Cream	*Buraki ze śmietaną*
Cabbage with Apples	*Kapusta z jabłkami*
Cabbage with Tomatoes	*Kapusta z pomidorami*
Savoy Cabbage with Caraway	*Kapusta włoska z kminkiem*
Cabbage with Bacon	*Kapusta z boczkiem*
Stewed Sauerkraut	*Kapusta kiszona, duszona*
Stewed Sauerkraut with Mushrooms	*Kapusta kiszona z grzybami*
Red Cabbage with Caraway	*Czerwona kapusta z kminkiem*
Creamed Spinach	*Szpinak*
Potato Pancakes	*Placki kartoflane*
Potato Cutlets	*Kotlety kartoflane*
Potato Dumplings	*Kluski kartoflane*

Green Potato Dumplings	*Kopytka*
Potato Dumplings Country Style	*Pyzy*
Potato Croquettes	*Kartoflane krokiety*
Asparagus au Gratin	*Szparagi zapiekane*
Cauliflower au Gratin	*Kalafior zapiekany*
Potatoes au Gratin	*Kartofle zapiekane*
Vegetable and Macaroni Casserole	*Zapiekanka z jarzyn i makaronu*

BRUSSELS SPROUTS POLONAISE
Brukselka po polsku

1½ *pounds Brussels sprouts*
Salt
1½ *tablespoons butter*
1½ *tablespoons toasted bread crumbs*

Wash and clean the vegetable. Place in a saucepan with a small amount of boiling salted water. Bring to a boil. Cook uncovered for 3 minutes. Cover and cook on low heat for 20 minutes. Drain. Place in a warmed serving dish.
Melt the butter over low heat. Add the bread crumbs, fry for a few minutes until golden, stirring. Pour over the vegetable.
Serves 6.

SAVOY CABBAGE POLONAISE
Kapusta włoska po polsku

1 *small head* (1½ *pounds*) *savoy cabbage, cut into 6 portions*
Salt
1½ *tablespoons butter*
1½ *tablespoons toasted bread crumbs*

Rinse the cabbage and place in a kettle with a small amount of boiling salted water. Bring to a boil. Cook uncovered for 3 minutes. Cover and cook on low heat for 15 minutes. Drain and place in a warmed serving dish.
Prepare the butter and bread crumb mixture as for Brussels Sprouts Polonaise*. Pour over the cabbage.
Serves 6.

YOUNG CARROTS POLONAISE
Karotka

3 bunches (1½ pounds) small, young carrots
Salt
½ teaspoon sugar
1½ tablespoons butter
1½ tablespoons toasted bread crumbs

Scrub the carrots with a brush and rinse well. Cook in a small amount of boiling, salted water with sugar for 10 minutes.
Drain, place in a warmed serving dish. Prepare the butter and bread crumb mixture as for Brussels Sprouts Polonaise*. Pour over the carrots.
Serves 6.

GREEN OR YELLOW STRING BEANS POLONAISE
Fasolka szparagowa po polsku

1½ pounds string beans
Salt
½ teaspoon sugar
1½ tablespoons butter
1½ tablespoons toasted bread crumbs

Cut off the ends, rinse and cook the beans in a small amount of boiling salted water with sugar for 15 minutes.
Drain, place in a warmed serving dish. Prepare the butter and bread crumb mixture as for Brussels Sprouts Polonaise*. Pour over the string beans.
Serves 6.

CAULIFLOWER POLONAISE
Kalafior po polsku

1 cauliflower (3 pounds)	*2 tablespoons butter*
Salt	*2 tablespoons toasted*
½ teaspoon sugar	*bread crumbs*

Soak the cauliflower in salted water for 1 hour.
Place in a kettle, pour boiling water over cauliflower to cover.
Add salt and sugar. Bring to a boil. Cook uncovered for 3 minutes. Cover and cook 25 minutes. Drain.
Place on a warmed serving platter. Prepare the butter and bread crumb mixture as for Brussels Sprouts Polonaise*. Pour over cauliflower.
Serves 6.

LEEK POLONAISE
Pory z wody

1½ pounds leeks
Salt
½ teaspoon sugar
1½ tablespoons butter
1½ tablespoons toasted bread crumbs

Rinse the leeks. Cut out the roots and the green leaves. Cover the yellow stems with boiling water, add salt and sugar. Cook for 10 minutes. Drain.
Place on a warmed serving platter. Prepare the butter and bread crumb mixture as for Brussels Sprouts Polonaise*. Pour over the leeks.
Serves 6.

ASPARAGUS POLONAISE
Szparagi po polsku

3 pounds asparagus	1½ tablespoons butter
Salt	1½ tablespoons toasted
½ teaspoon sugar	bread crumbs

Wash the asparagus very well. Cut out the hard parts. Place in a kettle, cover with small amount of boiling water, add salt and sugar. Cook 15 minutes. Drain.

Place on a warmed serving platter. Prepare the butter and bread crumb mixture as for Brussels Sprouts Polonaise*. Pour over the asparagus.

Serves 6.

VEGETABLE BOUQUET
Bukiet z jarzyn

1 pound small, young potatoes
½ pound green beans
½ pound young carrots
1½ pounds cauliflower
½ pound green peas
Salt and sugar for cooking vegetables
1 tablespoon dill leaves
3 tablespoons butter
3 tablespoons bread crumbs

8 slices white bread
1½ tablespoons soft butter

Cook each vegetable separately. Arrange on a large, warmed serving platter. Sprinkle the potatoes with dill. Prepare the butter and bread crumb mixture as in Brussels Sprouts Polonaise* and pour over the vegetables.

Spread the bread with butter, cut each slice in two. Place in a

hot 450° F. oven for 5 minutes or until golden. Divide the vegetables with pieces of toast.
Serve with ham on spring days.
Serves 8.

CARROTS AND PEAS
Marchewka z groszkiem

1 cup canned diced carrots, drained
½ cup canned small peas, drained
1½ tablespoons soft butter
1½ tablespoons instant flour
½ cup chicken cube bouillon
1 teaspoon chopped green parsley
¼ teaspoon sugar
½ teaspoon lemon juice
Salt to taste

Combine the carrots with the peas in a saucepan.
Combine the butter with the flour, add hot bouillon by spoonfuls, mixing thoroughly. Add to the vegetables, bring to a boil. Add green parsley, sugar, and lemon juice. Season with salt.
Serve with Hamburgers Polish Style*.
Serves 3.

DILL PICKLES
Kiszenie ogórków

10 medium cucumbers
4 large twigs dill
½ horseradish root, sliced
2 oak leaves
2 cherry or peach leaves
½ clove garlic
Salted water (use 1½ tablespoons salt for 1 quart)

Wash the cucumbers and place in 1 or 2 jars. Place dill, horse-radish, and the leaves among cucumbers. Cover with boiled and cooled salted water.

Close the jars and let stand at room temperature for 2 days. Refrigerate for at least 1 week.

Yields 10 pickles.

RED BEETS WITH HORSERADISH
Ćwikła

2 *1-pound jars canned red beets, drained, coarsely chopped*
5 *ounces prepared horseradish*
2 *teaspoons sugar*

Combine the ingredients. Return to the jars, cover, refrigerate for 3 days.

Serve with cold meats.

This is a traditional Easter relish.

Serves 10.

RED BEETS WITH APPLES
Buraki z jabłkami

1 *1-pound can red beets, drained, chopped*
2 *tablespoons beet juice*
1½ *tablespoons instant flour*
Salt
¼ *teaspoon sugar*
1 *large apple, peeled, shredded*
½ *cup sour cream*
1 *tablespoon lemon juice*

Heat the beets. Add the beet juice mixed with flour. Bring to a boil. Season with salt and sugar. Add the apple, sour cream, and lemon juice. Heat, but do not boil.

Serve with Pot Roast Marinated*, lamb, or Venison*.

Serves 3.

RED BEETS WITH SOUR CREAM
Buraki ze śmietaną

1 1-pound can red beets, drained, coarsely chopped
2 tablespoons beet juice
1½ tablespoons instant flour
Salt
¼ teaspoon sugar
½ cup sour cream
1 tablespoon lemon juice

Heat the beets. Add the juice mixed with flour. Bring to a boil.
Remove from the heat.
Add salt, sugar, sour cream, and lemon juice.
Serve with roasts and Venison*.
Serves 3.

CABBAGE WITH APPLES
Kapusta z jabłkami

1½ pounds cabbage, finely sliced
3 apples, peeled, shredded
Salt
¼ teaspoon sugar
2 tablespoons lemon juice
1½ tablespoons instant flour
2 tablespoons water
½ cup sour cream
1 teaspoon dill leaves
1 teaspoon chopped green parsley

Place the cabbage in a kettle. Add a small amount of boiling
water. Bring to a boil. Cook uncovered for 3 minutes. Cover
and cook 15 minutes.
Add the apples, cook another 10 minutes. Add salt, sugar, lemon
juice, and flour mixed with 2 tablespoons water. Bring to a boil.
Add sour cream, dill, and parsley.
Serve with pork chops, pork, or veal roasts.
Serves 6.

CABBAGE WITH TOMATOES
Kapusta z pomidorami

1½ pounds cabbage, finely sliced
2 apples, peeled, shredded
2 tomatoes, quartered, or ¾ cup canned tomato purée
1 onion, chopped
2½ tablespoons butter
2 tablespoons instant flour
Salt
¼ teaspoon sugar

Cook the cabbage as in Cabbage with Apples*. Add the apples and the tomatoes, cook another 10 minutes.
Brown the onions in 1 tablespoon butter. Add the rest of the butter and the flour. Fry stirring till golden. Dilute with the liquid from the cabbage. Add to the cabbage, bring to a boil. Season with salt and sugar.
Serve with pork.
Serves 6.

SAVOY CABBAGE WITH CARAWAY
Kapusta włoska z kminkiem

1½ pounds savoy cabbage, sliced
1 teaspoon caraway seeds
2 apples, peeled, shredded
1 onion, chopped
2 tablespoons butter
1½ tablespoons instant flour
Salt

Cook the cabbage as in Cabbage with Apples*. Add the caraway seeds together with the apples, cook another 10 minutes.
Brown the onions in 1 tablespoon butter. Add the rest of the butter

and the flour. Fry till golden, stirring. Dilute with the liquid from the cabbage. Add to the cabbage, bring to a boil. Season with salt. Serve with pork and fried meats.
Serves 6.

CABBAGE WITH BACON
Kapusta z boczkiem

1½ pounds cabbage, sliced	Salt and pepper
4 slices bacon, cut up	½ teaspoon sugar
2½ tablespoons instant flour	1 tablespoon lemon juice

Place the cabbage in a kettle. Add a small amount of boiling water. Bring to a boil. Cook uncovered for 3 minutes. Cover and cook for 20 minutes.
Fry the bacon till golden. Add the flour, fry some more, stirring. Dilute with the liquid from the cabbage. Add to the cabbage. Bring to a boil. Season with salt, pepper, sugar, and lemon juice. Serve with pork roasts and boiled potatoes.
Serves 6.

STEWED SAUERKRAUT
Kapusta kiszona, duszona

1½ pounds sauerkraut, rinsed and squeezed
1 teaspoon caraway seeds
4 slices bacon, cut up
1 large onion, diced
2½ tablespoons instant flour
Salt
½ teaspoon sugar

Cook sauerkraut with caraway seeds following cooking directions for cabbage in Cabbage with Bacon*.
Fry the bacon till golden. Add to sauerkraut. Fry the onions in the drippings, add the flour, fry some more, stirring. Dilute with

the liquid from sauerkraut. Add to sauerkraut. Simmer 10 minutes.
Season with salt and sugar.
Serve with roasts, boiled potatoes, or noodles.
Serves 6.

STEWED SAUERKRAUT WITH MUSHROOMS
Kapusta kiszona z grzybami

1 ounce dried mushrooms or ¼ pound fresh ones and
*   3 tablespoons water*
½ cup water
1½ pounds sauerkraut, rinsed and squeezed
1 large onion, diced
2½ tablespoons shortening
2½ tablespoons instant flour
Salt

Soak the dried mushrooms in ½ cup water for 1 hour.
Cook sauerkraut with mushrooms and their water following cooking directions for cabbage in Cabbage with Bacon*. Slice the mushrooms.
Simmer the fresh mushrooms (sliced) in 3 tablespoons water for 5 minutes, add to cooked sauerkraut.
Brown the onions in 1 tablespoon shortening. Add the rest of the shortening and the flour, fry some more, stirring. Dilute with the liquid from sauerkraut. Add to sauerkraut and simmer 10 minutes.
Season.
Serve with fish. It is a traditional Christmas Eve dish.
Serves 6.

RED CABBAGE WITH CARAWAY
Czerwona kapusta z kminkiem

1 small onion, chopped
3 tablespoons bacon drippings
2½-pound head red cabbage, coarsely shredded
2 tart apples, peeled, shredded
1 teaspoon caraway seeds
1 teaspoon sugar
2 tablespoons lemon juice
½ teaspoon salt

Sauté the onions in the drippings in a saucepan. Add the cabbage, and barely cover with boiling water. Bring to a boil. Add the apples and the caraway seeds. Simmer 30 minutes. Add sugar, lemon juice, and salt. Mix well.
Serve with roast meats.
Serves 8.

CREAMED SPINACH
Szpinak

1½ pounds spinach
Salt
2 tablespoons butter

2 tablespoons instant flour
¾ cup milk
Dash garlic powder

Wash the spinach very well. Cover with boiling salted water. Cook vigorously for 5 minutes. Drain. Chop very finely or grind.
Melt the butter, add the flour, and fry for few minutes, stirring. Add milk in a thin stream, stirring constantly.
Add the spinach, season with salt and garlic. Heat and serve.
Serve with veal chops or veal roast.
Serves 4.

POTATO PANCAKES
Placki kartoflane

8 large potatoes, peeled, cut up, and grated (in a blender)
1 large onion, cut up and grated (in a blender)
1 egg
3 tablespoons flour
Salt
⅓ cup bacon drippings

Combine the potatoes with the onions, egg, and flour. Season with salt.
Heat the bacon in a large skillet. Drop batter by spoonfuls into fat. Flatten with a fork. Fry 3 pancakes at one time on high heat on both sides till golden.
Serve with mushrooms and salad.
Serves 6.

POTATO CUTLETS
Kotlety kartoflane

6 large boiled potatoes, ground
2 eggs
½ cup flour
1 onion, chopped
3½ tablespoons bacon drippings
Salt and pepper
3 tablespoons bread crumbs
Onion*, Tomato*, or Dill Pickle Sauce*

Combine the potatoes with the eggs, flour, and onions which have been sautéed in 1 tablespoon drippings. Season. Form a roll and slice.
Roll the cutlets in bread crumbs, and fry in hot drippings on high heat on both sides till golden.
Serve with Onion*, Tomato*, or Dill Pickle Sauce* and salad.
Serves 6.

POTATO DUMPLINGS
Kluski kartoflane

2 cups ground boiled
   potatoes
1 cup flour
1 egg
Salt

1½ tablespoons bread
   crumbs
1½ tablespoons butter,
   melted

Combine the potatoes with the flour and the egg. Season with salt. Form long thin rolls on a floured board. Cut each roll into small dumplings.

Cook in a large kettle in boiling water for 5 minutes. Remove with a colander spoon onto a warmed serving platter.

Add the bread crumbs to the butter, fry for a few minutes, stirring. Pour over the dumplings.

Use fried bacon crumbs and drippings instead of the butter for change.

It is an excellent way to use leftover potatoes.

Serves 3.

GREEN POTATO DUMPLINGS
Kopytka

4 medium ground boiled potatoes
1 cup flour
3 eggs
1 tablespoon grated cheese
2 tablespoons chopped green parsley
Salt
2 slices bacon, diced, fried

Combine the potatoes with the flour, eggs, cheese, and parsley. Form long, thin rolls on a floured board. Cut each roll into small dumplings.

Cook as in Potato Dumplings*. Pour the bacon with drippings over the dumplings.

Serves 3.

POTATO DUMPLINGS COUNTRY STYLE
Pyzy

2 cups peeled and grated (in a blender) potatoes
2 cups ground boiled potatoes
1 egg
Salt
¾ cup flour
3 slices bacon, diced
1 onion, diced

Drain and squeeze the raw potatoes well. Combine with boiled ones, egg, and salt. Form small balls. Roll each in flour.
Drop the dumplings into a large kettle with boiling, salted water. Cover, bring to a boil. Cook uncovered on high heat until they float. Transfer with a colander spoon onto a warmed serving platter. Fry the bacon with the onions till golden. Pour over the dumplings. Serve with braised meats.
Serves 4.

POTATO CROQUETTES
Kartoflane krokiety

Prepare the mixture using the ingredients of and following directions for Potato Cutlets*. Form a long, thin roll. Roll in bread crumbs. Cut into finger-like pieces.
Fry in hot drippings on high heat on both sides till golden.
Serve with Mushroom* or Tomato Sauce* and salads.
Serves 6.

ASPARAGUS AU GRATIN
Szparagi zapiekane

2½ *pounds asparagus*
Salt
½ *teaspoon sugar*
1 *cup Béchamel Sauce**

3 *tablespoons grated cheese*
2 *tablespoons bread crumbs*
1 *tablespoon butter, melted*

Cook the asparagus, with salt and sugar, as in Asparagus Polonaise*. Place in a baking dish. Pour the sauce over the vegetable. Sprinkle with cheese, bread crumbs, and butter.
Place under broiler for a few minutes until golden.
Serve with ham.
Serves 6.

CAULIFLOWER AU GRATIN
Kalafior zapiekany

1 *cauliflower* (2½ *pounds*)
Salt
½ *teaspoon sugar*
1 *cup Béchamel Sauce**
3 *tablespoons grated cheese*
2 *tablespoons bread crumbs*
1 *tablespoon butter, melted*

Cook the cauliflower, with salt and sugar, as in Cauliflower Polonaise*. Separate the flowers. Arrange in a baking dish. Pour the sauce over the vegetable. Sprinkle with cheese, bread crumbs, and butter.
Place under broiler for a few minutes until golden.
Serve with veal.
Serves 6.

POTATOES AU GRATIN
Kartofle zapiekane

4 *large boiled potatoes, sliced*
1 *pound asparagus, cooked as in Asparagus Polonaise**
1 *cup Béchamel Sauce**
3 *tablespoons grated cheese*
2 *tablespoons bread crumbs*
1 *tablespoon butter, melted*
1 *teaspoon dill leaves*
1 *teaspoon chopped green parsley*

Place half of the potatoes in a baking dish. Cover with cut up asparagus, cover with the rest of the potatoes. Pour the sauce over. Sprinkle with cheese, bread crumbs, and butter.
Bake in a hot 450° F. oven for 10 minutes. Sprinkle with dill and parsley before serving.
Serve with steaks and tomato salad.
Serves 6.

VEGETABLE AND MACARONI CASSEROLE
Zapiekanka z jarzyn i makaronu

2 *cups cooked elbow macaroni*
2 *cups frozen mixed vegetables*
2 *hard-boiled eggs, chopped*
1½ *tablespoons butter, melted*
4 *tablespoons grated cheese*
½ *cup sour cream*
1 *egg yolk*
Salt

Combine the macaroni, cooked vegetables, the eggs, and the butter in a baking dish.
Combine half of the cheese with sour cream and egg yolk. Season with salt. Pour over the casserole. Sprinkle with the rest of the cheese.
Place in a hot 450° F. oven for 10 minutes or until golden.
Serve with broiled veal chops.
Serves 4.

SAUCES

In the top French restaurants, the highest salary is paid to the chef in charge of the sauces, because it is believed that the sauce makes the dish. Polish sauces are tasty, but not that numerous or complicated to prepare, and Polish housewives do not feel that they need a Cordon Bleu diploma.

The key to success lies in good proportions of fat, flour, liquids, and patience. Cook the sauce over low heat, stir vigorously. Instant flour is a blessing because it does not lump easily. A rotary beater or portable mixer is a great help.

Do not add the flour to the sauce, but the sauce to the flour, spoon by spoon, stirring constantly. Add the sauce to sour cream the same way, until it doubles its volume. Never sour cream to the sauce.

A lumpy sauce still is not a cause to despair, even when the guests are waiting in the living room for dinner to be served. Usually the mixer will save the reputation of our cooking skills. The most stubborn cases respond to a rubbing through a sieve.

Never bring a sauce with sour cream added to a boil. It will separate. But if it happens accidentally, hold your tears. The sauce may be saved by adding some more sour cream in the proper way. Be sure that the sour cream is fresh.

Chicken or beef stock is best, but a bouillon from a cube can be substituted. In preparing a sauce for a fish dish, use Vegetable Fish Bouillon* rather than meat stock.

Cold sauces never pose problems, and the preparation only takes minutes. Even the favorite Polish dressing—mayonnaise, which used to be so tricky, is always smooth and fluffy from a mixer. If it tends to become too thick, just add some cold water.

SAUCES	SAUCES
Cold Horseradish Sauce	*Sos chrzanowy zimny*
Mustard Sauce	*Sos musztardowy*
Sour Cream Sauce	*Sos śmietanowy*
Cold Green Onion Sauce	*Sos szczypiorkowy zimny*
Mayonnaise	*Sos majonezowy*
Tartar Sauce	*Sos tatarski*
Cumberland Sauce	*Sos Cumberland*
Onion Sauce	*Sos cebulowy*
Hot Horseradish Sauce	*Sos chrzanowy gorący*
Dill Sauce	*Sos koperkowy*
Hot Green Onion Sauce	*Sos szczypiorkowy gorący*
Tomato Sauce	*Sos pomidorowy*
Mushroom Sauce	*Sos grzybowy*
Dried Mushroom Sauce	*Sos z suszonych grzybów*
Béchamel Sauce	*Sos Beszamel*
Dill Pickle Sauce	*Sos ogórkowy*
Sauce Hollandaise	*Sos holenderski*

COLD HORSERADISH SAUCE
Sos chrzanowy zimny

5 ounces prepared
  horseradish
1 large apple, peeled,
  shredded

1 cup sour cream
Salt to taste
¼ teaspoon sugar

Mix the horseradish with the apples. Add sour cream. Season
with salt and sugar.
Serve with cold cuts, boiled eggs, and fish.
Yields 2 cups.

MUSTARD SAUCE
Sos musztardowy

2 tablespoons prepared mustard
1 cup sour cream
Salt to taste
¼ teaspoon sugar

Mix all the ingredients well.
Serve with cold pork loin, ham, or boiled eggs.
Yields 1 cup.

SOUR CREAM SAUCE
Sos śmietanowy

1 cup sour cream
2 hard-boiled eggs,
  finely chopped

1 teaspoon prepared mustard
Salt to taste
¼ teaspoon sugar

Beat sour cream with the eggs in a mixer at low speed for 5
minutes. Add mustard, salt, and sugar. Mix well.
Serve with the Easter ham or cold veal roast.
Yields 1½ cups.

COLD GREEN ONION SAUCE
Sos szczypiorkowy zimny

1 cup sour cream
2 hard-boiled eggs, chopped
4 tablespoons chopped green onions
¼ teaspoon sugar
1 teaspoon lemon juice
Salt to taste

Mix all the ingredients well.
Serve with cold cuts.
Yields 1¾ cups.

MAYONNAISE
Sos majonezowy

1 egg yolk
1 tablespoon lemon juice
1 cup salad oil
2–3 tablespoons water if needed
Salt to taste
¼ tablespoon sugar

Beat the egg yolk in the mixer at low speed. Add the lemon juice in 4 parts, beating all the time. Add the oil in a thin stream. Add 2–3 tablespoons water if the sauce is too thick. Season.
Use for salads and various hors d'oeuvres.
Yields 1 cup.

TARTAR SAUCE
Sos tatarski

2 hard-boiled eggs, separated
2 egg yolks
½ cup salad oil
2 tablespoons prepared mustard
½ cup sour cream
1 teaspoon lemon juice
¼ teaspoon sugar
Salt to taste
2 tablespoons finely chopped dill pickles
2 tablespoons finely chopped pickled mushrooms

Beat the cooked egg yolks with the raw ones in a mixer at low speed adding the oil in a thin stream. Beat 3 minutes.
Add chopped egg whites and all the other ingredients. Mix well.
Excellent with cold cuts and fish.
Yields 2 cups.

CUMBERLAND SAUCE
Sos Cumberland

2 tablespoons prepared horseradish
Juice 1 orange
Orange peel 1 orange, finely chopped
2 tablespoons currant jelly
1 tablespoon prepared mustard
½ cup red wine

Combine all the ingredients.
Use with cold chicken or turkey.
Yields 1 cup.

ONION SAUCE
Sos cebulowy

4 onions (7 ounces), sliced
1 cup water
½ cup chicken or beef bouillon, homemade or from a cube
3¼ tablespoons instant flour
½ cup coffee cream
Salt to taste
¼ teaspoon sugar

Cook the onions in 1 cup water for 15 minutes. Mix in a blender, add the bouillon and flour.
Bring to a boil, stirring constantly. Stir in the cream. Season with salt and sugar.
Use over hard-boiled eggs or boiled beef.
Yields 3 cups.

HOT HORSERADISH SAUCE
Sos chrzanowy gorący

1 cup chicken or beef bouillon, homemade or from a cube
2½ tablespoons instant flour
3 ounces prepared horseradish
½ cup table cream
Salt to taste
¼ teaspoon sugar

Stir the bouillon into the flour gradually. Bring to a boil, stirring constantly. Stir in the horseradish and cream. Season with salt and sugar.
Use with boiled fish, beef, and casseroles.
Yields 2 cups.

DILL SAUCE
Sos koperkowy

1 cup chicken or beef bouillon, homemade or from a cube
3 tablespoons instant flour
2½ tablespoons dill leaves
Salt to taste
½ cup sour cream

Stir the cold bouillon into the flour gradually. Bring to a boil, stirring constantly. Add the dill. Remove from the heat, season with salt. Add sour cream.
Serve with boiled and braised meats and casseroles.
Yields 3 cups.

HOT GREEN ONION SAUCE
Sos szczypiorkowy gorący

Prepare as Dill Sauce* using chopped green onions instead of dill. Serve with boiled and braised meats and casseroles.
Yields 3 cups.

TOMATO SAUCE
Sos pomidorowy

1 cup canned heavy tomato purée
1 tablespoon butter
1 onion bouillon cube
½ cup water
1 cup chicken or beef bouillon, homemade or from a cube
2½ tablespoons instant flour
Salt to taste
½ teaspoon sugar
½ cup sour cream

Simmer the tomato purée for 15 minutes with the butter and bouillon cube dissolved in ½ cup boiling water.

Stir the cold broth into the flour. Add to tomatoes, bring to a boil, stirring constantly. Remove from the heat. Season with salt and sugar. Add sour cream.

Serve with braised meats and casseroles.

Yields 3 cups.

MUSHROOM SAUCE
Sos grzybowy

1 pound mushrooms, sliced
1 large onion, chopped
1 cup chicken or beef bouillon, homemade or from a cube
2½ tablespoons instant flour
2 tablespoons cold water
Salt and pepper
1 teaspoon lemon juice
½ cup sour cream

Simmer the mushrooms with the onions and bouillon for 15 minutes.

Stir in the flour mixed with 2 tablespoons cold water. Bring to a boil, stirring. Remove from the heat. Season with salt, pepper, and lemon juice. Add sour cream.

Yields 3 cups.

DRIED MUSHROOM SAUCE
Sos z suszonych grzybów

1 ounce dried mushrooms   *4 tablespoons cold water*
1 cup water   *Salt and pepper*
3½ tablespoons instant flour   *½ cup sour cream*

Scrub the mushrooms with a brush. Soak in 1 cup water for 1 hour. Simmer in the same water for 45 minutes.

Slice the mushrooms. Combine the broth with the flour mixed with

4 tablespoons cold water. Fold in the mushrooms, bring to a boil, stirring. Remove from the heat. Season and add sour cream. Excellent with meat loaf, meatballs, and braised meats. Yields 1½ cups.

BÉCHAMEL SAUCE
Sos Beszamel

2 tablespoons butter, melted	*Salt to taste*
3 tablespoons instant flour	*½ teaspoon lemon juice*
1½ cups milk	*2 egg yolks*

Mix the butter with the flour over low heat. Gradually stir in the milk. Bring to a boil, stirring constantly. Remove from the heat. Season with salt and lemon juice.
Stir a few tablespoons of the sauce into the egg yolks, then combine.
Excellent on vegetables, fish, and casseroles.
Yields 1¾ cups.

DILL PICKLE SAUCE
Sos ogórkowy

1½ tablespoons butter, melted
2 tablespoons instant flour
½ cup beef bouillon, homemade or from a cube
½ cup pickle liquid from jar
3 large dill pickles, shredded
½ cup sour cream
Salt

Mix the butter with the flour over low heat. Stir in the hot bouillon gradually; stir in the pickle liquid. Bring to a boil, stirring constantly.
Add the pickles and sour cream. Heat, but do not boil. Season with salt.
Excellent on boiled beef and boiled potatoes.
Yields 3 cups.

SAUCE HOLLANDAISE
Sos holenderski

½ *cup beef or fish bouillon, homemade or from a cube*
½ *cup white table wine*
4 *egg yolks*
Salt to taste

Heat the bouillon with the wine.
Beat the egg yolks with a portable mixer at low speed in a small saucepan. Add the hot bouillon mixture in a thin stream, mixing. Heat over low heat or in a double boiler, stirring constantly till it thickens. Do not bring to a boil. Season with salt.
Serve immediately with fish, veal, cauliflower, or asparagus.
Yields 1 cup.

SWEET DISHES AND DESSERTS

Most busy housewives have a tendency of falling into a routine of ten to fifteen habitual family dishes. Preparing the favorite ones often may be satisfactory at the beginning, but turns quickly into a boring monotony.

There are many delicious gelatin or pudding mixes and canned fruits on the American market, therefore I have omitted from my book all similar Polish recipes. The few listed on the next pages are definitely different, and may provide a needed variety to our usual meals.

Many of the following sweet dishes may serve as a main course and a dessert at the same time. They should be served after a nourishing soup containing vegetables. Polish people used them to break the monotony of fish dinners during Lent, and on hot summer days when heavier meat dishes are not welcomed. They can also provide attractive luncheons or light Sunday suppers.

Sugar is not necessarily an evil to be avoided at all times.

Children need it in larger amounts than grown-ups, but it also has a place in any well-balanced diet of older people. Sensible menus will never provoke obesity, when one eats with moderation. A real gourmet is seldom fat. It is a characteristic of persons who eat with less discrimination. And a dinner without dessert—is like lingerie without lace.

SWEET DISHES AND DESSERTS	SŁODKIE DANIA I DESERY
Rice with Plums or Peaches	*Ryż ze śliwkami lub brzoskwiniami*
Rice and Apple Casserole	*Ryż zapiekany z jabłkami*
Rice and Cheese Baba	*Babka z ryżu i sera*
Rice Pudding	*Budyń z ryżu*
Plum Dumplings	*Knedle ze śliwkami*
Apple Dumplings	*Knedle z jabłkami*
Pierogi with Sweet Cheese	*Pierożki z serem słodkie*
Pierogi with Cherries, Blueberries, or Apples	*Pierogi z czereśniami, jagodami lub jabłkami*
Apples in Blankets	*Jabłuszka w cieście*
Sweet Cheese Dumplings	*Leniwe pierożki*
Omelet with Strawberry Preserves	*Omlet z konfiturą truskawkową*
Pancakes with Cheese	*Naleśniki z serem*
Pancakes with Jam	*Naleśniki z marmoladą*
Noodles with Cheese	*Kluski z serem*
Noodles with Poppy Seeds	*Kluski z makiem*
Bread and Apple Baba	*Babka z bułki i jabłek*
Cheese Pascha from Lwow	*Pascha ze Lwowa*
Dried Fruit or Prune Compote	*Kompot z suszu*
Summer Compote	*Kompot letni*
Apple Compote	*Kompot z jabłek*
Pears in Vanilla Sauce	*Gruszki w sosie waniliowym*
Baked Apples	*Pieczone jabłka*
Cranberry Pudding	*Kisiel żurawinowy*
Strawberry Cream	*Krem truskawkowy*

Strawberry Dessert	*Deser truskawkowy*
Strawberry Mousse	*Mus truskawkowy*
Apricot Mousse	*Mus morelowy*
Plum Jam	*Powidła*
Preserves	*Konfitury*

RICE WITH PLUMS OR PEACHES
Ryż ze śliwkami lub brzoskwiniami

2 cups cooked rice
2 cups plums or peaches, peeled and sliced
½ teaspoon cinnamon
4 tablespoons sugar
¾ cup sour cream

Arrange the rice and the fruits in layers: rice, fruits, rice, fruits, and rice. Sprinkle each layer of fruits with cinnamon and 1 tablespoon sugar. Refrigerate for 2 hours.
Beat sour cream with the rest of the sugar. Pour over the rice and serve after a nourishing vegetable soup.
Serves 4.

RICE AND APPLE CASSEROLE
Ryż zapiekany z jabłkami

2 cups cooked rice
2 cups peeled, shredded apples
1 teaspoon cinnamon
4 tablespoons sugar
¾ cup sour cream

Arrange the rice and the apples in layers. Start and top with the rice. Sprinkle each layer of apples with cinnamon and sugar. Use half of the sugar.
Place in a baking dish. Cover and bake in moderate 375° F. oven for 35 minutes.
Beat sour cream with the rest of the sugar. Serve in a separate bowl.
Serve after a nourishing vegetable soup.
Serves 4.

RICE AND CHEESE BABA
Babka z ryżu i sera

2 eggs, separated
3 tablespoons sugar
10 ounces farmer cheese or ricotta cheese
2 cups cooked rice
Bread crumbs
¾ cup apricot nectar

Beat the egg yolks with sugar. Combine with the cheese. Add to the rice. Fold in whipped, stiff egg whites.
Place in a buttered and sprinkled with bread crumbs tube pan with removable bottom. Bake in 400° F. oven for 30 minutes. Remove from pan. Serve hot or cold. Sprinkle with apricot nectar before serving.
Serves 3.

RICE PUDDING
Budyń z ryżu

4 eggs, separated
½ cup sugar
4 cups cooked rice
2 tablespoons finely chopped candied orange peel
Grated rind 1 lemon
3 tablespoons raisins
½ cup sour cream
Apricot or cranberry nectar

Beat egg yolks with the sugar till fluffy. Fold in rice, whipped stiff egg whites, orange peel, lemon rind, raisins, and sour cream. Mix lightly.
Place in a baking dish. Bake in a moderate 375° F. oven for 30 minutes.
Serve warm sprinkled with apricot or cranberry nectar.
Serves 4.

PLUM DUMPLINGS
Knedle ze śliwkami

DOUGH

2 cups ground boiled, peeled potatoes
1 cup flour
1 egg
Salt

STUFFING

15 small prune plums or 15 tablespoons plum jam

TOPPING

1½ tablespoons bread crumbs
1½ tablespoons butter, melted
⅓ cup confecioners' sugar

Mix all the ingredients and knead the dough. Form circles about 2 inches in diameter.

To make stuffing: Wash and dry the plums. Place a plum or 1 tablespoon jam in the center of a circle and fold over. Seal the edges, smooth, rolling in your palms.
Cook in a large kettle with salted boiling water until they float to the surface. Transfer to a warmed platter.

To make topping: Add the bread crumbs to the butter, fry for 1 minute, pour over the dumplings. Sprinkle with sugar.
Serves 3.

APPLE DUMPLINGS
Knedle z jabłkami

DOUGH

3¼ cups flour
1 egg
Salt
About ½ cup water

STUFFING

½ pound apples, peeled, cored, cut up in small pieces

TOPPING

1½ tablespoons butter
1½ tablespoons bread crumbs
⅓ cup confectioners' sugar

To make dough: Combine the flour with the egg, dash of salt, and as much water as needed to knead a smooth, loose dough.

Roll out on a floured board ¼ inch thick. Cut out small circles. Place a piece of apple in the center of each circle and fold over. Seal the edges, roll in the palms.
Cook, make topping, and serve as for Plum Dumplings*.
Serves 4.

PIEROGI WITH SWEET CHEESE
Pierożki z serem słodkie

DOUGH

Prepare as for Apple Dumplings*

STUFFING

1 pound farmer cheese, ground, or ricotta cheese
1 teaspoon vanilla
2 tablespoons sugar
1 egg yolk

TOPPING

1 tablespoon butter, melted
1 cup sour cream
½ cup confectioners' sugar

To make dough: Knead the dough and roll very thin. Cut out circles 2 inches in diameter.

To make stuffing: Mix the cheese with vanilla, sugar, and egg yolk. Spoon the stuffing on each circle, fold. Seal the edges. Cook in a large kettle in boiling water for 5 minutes till they float. Remove with a colander spoon to a warmed serving platter.

To make topping: Pour the butter over. Beat sour cream with sugar. Serve in a separate bowl.
Serves 5.

PIEROGI WITH CHERRIES, BLUEBERRIES, OR APPLES
Pierogi z czereśniami, jagodami lub jabłkami

DOUGH

Prepare as for Apple Dumplings*

STUFFING

1½ pounds cherries, pitted
  OR
1 quart blueberries
  OR
1 pound apples, peeled, cored, cut up in small pieces
2 tablespoons bread crumbs

TOPPING

1 tablespoon butter
1 cup sour cream
½ cup confectioners' sugar

To make dough: Knead the dough and roll out very thin. Cut out circles 2 inches in diameter.
To make stuffing: Mix the fruits with bread crumbs. Spoon over each circle. Fold, seal the edges.
Cook, prepare topping, and serve as in Pierogi with Sweet Cheese*. Serves 5.

APPLES IN BLANKETS
Jabłuszka w cieście

1 pound apples, peeled	*5 tablespoons sour cream*
2 eggs	*Dash salt*
¼ cup sugar	*3 tablespoons shortening*
1¼ cups flour	*⅓ cup confectioners' sugar*

Cut the apples in thick slices, core.

Beat the eggs with the sugar very well. Add the flour and sour cream, beat some more. Season with salt.

Dip the apple slices in the batter and fry in hot shortening on both sides till golden. Place on a warmed serving platter, sprinkle with sugar.

Serves 4.

SWEET CHEESE DUMPLINGS
Leniwe pierożki

1 pound *farmer cheese, ground or dry cottage cheese
    ground and 1 tablespoon butter*
1 tablespoon *soft butter*
4 eggs, *separated*
1½ cups *flour*
2 tablespoons *butter, melted*
1 teaspoon *cinnamon*
3 tablespoons *sugar*

Combine the cheese with butter and egg yolks. Beat the egg whites until stiff. Add the flour alternately with egg whites. Mix slightly. Form 3 long rolls 1 inch wide on a floured board. Cut into small dumplings.

Cook in a large kettle with boiling salted water until they float. Remove with a colander spoon to a warmed serving platter. Pour over the butter. Sprinkle with cinnamon and sugar.

Serves 4.

OMELET WITH STRAWBERRY PRESERVES
Omlet z konfiturą truskawkową

6 *eggs*	*Salt*
2 tablespoons *sugar*	1½ tablespoons *butter*
4 tablespoons *sour cream*	4 tablespoons *strawberry*
⅓ cup *flour*	*preserves*

Beat the eggs with the sugar very well. Add sour cream. Sift the flour and dash of salt over the eggs. Mix slightly.

Heat the butter in a large skillet. Fold in the egg mixture. Fry on medium heat until the bottom is set. Place in a hot 500° F. oven for 5 minutes.

Spread with preserves, cut into serving portions in the skillet. Serve immediately.

This is a children's favorite. Serve after Vegetable Beef Soup*. Serves 4.

PANCAKES WITH CHEESE
Naleśniki z serem

BATTER

1 cup milk
2 eggs
1 cup flour
½ cup water
Salt

STUFFING

1 cup creamed cottage cheese
¼ cup sugar
1 teaspoon vanilla
1 tablespoon grated orange or lemon rind
2 tablespoons salad oil

TOPPING

½ cup sour cream
⅓ cup confectioners' sugar

Combine the batter in a mixer.
Combine the stuffing in a blender.
Heat a skillet 6 inches in diameter. Brush with oil. Pour in ¼ cup of the batter and tilt the pan immediately so the batter will spread over entire bottom of the pan. Cook the pancake on both

sides. Repeat until all pancakes are cooked, stacking them on a plate.

Stuff each pancake and fold in four. Reheat in a hot 450° F. oven.

Serve with sour cream mixed with confectioners' sugar.

Yields 10 pancakes. Serves 3–4.

PANCAKES WITH JAM
Naleśniki z marmoladą

Prepare 10 pancakes as for Pancakes with Cheese*
6 ounces jam

Spread each pancake with jam and fold in four.

Yields 10 pancakes. Serves 3–4.

NOODLES WITH CHEESE
Kluski z serem

3 cups cooked egg noodles
1 tablespoon butter
1 pound cottage cheese
1 small package frozen strawberries
½ cup heavy cream
2 tablespoons confectioners' sugar
1 teaspoon vanilla

Combine the warm noodles with butter. Cool. Combine with cheese.

Arrange on a serving platter in 3 layers, sprinkling each layer with strawberries. Pour whipped cream mixed with sugar and vanilla over the top.

Serves 3.

NOODLES WITH POPPY SEEDS
Kluski z makiem

2 cups cooked egg noodles
1 tablespoon butter, melted
1 cup poppy seed pastry filling
1 tablespoon vanilla
Grated rind 1 lemon
⅓ cup raisins, steamed

Combine the noodles with the butter.
Combine the poppy seeds with vanilla, lemon rind, and raisins.
Add to the noodles. Heat.
Serve warm. This is a centuries-old traditional Christmas Eve
treat.
Serves 6.

BREAD AND APPLE BABA
Babka z bułki i jabłek

2 cups milk
2 eggs
1 tablespoon sugar
12 slices Vienna bread, toasted
8 apples, peeled, cored, sliced
2 tablespoons finely chopped candied orange peel
1 teaspoon vanilla
3 tablespoons confectioners' sugar
Bread crumbs

Beat the milk with the eggs and sugar. Dip each toast and place
on a platter. Pour over the rest of the milk mixture.
Sprinkle the apples with orange peel, vanilla, and sugar.
Arrange in 3 layers, starting and ending with toast, in a baking
dish buttered and sprinkled with bread crumbs.
Bake in a hot 400° F. oven for 40 minutes.
Remove to a serving platter. Serve hot with fruit nectars.
Serves 4.

CHEESE PASCHA FROM LWOW
Pascha ze Lwowa

5 egg yolks
2¾ cups sugar
1 cup coffee cream
2 pounds white farmer cheese
½ pound unsalted soft butter
1 tablespoon vanilla
4 ounces almonds, peeled, chopped
4 ounces small raisins, steamed
Grated rind 1 orange

Beat the egg yolks with the sugar until thick and creamy. Add half of the cream. Heat stirring almost to the boiling point, but do not boil. Remove from the heat.

Combine in a blender the cheese with the butter, the rest of the cream and vanilla. Fold in the egg mixture, mix well. Add the almonds, raisins, and orange rind.

Refrigerate for 4 hours. Place in a corner of a small sack (pillowcase). Hang in a cold place, and let the liquid drain for 24 hours.

Serve very cold. Cut small slices.

It is an old, traditional Easter delicacy from the eastern regions of Poland.

Serves 10.

DRIED FRUIT OR PRUNE COMPOTE
Kompot z suszu

½ pound mixed dried fruits or prunes
2 cups water
1 cup sugar
1 tablespoon lemon juice
Grated rind 1 lemon

Rinse the fruits and soak in 2 cups water for 24 hours. Remove

the fruits. Heat the liquid with the sugar till dissolved. Pour over the fruits. Add lemon juice and rind. Refrigerate.
This is a traditional Christmas Eve dessert.
Serves 6.

SUMMER COMPOTE
Kompot letni

1 cup sugar
2 cups water
½ cup white wine
1 cup strawberries, quartered
½ cup raspberries
½ cup quartered peeled yellow plums

Dissolve the sugar in 2 cups hot water. Cool, mix with wine. Pour over the fruits.
Ideal for summer dinner parties.
Serves 6.

APPLE COMPOTE
Kompot z jabłek

3 cups water
1¼ cups sugar
1 teaspoon cinnamon
½ teaspoon lemon rind
6 apples, peeled, cored, quartered

Bring to a boil 3 cups water with the sugar, cinnamon, and the lemon rind. Add the apples. Simmer 15 minutes.
Serve very cold.
Serves 6.

PEARS IN VANILLA SAUCE
Gruszki w sosie waniliowym

4 large pears, peeled, cut into halves
½ cup water
½ cup sugar
1 package vanilla instant pudding
2 cups milk

Cook the pears in ½ cup water with the sugar for 15 minutes. Prepare the pudding with milk as usual, add the cold liquid from the pears. Mix. Pour over the pears. Chill.
Serves 4.

BAKED APPLES
Pieczone jabłka

4 cooking apples
4 teaspoons pure preserves

Cut the tops off the apples. Remove the seeds. Fill the holes with preserves. Cover with the tops.
Bake in moderate 375° F. oven for ½ hour.
Serves 4.

CRANBERRY PUDDING
Kisiel żurawinowy

1 pound cranberries
1½ cups water
4 tablespoons cornstarch

3 tablespoons cold water
¾ cup sugar
Coffee cream

Cook the cranberries in 1½ cups water till tender. Rub through a sieve or use a blender.
Add the cornstarch mixed with 3 tablespoons cold water, and the

sugar. Bring to a boil stirring. Cool. Serve with coffee cream. Serves 6.

STRAWBERRY CREAM
Krem truskawkowy

1 cup frozen strawberries, thawed
1 envelope gelatin
1 tablespoon water
1 cup heavy cream, whipped

Strain the strawberry juice and heat. Soak the gelatin in 1 tablespoon water for 3 minutes, add to the juice. Heat, stirring till dissolved. Cool until it begins to thicken.
Add the strawberry juice and the strawberries to the whipped cream in small portions, beating all the time at slow speed.
Line a mold with plastic wrap. Pour in the cream. Refrigerate for several hours. Unmold before serving.
Serves 6.

STRAWBERRY DESSERT
Deser truskawkowy

½ pint vanilla ice cream, softened
2 tablespoons lemon juice
3 tablespoons any fruit-flavored cordial
½ cup heavy cream, whipped
1 quart strawberries, washed and hulled
Cookies

Whip the ice cream until fluffy. Mix with the lemon juice and the cordial. Fold in the whipped cream. Fold in the berries gently.
Serve with tiny, elegant cookies. It is a gourmet treat.
Serves 4.

STRAWBERRY MOUSSE
Mus truskawkowy

2 envelopes unflavored gelatin
½ cup cold water
½ cup boiling water
1 quart strawberries, washed and hulled
½ cup sugar
½ cup wine
2 cups heavy cream, whipped

Soak the gelatin in ½ cup cold water. Add ½ cup boiling water, stir till dissolved. Cool.

Reserve a few strawberries. Rub the rest through a sieve or use a blender. Add sugar, wine, and gelatin, mix well. Refrigerate till it begins to thicken.

Beat in a mixer for few minutes. Fold in the whipped cream.

Line a 2-quart mold with a plastic wrap. Fold in the mousse. Refrigerate for several hours.

Unmold onto a chilled platter before serving. Garnish with strawberries.

Beautiful dessert for a springtime dinner party.

Serves 8.

APRICOT MOUSSE
Mus morelowy

1 teaspoon unflavored gelatin
1 tablespoon cold water
2 tablespoons boiling water
3 tablespoons apricot preserves
4 egg whites, whipped stiff
3 tablespoons confectioners' sugar
Grated rind 1 lemon

Soak the gelatin in 1 tablespoon cold water for 5 minutes. Add 2 tablespoons boiling water, stir till dissolved.

Add the gelatin and the preserves to the egg whites in small portions, beating at low speed. Add the sugar by spoonfuls. Add the rind. Chill for 1 hour and serve.

Fresh raspberries or strawberries may be used instead of preserves. This is an excellent use of leftover egg whites, and a tasty Sunday dessert.

Serves 4.

PLUM JAM
Powidła

10 pounds prune plums, rinsed, pitted
4 cups sugar

Place the fruits and the sugar in a large kettle. Keep in a hot 450° F. oven for about 15 minutes or until some juice forms.

Remove from the oven, bring to a boil. Simmer, stirring often for 2½ hours until the jam is thick.

Transfer the jam into clean, dry jars. Place uncovered in a warm 300° F. oven for 1 hour. Cover. Store in a cool place.

Yields 10 pounds jam.

PRESERVES
Konfitury

10 pounds cherries (pitted), strawberries, raspberries, or
   currants
10 pounds sugar
2½ quarts boiling water

Rinse the fruits. Place the sugar in a large kettle. Add 2½ quarts boiling water. Bring to a boil, add the fruits. Bring to a boil and cook uncovered at medium heat for ½ hour. Do not stir, just shake the kettle from time to time.

Remove from the heat and let stand overnight.

Cook on low heat for 2 hours. Cool. Transfer to clean, dry jars. Cover. Store in a cool place.

Yields 20 pounds preserves.

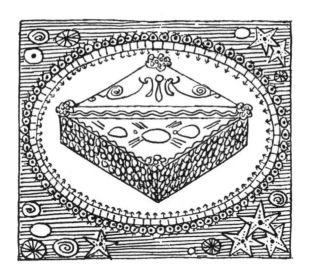

PASTRIES

Polish people do not try to hide the fact that they have a sweet tooth. In spite of economic difficulties, even now Poland can offer exceptional pastries, and all kinds of goodies are produced in each home almost everyday.

In the prewar days, Warsaw and all the large cities had a bakery at every second corner, and each one had an impressive variety of cakes, tarts, and cookies. They were so tasty that city ladies did not undertake baking at home very often.

Baking traditions were more rooted in the country. An unexpected visitor was always sure to be treated with elegant home-baked goods in each country manor. Talented housewives were famous all over the country, and a lass who could produce an excellent torte could expect an excellent marriage.

When I was a little girl, I often wondered, why mazurka cakes appeared on the table only on Easter day, why we had to wait till Christmas to eat Poppy Seed Rolls*, or why jelly doughnuts were never served in July. My nanny used to say that eating traditional dishes at the wrong times brings bad luck. Mother smiled at these superstitions, but she never served Easter Cheese Pascha* in September.

Now I know the deep meaning of my nanny's words. Although I do not expect to break my leg after eating a delicious Gypsy Mazurka* in May, I believe that being able to have everything at all times and at a whim brings boredom and satiety. We do not savor traditional delicacies with the same gusto as when we conform, and in a harmony with nature we change our eating habits with the changing seasons.

How delicious are the rosy strawberry tarts after a long winter of heavy, nutty cakes! There is no time for ennui when they are soon followed by cherry and blueberry squares, prune plums juicy under a silvery icing. With the first leaves falling from the trees, comes the time for innumerable apple pastry recipes. When Christmas approaches, what a joy to bake a spicy Honey Cake*, to hang Honey Hearts* on the Christmas tree, and to wrap gifts in a home smelling of the rising yeast dough.

Winter parties call for the Favors* light and crumbly, Polish Doughnuts* piled high on crystal platters, and elegant tortes invented by the wizards of the culinary art. Tall babas in their icing caps, snowy-like church domes, adorn Polish Easter tables in the company of thin, delicate, and sweet shapes of mazurkas in endless variety.

In the old times baking was not only an art, but a difficult skill. Nowadays with modern ovens and regulated temperatures everyone can come out with a perfect result. A good recipe and a measuring cup do the trick. Do not use instant flour for pastries that require rolling out. Check from time to time whether the oven thermostat works properly. Do not change the order of the ingredients when adding them to the mixing bowl. Be sure that your yeast is always fresh.

PASTRIES	CIASTA
Almond Cookies	*Ciasteczka z migdałami*
Walnut Cookies	*Ciasteczka z orzechami*
Chocolate Sandwiches	*Ciasteczka z czekoladą*
Poppy Seed Cookies	*Ciasteczka z makiem*
Cookies and Poppy Seeds	*Łamańce z makiem*
Chestnuts	*Kasztanki*
Meringues	*Bezy*
Macaroons	*Makaroniki*
Cheese Cookies	*Ciasteczka z serem*
Christmas Honey Cookies	*Piernikowa krajanka świąteczna*
Honey Kisses	*Całuski*
Honey Cake Hearts	*Piernikowe serduszka*
Chocolate Honey Hearts	*Pierniczki w czekoladzie*
Honey Cake from Warsaw	*Piernik warszawski*
Sand Baba	*Babka piaskowa*
Baba with Raisins	*Babka z rodzynkami*
Light Fruit Cake from Warsaw	*Keks warszawski*
Christmas Bread	*Placek świąteczny*
Walnut Ring	*Orzechowy wieniec*
Quick Fruit Cake	*Keks szybki*
Nut Rolls	*Strucle z orzechami*
Poppy Seed Rolls	*Strucle z makiem*
Spanish Torte	*Tort hiszpański*
Mocha Torte	*Tort mocca*
Orange Nut Torte	*Tort pomarańczowo-orzechowy*
Chocolate Torte	*Tort czekoladowy*
Walnut Torte	*Tort orzechowy*
Almond Torte	*Tort migdałowy*
Brazil Nut Torte	*Tort orzechowy ciemny*
Torte Provençe	*Tort prowancki*
Poppy Seed Coffee Torte	*Tort makowy z kawą*
Torte Stephanie	*Tort Stefanka*
Poppy Seed Torte	*Torcik z makiem*
Date Torte	*Tort daktylowy*

Pumpernickel Torte	*Tort z razowca*
Lemon Torte	*Tort cytrynowy*
Favors	*Chrust-Faworki*
Polish Doughnuts	*Pączki*
Chocolate Roll	*Rolada czekoladowa*
Coffee Roll	*Rolada kawowa*
Cream Puffs	*Ptysie z kremem*
Coffee Éclairs	*Eklery kawowe*
Tiny Babas	*Babeczki śmietankowe*
Nut Cups	*Babeczki orzechowe*
Chocolate Squares	*Czekoladowe ciastka*
Almond Squares	*Migdałowe ciastka*
Easter Baba	*Babka wielkanocna*
Poppy Seed Yeast Cake	*Placek drożdżowy z makiem*
Cheese Yeast Cake	*Placek drożdżowy z serem*
Cheese Bread	*Strucla z serem*
Country Cheese Cake	*Serowiec*
Grandmother's Cheese Cake	*Sernik babci*
Easter Cheese Cake	*Sernik wielkanocny*
Cheese Cake from Krakow	*Sernik krakowski*
Royal Mazurka I	*Mazurek królewski I*
Royal Mazurka II	*Mazurek królewski II*
Chocolate Mazurka	*Mazurek czekoladowy*
Gypsy Mazurka	*Mazurek cygański*
All Fruit Mazurka	*Mazurek bakaliowy*
Fig Mazurka	*Mazurek figowy*
Prune Mazurka	*Mazurek śliwkowy*
Date Mazurka	*Mazurek daktylowy*
Mazurka from Wilno	*Mazurek wileński*
Walnut Mazurka	*Mazurek orzechowy*
Cinnamon Cake	*Placek z cynamonem*
Egg White Cake	*Placek z białek*
Strawberry Shortcake	*Torcik z truskawkami*
Strawberry Tarts	*Ciastka z truskawkami*
Strawberry Torte	*Tort z truskawkami*
Cherry Pie	*Placek z czereśniami*
Plum Cake	*Placek ze śliwkami*
Plum Tarts	*Ciastka ze śliwkami*
Peach Tarts	*Ciastka z brzoskwiniami*

Raspberry Pie	*Torcik z malinami*
Orange Cake	*Ciasto pomarańczowe*
Blueberry Squares	*Placek z jagodami*
Peach Meringue	*Beza z brzoskwiniami*
Pineapple Squares	*Ciastka z ananasem*
Apple Squares	*Placek z jabłkiem*
Apple Cake	*Ciasto z jabłkiem*
Charlotte	*Szarlotka*
Apple Raisin Cake	*Ciasto z jabłkiem i rodzynkami*
Poppy Seed Squares	*Ciastka z makiem*

ALMOND COOKIES
Ciasteczka z migdałami

1 cup soft butter
1¾ cups pre-sifted flour
⅔ cup confectioners' sugar, sifted
4 ounces almonds, peeled, ground

Cut the butter into the flour with a knife, and rub in with finger-
tips. Add the sugar and knead for a few minutes. Add the almonds.
Roll out the dough as thin as you can. Place on a cookie sheet.
Roll till it is ¼ inch thick. Cut out small squares. Bake in a hot
450° F. oven for 8–10 minutes till golden.
Remove from the cookie sheet with a knife immediately.
Yields 3 dozen.

WALNUT COOKIES
Ciasteczka z orzechami

⅔ cup butter
1 cup sugar
1 egg
1 teaspoon vanilla
2¼ cups pre-sifted, all purpose flour
1 teaspoon baking powder
¾ cup finely chopped walnuts

Cream the butter with the sugar very well. Add the egg and
vanilla. Beat for 5 minutes. Blend in the flour mixed with baking
powder. Combine with walnuts.
Divide the dough in half. Shape into 2 rolls. Wrap in wax paper.
Refrigerate overnight.
Slice ⅛ inch thick. Bake on a buttered cookie sheet in a hot
425° F. oven for 5–7 minutes.
Yields 7 dozen.

CHOCOLATE SANDWICHES
Ciasteczka z czekoladą

DOUGH

¼ *pound butter*
2¾ *cups pre-sifted, all purpose flour*
⅔ *cup confectioners' sugar*
2 *teaspoons baking powder*
1 *egg*
2 *egg yolks*
3 *tablespoons sour cream*

FILLING

2 *eggs*
⅔ *cup sugar*
⅔ *cup sweet butter, creamed*
½ *teaspoon vanilla extract*
1 *tablespoon vodka*
3 *tablespoons cocoa*

To make dough: Cut the butter into the flour with a knife, and rub in with fingertips. Add the rest of the ingredients. Knead the dough for a few minutes. Refrigerate for 15 minutes.
Roll out ⅛ inch thick. Cut out small circles. Bake on a buttered cookie sheet in a moderate 375° F. oven for 10 minutes or until golden. Remove from the baking sheet, cool.
To make filling: Beat the eggs with the sugar very well. Add to the butter in small portions beating at low speed. Add the rest of the ingredients. Spread 1 teaspoon of the filling over 1 cookie, cover with another. Refrigerate for 1 hour.
Yields 4 dozen.

POPPY SEED COOKIES
Ciasteczka z makiem

Prepare dough as for Chocolate Sandwiches*
3 tablespoons poppy seeds

Combine the dough with the poppy seeds. Roll out, cut out, and bake as in Chocolate Sandwiches*.
Yields 8 dozen.

COOKIES AND POPPY SEEDS
Łamańce z makiem

DOUGH

½ cup butter
2¾ cups pre-sifted, all purpose flour
⅔ cup confectioners' sugar
2 teaspoons baking powder
2 eggs
1 egg yolk
1 teaspoon vanilla
2 tablespoons sour cream

SPREAD

2 cups poppy seed pastry filling
1 teaspoon vanilla extract
½ cup raisins, steamed

Prepare and knead the dough as in Chocolate Sandwiches*. Roll out ⅛ inch thick in large rectangles. Place on a buttered cookie sheet. Cut out into 1 inch squares.
Bake in a hot 400° F. oven for 15 minutes. Remove immediately from the sheet.
Combine the ingredients of the spread. Form a ball on a serving platter. Stick the cookies in.
This is a traditional Christmas Eve dessert.
Yields 5 dozen.

CHESTNUTS
Kasztanki

⅔ cup butter
1 teaspoon vanilla extract
3 tablespoons sugar

1 cup flour
1 cup ground walnuts
3 tablespoons cocoa

Beat the butter with vanilla and sugar for 5 minutes. Combine with the flour mixed with nuts. Roll into marble-sized balls.
Bake on a buttered cookie sheet in a moderate 375° F. oven for 12 minutes.
Roll warm cookies in cocoa.
Yields 2 dozen.

MERINGUES
Bezy

6 egg whites
2 cups sugar
1 teaspoon vinegar

½ teaspoon vanilla extract
Whipped cream or ice cream

Beat the egg whites till stiff. Add sugar by spoonfuls gradually, beating constantly; add vinegar and vanilla; beat 10 more minutes. Line a cookie sheet with brown paper. Drop small amounts of egg white mixture from a spoon. Bake in a slow 275° F. oven for 1 hour. Turn off the heat, and leave the meringues in the oven till cold.
Serve with whipped cream or ice cream.
Yields 7 dozen.

MACAROONS
Makaroniki

2 eggs
¾ cup sugar
1 tablespoon butter, melted
1 teaspoon grated lemon
  rind

1 teaspoon vanilla
½ cup pre-sifted flour
2 cups flaked coconut
6 ounces chocolate morsels

Beat the eggs with the sugar for 6 minutes at high speed. Add the butter, lemon rind, vanilla, and flour. Beat 3 more minutes.
Combine with the coconut and chocolate morsels. Drop by rounded teaspoonfuls onto a buttered and floured cookie sheet. Bake in a slow 325° F. oven for 15 minutes.
Yields 3 dozen.

CHEESE COOKIES
Ciasteczka z serem

½ pound farmer cheese, ground, or ricotta cheese
½ pound soft butter
2 cups all purpose pre-sifted flour
½ cup orange marmalade

Combine the cheese with butter and flour. Knead the dough. Roll out on a floured board ⅛ inch think. Cut out into 2½-inch squares. Place ¼ teaspoon marmalade on each square. Fold the corners over, and seal together.
Place on a buttered and floured cookie sheet. Bake in a hot 400° F. oven for 20 minutes.
They are best when fresh.
Yields 5 dozen.

CHRISTMAS HONEY COOKIES
Piernikowa krajanka świąteczna

DOUGH

1 cup sugar	*4 teaspoons margarine*
¼ cup water	*4 cups flour*
½ pound honey	*1 egg*
2 teaspoons allspice	*2 teaspoons baking soda*
1 teaspoon cinnamon	*⅓ cup water*
½ teaspoon cloves	*1 egg yolk*
½ teaspoon nutmeg	

SPREAD

½ cup heavy cream, hot
1 teaspoon vanilla extract
1¼ cups confectioners' sugar
6 ounces chocolate, melted
6 ounces almonds, toasted, ground

To make dough: Brown 2 tablespoons sugar in a saucepan. Add ¼ cup water and stir till dissolved. Add the rest of the sugar, honey, spices, and margarine. Bring to a boil stirring. Remove from the heat, cool.

Add the flour, the egg, baking soda, and about ⅓ cup water. Knead the dough for few minutes. Cover and let stand for 20 minutes.

Roll out a rectangle on a floured board to fit a 12×15 cookie sheet, buttered and floured. Spread dough with egg. Bake in a moderate 350° F. oven for 15 minutes.

Cool. Cut into two halves widthwise.

To make spread: Mix the ingredients of the spread well. Spread over the bottom side of ½ of the cake. Cover with the bottom part of the second half. Place a heavy book over it. Cover, and let stand overnight.

Cut out into small rectangular cookies. Store in an airtight box to prevent drying. They are best after a few days.

This is an old traditional recipe.

Yields 4 dozen.

HONEY KISSES
Całuski

Prepare dough as for Christmas Honey Cookies *

ICING

1 cup confectioners' sugar
2 tablespoons water
A few drops peppermint extract
Red, green, and yellow food coloring

Form small balls (walnut size). Bake on a buttered cookie sheet in a moderate 350° F. oven for 7 minutes. Cool.
Mix the ingredients of the icing. Divide into 4. Add food coloring. Spread some cookies with white icing, some with pink, green, or yellow. Store for a few days in an airtight box.
This is a favorite from the city of Toruń.
Yields 5 dozen.

HONEY CAKE HEARTS
Piernikowe serduszka

Prepare dough as for Christmas Honey Cookies *
1 egg
4 ounces almonds, peeled, divided in halves

Roll out the dough ⅛ inch thick. Cut out heart-shaped cookies. Spread with egg. Decorate with almonds.
Bake on a buttered cookie sheet in a moderate 350° F. oven for 7 minutes. Store for a few days in an airtight box.
Polish children like to hang these cookies on the Christmas tree.
Yields 5 dozen.

CHOCOLATE HONEY HEARTS
Pierniczki w czekoladzie

Prepare dough as for Christmas Honey Cookies*

ICING

4 *ounces chocolate, melted*
⅓ *cup cream*
¼ *cup confectioners' sugar*

Roll out dough ⅛ inch thick. Cut out heart-shaped cookies. Bake on a buttered cookie sheet in a moderate 350° F. oven for 7 minutes.
To make icing: Combine the chocolate with cream and sugar. Spread over the cookies. Store for a few days in an airtight box. Serve with yogurt or buttermilk.
Yields 5 dozen.

HONEY CAKE FROM WARSAW
Piernik warszawski

BATTER

1 *cup sugar*
3 *tablespoons water*
2 *tablespoons butter*
1 *cup honey*
1 *cup sour cream*
3 *egg yolks*
1 *teaspoon allspice*

1 *teaspoon cinnamon*
1 *teaspoon cloves*
1 *teaspoon grated orange rind*
1 *teaspoon baking soda*
4 *cups flour*

SPREAD

½ *cup jam*

ICING

6 *ounces chocolate*
2 *tablespoons butter*
¼ *cup coffee cream, hot*

To make batter: Brown 1 tablespoon sugar in a saucepan. Add 3 tablespoons water and stir till dissolved. Add the rest of the sugar, butter and honey. Bring to a boil. Remove from the heat. Add sour cream, egg yolks, spices, and orange rind. Mix well. Add the soda and flour. Beat at low speed for a few minutes. Fold into a buttered pan (9×12) which has been sprinkled with bread crumbs. Bake in a moderate 350° F. oven for 1 hour.

Cool. Remove from the pan. Cut with a sharp, long knife into 2 layers. Spread the jam over the bottom layer, cover with top layer.

To make icing: Melt the chocolate and the butter in the cream over low heat. Do not boil. Spread over the cake. Cut before serving into long narrow pieces.

This cake is better the next day. Keep covered.

Yields 32 rectangles.

SAND BABA
Babka piaskowa

⅓ *cup butter*
¾ *cup sugar*
4 *eggs*
½ *cup milk*
½ *teaspoon almond extract*
1 *teaspoon vanilla extract or rum flavoring*
1½ *cups flour*
2 *teaspoons baking powder*

Cream the butter with the sugar. Add the eggs one at a time beating at high speed. Add the milk and the flavorings, beat 3 minutes more. Add the flour and baking powder, beat 5 minutes more.

Bake at 375° F. for 50 minutes in a well-buttered baba pan which has been sprinkled with bread crumbs.

Yields 1 baba.

Serves 8.

BABA WITH RAISINS
Babka z rodzynkami

1 cup butter
1½ cups confectioners' sugar
4 eggs, separated
Juice ½ lemon
4 tablespoons coffee cream
2 tablespoons grated orange rind
2 tablespoons baking powder
1 cup cornstarch, sifted
1½ cups pre-sifted flour
⅓ cup raisins, mixed with 1 tablespoon flour
⅓ cup confectioners' sugar

Cream the butter with 1½ cups sugar very well. Add the egg yolks, beat for 5 minutes. Add lemon juice, cream, orange rind, and baking powder. Beat for 3 minutes. Fold in whipped stiff egg whites in small parts alternately with cornstarch mixed with flour. Add the raisins, mix slightly.
Bake at 375° F. for 45 minutes in a large baba or ring pan which has been buttered and sprinkled with bread crumbs.
Sprinkle the hot baba with confectioners' sugar through a sieve.
Serves 10.

LIGHT FRUIT CAKE FROM WARSAW
Keks warszawski

5 eggs
1½ cups confectioners' sugar
⅔ cup butter, creamed
1 teaspoon vanilla extract
2 teaspoons baking powder
2¾ cups flour
3 ounces candied orange rind, finely chopped
3 ounces raisins, steamed
2 ounces walnuts, finely chopped
2 ounces figs, finely sliced
2 ounces prunes, finely sliced
1 teaspoon cornstarch

Beat the eggs with the sugar for 7 minutes. Add to the butter by small portions, still beating. Add vanilla, baking powder, and flour. Beat another 10 minutes at medium speed.

Fold in the fruits mixed with cornstarch. Bake in a long, narrow loaf pan, buttered and sprinkled with bread crumbs, at 375° F. for 50 minutes. Serve thinly sliced.

Yields 1 loaf.

Serves 10.

CHRISTMAS BREAD
Placek świąteczny

5 *eggs*
2 *cups confectioners' sugar*
½ *pound margarine, creamed*
3 *tablespoons vodka*
1 *teaspoon vanilla extract*
1 *tablespoon grated lemon rind*
2 *teaspoons baking powder*
2¼ *cups flour*
¾ *cup finely chopped walnuts*
⅔ *cup raisins*
4 *ounces candied orange rind, finely chopped*
1 *teaspoon cornstarch*

Beat the eggs with the sugar for 5 minutes at high speed. Add to the margarine by small portions. Add vodka, vanilla, and lemon rind beating constantly. Add baking powder and flour, beat 5 more minutes. The batter is thick.

Mix the nuts, raisins, orange rind, and cornstarch. Combine with the batter.

Bake at 350° F. for 1 hour in a loaf or ring pan which has been buttered and sprinkled with bread crumbs.

It is better on the second day. Serve thinly sliced.

Yields 1 loaf.

Serves 12.

WALNUT RING
Orzechowy wieniec

BATTER

4 eggs
2 cups confectioners' sugar
⅔ cup butter or margarine, creamed
2¾ cups pre-sifted flour
2 teaspoons baking powder
⅓ cup rum, or vodka and rum flavoring
1½ cups ground walnuts
½ cup chopped chocolate chips

ICING

1½ cups confectioners' sugar
¼ cup cocoa
2 tablespoons butter
2 tablespoons milk, boiling
12 walnut halves

To make dough: Beat the eggs with the sugar for 5 minutes at high speed. Add to the butter in small portions. Beat another 3 minutes.
Add the flour, baking powder, and rum. Beat 5 minutes more. The batter is thick.
Combine with walnuts and chocolate chips. Fold into a tube pan which has been buttered and sprinkled with bread crumbs. Bake in a moderate 350° F. oven for 1 hour and 10 minutes.
Cool slightly. Remove from the pan.
To make icing: Mix the sugar with the cocoa and the butter melted in the milk. Spread over the cake. Decorate with walnut halves.
Serve with coffee on winter afternoons.
Yields 1 ring cake.
Serves 15.

QUICK FRUIT CAKE
Keks szybki

BATTER

½ cup raisins
6 ounces candied fruits, finely chopped
½ cup finely chopped walnuts
1 tablespoon grated orange rind
¼ cup flour
1 package date bread mix
1 egg
1 cup water

ICING

1 cup confectioners' sugar
2 tablespoons orange juice
16 almonds, peeled, divided into halves

Combine the fruits, walnuts, and orange rind with the flour.
To make batter: Combine the date bread mix with 1 egg mixed with 1 cup water. Mix for 5 minutes with a spoon. Fold in the fruit mixture.
Grease a 9×5 loaf pan and line with wax paper. Fold in the batter. Bake in a moderate 350° F. oven for 1 hour and 15 minutes. Cool in the pan. Remove, wrap in foil. Refrigerate overnight.
To make icing: Mix the icing sugar with orange juice. Spread over the cake, decorate with almonds.
Yields 1 fruit cake.
Serves 12.

NUT ROLLS
Strucle z orzechami

DOUGH

5 cups flour
8 tablespoons sugar
1 pound margarine
4 egg yolks
1 cup milk
2 ounces yeast
1 tablespoon vinegar

STUFFING

4 egg whites
1 cup sugar
2 teaspoons lemon juice
1 pound walnuts, ground

SPREAD

1 egg white

To make dough: Combine the flour with the sugar. Cut the margarine into the flour with a knife, and rub in with fingertips. Add the egg yolks mixed with ½ cup cold milk, and yeast mixed with ½ cup warm milk. Knead the dough. Add the vinegar and knead some more. Form a ball, cover, and refrigerate overnight.
To make stuffing: Beat the egg whites till stiff, add the sugar by spoonfuls, beating constantly. Add lemon juice, beat 1 minute more. Add the walnuts and mix slightly.
Roll out 5 rectangles from the dough. Spread the stuffing on each. Roll on the long side, and seal the ends.
Place on a buttered cookie sheet seam down. Spread with egg white. Bake in a moderate 375° F. oven for 40 minutes.
Yields 5 rolls. Serves 20.

POPPY SEED ROLLS
Strucle z makiem

DOUGH

⅔ cup butter
4¼ cups pre-sifted, all purpose flour
1 cup confectioners' sugar, sifted
2 eggs
3 egg yolks
½ cup sour cream or coffee cream
1 teaspoon vanilla extract
1 tablespoon grated lemon rind
2 ounces yeast
1 tablespoon sugar

FILLING

2 tablespoons butter
10 ounces poppy seeds, ground twice
    (*may be purchased ground in many delicatessen stores*)
⅔ cup sugar
2 tablespoons honey
2 tablespoons finely chopped candied orange rind
2 tablespoons finely chopped almonds
1 tablespoon grated lemon rind
1 teaspoon vanilla extract
¼ cup raisins, steamed
1 egg white, whipped stiff

ICING

1 cup confectioners' sugar
2 tablespoons lemon juice

To make dough: Cut the butter in the flour with a knife, and rub in with fingertips. Combine with confectioners' sugar. Add all the other ingredients and yeast mixed with sugar. Knead the dough. Roll out 2 12-inch squares.

To make filling: Heat the butter in a saucepan. Add the poppy seeds, fry for few minutes. Add all the rest of the ingredients. Mix. Spread the stuffing over the dough. Roll. Place seam down in buttered long loaf pans, or on a cookie sheet. Place in the oven heated to 100° F. Cover with a towel, leave the oven door half open. Let stand till it doubles in size—about 1½ hours. Bake in a moderate 350° F. oven for 45 minutes. Cool. Spread with the confectioners' sugar mixed with lemon juice. Yields 2 long rolls. Serves 20.

SPANISH TORTE
Tort hiszpański

3½ dozen Meringues*	*1¼ cups confectioners' sugar*
1 pound mixed candied fruits	*1 teaspoon vanilla extract*
1 pint whipping cream	

Arrange ⅓ of the meringues in a circle on a serving platter. Sprinkle with ⅓ of the fruits. Cover with ⅓ of the cream whipped with sugar and vanilla. Place the second layer of meringues, fruits, and cream over it. Place the third layer of meringues and cream over it. Sprinkle with the rest of the fruits.
Serve immediately.
Yields 1 large torte. Serves 12.

MOCHA TORTE
Tort mocca

BATTER	ICING
12 egg whites	*1¼ cups sweet butter*
3½ cups confectioners' sugar	*2 egg yolks*
Juice ½ lemon	*⅓ cup confectioners' sugar*
1 pound almonds, ground	*2 tablespoons instant coffee*
	4 tablespoons vodka

To make batter: Beat egg whites until stiff. Add sugar by spoonfuls, beat for 3 minutes. Add lemon juice, beat 5 more minutes. Add the almonds, mix slightly.

Spread the batter in 3 brown-paper-lined 9-inch round cake pans. Bake in a slow 275° F. oven for 1½ hours. Turn off the heat and leave the cake in the oven until cold.

To make icing: Cream the butter with egg yolks and confectioners' sugar. Dissolve the instant coffee in the vodka, mix with the cream icing, adding gradually.

Spread the icing between the layers, on the top and on the sides of the torte.

Yields 1 9-inch round torte. Serves 12.

ORANGE NUT TORTE
Tort pomarańczowo-orzechowy

DOUGH

½ pound butter
2¾ cups pre-sifted, all purpose flour
⅔ cup confectioners' sugar
3 egg yolks, cooked, rubbed through a sieve

ORANGE FILLING

2½ cups sugar
½ cup water
3 medium oranges, mashed in a blender, or coarsely
    grated
2 lemons, mashed in a blender, or coarsely grated

WALNUT FILLING

½ pound walnuts, ground
2 cups confectioners' sugar
½ cup sour cream
1 teaspoon vanilla extract

ICING

1 cup confectioners' sugar
1½ tablespoons lemon juice

Candied orange rind

To make dough: Cut the butter into the flour with a knife, and rub in with fingertips. Add the rest of the ingredients and knead the dough.

Spread the dough and bake at 400° F. for 15 minutes in 4 8-inch round pans which have been buttered and lined with wax paper. To make fillings: Cook the sugar with the water stirring till it thickens. Add the oranges and the lemons and cook at medium heat for 1½ hours. The filling should be thick and transparent. Cool slightly.

Combine the ingredients of the walnut filling.

Spread half of the orange filling on the first circle. Cover with the second. Spread with the walnut filling. Cover with the third circle. Spread with the rest of the orange filling. Cover with the fourth circle.

To make icing: Combine the confectioners' sugar with lemon juice. Spread over the top and sides of the torte. Decorate with candied orange rind. Refrigerate.

This is an elegant New Year's Eve torte.

Yields 1 tall 8-inch torte. Serves 20.

CHOCOLATE TORTE
Tort czekoladowy

BATTER

SPREAD

6 eggs, separated
⅔ cup confectioners' sugar
½ cup soft butter
1 tablespoon grated
 lemon rind
1 teaspoon cinnamon
½ teaspoon cloves
Dash salt
1 cup fine, toasted bread
 crumbs
1 cup instant chocolate

½ cup apricot jam

ICING

3 egg yolks
⅔ cup confectioners' sugar
1 cup soft sweet butter
6 ounces chocolate, melted
1 tablespoon instant coffee
2 tablespoons vodka

To make batter: Beat the egg yolks with the sugar for 5 minutes at high speed. Add the butter by small bits, beating constantly. Add lemon rind, cinnamon, and cloves, beat some more.

Add egg whites whipped with salt in small parts alternately with bread crumbs and chocolate. Mix slightly.

Bake in 2 8-inch pans, buttered and sprinkled with bread crumbs, at 325° F. for 30 minutes. Turn off the heat and leave the cake in the oven for 10 minutes. Cool.

Spread the jam between layers.

To make icing: Beat the egg yolks with the sugar for 5 minutes. Add the butter by small bits, beating constantly. Add the chocolate, beat some more. Combine with coffee dissolved in vodka. Spread on the top and on the sides of the torte.

Yields 1 8-inch torte. Serves 20.

WALNUT TORTE
Tort orzechowy

8 eggs, separated	*8 ounces walnuts, ground*
2 cups confectioners' sugar	*3 tablespoons bread crumbs*
Juice 1 lemon	*1 teaspoon vanilla extract*

COFFEE SPREAD

4 egg yolks	*2 tablespoons instant coffee*
1½ cups sugar	*1 teaspoon cocoa*
1 cup sweet butter, creamed	*4 tablespoons vodka*
1 teaspoon vanilla extract	
	Candied fruits

To make batter: Beat the egg yolks with the sugar for 4 minutes, add the lemon juice. Beat the egg whites until stiff. Fold in the walnuts, egg whites, bread crumbs, and vanilla extract alternately in small portions without mixing. Mix all together very slightly. Spread the batter in 3 buttered and wax-paper-lined 9-inch round cake pans. Bake in moderate 350° F. oven for 45 minutes. Remove from the oven, cool in the pan.

To make spread: Beat the egg yolks with the sugar, combine with butter. Add vanilla extract. Dissolve instant coffee and cocoa in the vodka, mix with the cream icing gradually. Spread between the layers, on the top and on the sides of the torte. Decorate with candied fruits.

Yields 1 9-inch torte. Serves 16.

ALMOND TORTE
Tort migdałowy

Use the same recipe as for Walnut Torte* using almonds instead
of walnuts and cornstarch instead of bread crumbs. Coffee spread
or chocolate icing (from the Chocolate Torte*) may be used.
Yields 1 9-inch torte. Serves 16.

BRAZIL NUT TORTE
Tort orzechowy ciemny

BATTER

6 eggs, separated
⅔ cup sugar
1 teaspoon instant coffee
2 tablespoons toasted bread crumbs
1 tablespoon vodka
2 cups ground Brazil nuts

CREAM

1½ cups whipping cream
3 tablespoons sugar
2 tablespoons instant coffee
1 tablespoon cold water
12 Brazil nut halves

To make batter: Beat the egg yolks with the sugar at high speed
for 6 minutes. Add the coffee, bread crumbs, and vodka. Beat
some more.
Beat the egg whites till stiff. Fold into the egg yolk mixture
alternately with nuts.
Bake in 2 8-inch cake pans, buttered and lined with wax paper,
in a moderate 350° F. oven for 35 minutes. Cool in the pans.
To make cream: Whip the cream, add the sugar, beat 1 more
minute at low speed. Add the coffee dissolved in 1 tablespoon
cold water. Spread between the layers, on the top and the sides

of the torte. Garnish with nut halves. Cut into 12 wedges and serve immediately.

Yields 1 8-inch torte. Serves 12.

TORTE PROVENÇE
Tort prowancki

BATTER

8 eggs, separated
2 cups confectioners' sugar
1 teaspoon vanilla extract
⅔ cup instant chocolate
3 tablespoons light bread crumbs
1⅔ cups ground almonds (ground in peels)

ICING

3 eggs
1 cup sugar
½ pound sweet butter, creamed
1 teaspoon rum
1 cup toasted ground almonds

To make batter: Beat the egg yolks with sugar and vanilla for 5 minutes at high speed. Whip the egg whites till stiff. Add the egg whites and the dry ingredients to the egg yolks alternately in small portions. Mix lightly.

To make icing: Bake in a moderate oven 375° F. for 1 hour in a 9-inch spring pan which has been buttered and sprinkled with bread crumbs. Turn off the heat, leave the oven door open, and let the torte stand for 10 minutes.

Beat the eggs with the sugar for 10 minutes at high speed. Add to the butter in small portions beating at low speed. Add the rum and fold in the almonds. Spread over the top and the sides of the torte. Refrigerate.

Yields 1 9-inch torte. Serves 20.

POPPY SEED COFFEE TORTE
Tort makowy z kawą

BATTER

8 eggs, separated
2 cups confectioners' sugar
1 tablespoon honey
1 teaspoon almond extract
1 teaspoon vanilla extract
1 teaspoon grated lemon rind
3 tablespoons light bread crumbs
3 ounces poppy seeds, ground twice

ICING

3 eggs
1 cup sugar
½ pound sweet butter, creamed
2 tablespoons instant coffee
1 tablespoon vodka

To make batter: Beat the egg yolks with the sugar for 5 minutes. Add honey, almond and vanilla extracts, beat some more. Add whipped stiff egg whites and dry ingredients alternately in small portions. Mix lightly. Bake as in Torte Provençe*.
To make icing: Beat the eggs with the sugar for 10 minutes at high speed. Add to the butter in small portions beating at low speed. Add coffee dissolved in vodka and beat some more.
Cut the torte horizontally into 2 layers. Spread the icing between the layers, on the top and the sides of the torte. Refrigerate.
Yields 1 9-inch torte. Serves 20.

TORTE STEPHANIE
Tort Stefanka

BATTER

6 eggs, separated
1¼ cups confectioners' sugar
½ tablespoon vinegar
1¼ cups pre-sifted, all purpose flour

FILLING

3 eggs
1¼ cups sugar
1¼ cups sweet butter, creamed
1 teaspoon vanilla extract
2 tablespoons grated orange rind
½ cup instant cocoa
3 ounces chocolate, melted

ICING

2 cups confectioners' sugar
3 tablespoons cocoa
3 tablespoons water
½ tablespoon lemon juice
12 almonds, peeled, divided into halves

To make batter: Beat the egg yolks with sugar for 5 minutes. Add the vinegar. Add whipped stiff egg whites, sift the flour over the egg mixture. Mix lightly.
Bake in 4 9-inch cake pans, buttered and lined with wax paper, in moderate 350° F. oven for 15 minutes or until golden. Cool.
To make filling: Beat the eggs with the sugar for 10 minutes. Add to the butter in small portions beating at low speed. Add vanilla, orange rind, and cocoa. Beat some more. Combine with chocolate. Spread between the layers of the torte. Refrigerate.
To make icing: Combine the sugar with cocoa mixed with water and lemon juice. Spread over the top and the sides of the torte. Decorate with almond halves. Refrigerate.
Yields 1 9-inch torte. Serves 16.

POPPY SEED TORTE
Torcik z makiem

½ cup poppy seeds
1 cup milk
1 teaspoon vanilla extract
¾ cup butter
1½ cups sugar
2 cups flour
2 teaspoons baking powder

4 egg whites
½ cup raspberry
 or apricot jam
1 cup whipping cream
2 teaspoons confectioners'
 sugar
Candied cherries

Soak the poppy seeds in milk and vanilla overnight.
Cream the butter with sugar. Add to the butter mixture flour, baking powder, and poppy seeds with the milk alternately. Mix well. Beat the egg whites until stiff, fold in, mix slightly.
Spread the batter in 2 8-inch pans which have been greased and sprinkled with bread crumbs. Bake in a moderate 350° F. oven for 40 minutes. Remove from the oven, cool for 5 minutes, remove from the pan. Spread the jam between the layers. Refrigerate.
Beat the cream, add the sugar. Spread on the top and on the sides of the torte. Serve immediately.
Yields 1 8-inch torte. Serves 12.

DATE TORTE
Tort daktylowy

6 eggs
2 cups confectioners' sugar
8 ounces dates, sliced
8 ounces almonds, peeled, ground
Juice ½ lemon
1 teaspoon vanilla extract
4 tablespoons fine bread crumbs

CHOCOLATE SPREAD

4 ounces melted chocolate
2 tablespoons butter

Beat the eggs with the sugar for 5 minutes. Add all the other ingredients, mix.

Spread the batter in 2 9-inch round cake pans which have been greased and lined with wax paper. Bake in moderate 375° F. oven for 45 minutes. Remove, cool.

Mix the chocolate with butter. Spread between the layers, thinly. Pour the rest of the chocolate over the top of the cake. Refrigerate for 1 hour.

Yields 1 9-inch torte. Serves 16.

PUMPERNICKEL TORTE
Tort z razowca

BATTER

10 eggs, separated
2½ cups confectioners' sugar
1 teaspoon cinnamon
1 teaspoon almond extract
Grated rind 1 lemon
Juice 1 lemon
¼ cup instant chocolate
2¼ cups ground walnuts
½ cup dried twice-ground pumpernickel

ICING

1½ cups confectioners' sugar
2 tablespoons lemon juice
9 maraschino cherries

Beat the egg yolks with sugar for 5 minutes. Add cinnamon, almond extract, lemon rind, and juice. Beat some more. Add whipped stiff egg whites alternately with chocolate, nuts, and pumpernickel in small parts, mix slightly.

Bake in a buttered, wax-paper-lined 9-inch spring pan in moderate 375° F. oven for 1 hour. Turn off the heat. Leave the cake in the oven with the door half open for 10 minutes. Cool.

Combine the confectioners' sugar with lemon juice. Spread over the top and sides of the torte. Decorate with cherries.
Yields 1 9-inch torte. Serves 20.

LEMON TORTE
Tort cytrynowy

BATTER

10 eggs, separated
2½ cups confectioners' sugar
1 tablespoon lemon juice
1 cup sifted all purpose flour
1 cup cornstarch, sifted

FILLING

2 egg yolks
⅔ cup confectioners' sugar
1 teaspoon lemon juice
¼ pound soft sweet butter
4 ounces almonds, toasted, ground

ICING

Prepare as for Pumpernickel Torte*

Candied lemon rind

To make batter: Prepare the batter as in Torte Stephanie*. Bake in 3 9-inch pans, buttered and lined with wax paper, at 350° F. for 40 minutes. Cool.
To make filling: Beat the egg yolks with sugar for 5 minutes. Add lemon juice and butter in small bits, beating constantly. Combine with almonds. Spread between the layers of the torte. Spread the icing over the top and sides. Decorate with lemon rind.
Yields 1 9-inch torte. Serves 20.

FAVORS
Chrust-Faworki

2 medium eggs
2 egg yolks
¼ teaspoon salt
½ cup confectioners' sugar
2 cups all purpose flour
¼ cup vodka
¼ cup soft butter
1 pound lard or shortening
⅔ cup confectioners' sugar (*mixed with powdered vanilla if you can get it*)

Beat the eggs and the egg yolks with salt until creamy. Add the ½ cup sugar and beat some more. Add the flour, vodka and butter. Knead the dough for 10 minutes.

Roll out small portion on a lightly floured board paper thin. Cut out 1½ × 6-inch strips. Cut a 2-inch-long hole in the middle of each strip, then pass one end of the strip through it.

Heat the lard in a large frying pan. Fry strips on high heat on both sides till golden. Place on tissue paper to cool. Sprinkle with confectioners' sugar through a sieve.

This is a traditional Polish treat for winter parties.

Yields 3 dozen.

POLISH DOUGHNUTS
Pączki

4 ounces yeast
⅔ cup sugar
8 cups pre-sifted, all purpose flour
2 cups milk
1 egg
7 egg yolks
2 teaspoons vanilla extract

Grated rind 1 lemon
Juice 1 lemon
¼ teaspoon salt
2 tablespoons vodka or rum
6 tablespoons salad oil
1 pound jam
3 pints lard or salad oil
⅔ cup confectioners' sugar

Combine the yeast with 1 tablespoon sugar, 1¾ cups flour, and 1 cup milk. Let stand in a warm place until doubled in size. Beat the egg and the egg yolks with the rest of the sugar. Add the rest of the flour and milk, vanilla, lemon rind and juice, salt, and vodka. Knead the dough till smooth. Add the oil in 3 parts, knead 10 more minutes. Place in the oven heated to 100° F., cover with a towel and leave the door half open, till the dough doubles in size.

Roll out ¾ inch thick. Cut out circles 1½ inches in diameter. Place 1 teaspoon jam on half of the circles. Cover with the rest of the circles. Seal the edges.

Heat the lard in an electric frying pan to 375° F., or test with a small piece of dough. It should float immediately. Fry the doughnuts on both sides, a few at a time. Remove and place on paper tissue.

Sprinkle warm doughnuts with confectioners' sugar sprinkled through a sieve.

Yields 65 doughnuts.

CHOCOLATE ROLL
Rolada czekoladowa

BATTER

5 egg yolks	*½ cup flour*
1 cup confectioners' sugar	*¾ cup ground walnuts*
1 tablespoon lemon juice	*7 egg whites, whipped stiff*

FILLING

2 eggs	*3 tablespoons cocoa*
1¼ cups sugar	*½ teaspoon vanilla extract*
⅔ cup sweet butter, creamed	*1 tablespoon vodka*

SPREAD

6 ounces mint chocolate, melted
2 tablespoons sweet butter

To make batter: Beat the egg yolks with sugar for 5 minutes. Add lemon juice and beat for another 2 minutes at high speed. Add the flour, walnuts, and egg whites in small parts alternately. Mix all slightly.

Spread the batter over a large cookie sheet (12×18 with edges) lined with buttered wax paper. Bake in a moderate 350° F. oven for 15–20 minutes or till golden. Cool.

To make filling: Beat the eggs with the sugar for 10 minutes. Add to the butter by small portions, beating at low speed. Add the rest of the ingredients and beat a few more minutes. Spread over the cake. Roll.

Spread with hot chocolate mixed with butter. Refrigerate for 1 hour. Slice before serving.

Yields 1 18-inch roll. Serves 20.

COFFEE ROLL
Rolada kawowa

BATTER

Prepare batter as for Chocolate Roll*

FILLING

Prepare filling as for Walnut Torte*

ICING

1 cup confectioners' sugar
1 tablespoon instant coffee
1½ tablespoons water

Prepare the Coffee Roll as Chocolate Roll*.
Yields 1 18-inch roll. Serves 20.

CREAM PUFFS
Ptysie z kremem

DOUGH

⅓ cup margarine   1½ cups flour
1 cup water   5 eggs
¼ teaspoon salt   1 teaspoon baking powder

FILLING

1½ cups heavy cream
1 teaspoon vanilla extract
½ cup confectioners' sugar

To make dough: Bring the margarine and the water to a boil.
Add salt and flour. Beat with a portable mixer at low speed till
smooth and shiny. Cool for a few minutes. Add the eggs one by
one, beating constantly till cold. Add baking powder.
Drop dough from a spoon (or use cookie gun) on a buttered cookie
sheet. Bake in a hot 450° F. oven for 10 minutes. Reduce the
heat to 375° F. Bake another 15 minutes. Cool.
To make filling: Whip the cream with vanilla and half of the
sugar. Cut each puff in two. Fill with cream. Cover. Sprinkle with
the rest of the sugar through a sieve.
Yields 25 puffs.

COFFEE ECLAIRS
Eklery kawowe

Prepare dough as for Cream Puffs*

FILLING

3 eggs   1 teaspoon vanilla
1½ cups confectioners' sugar   4 tablespoons instant coffee
2 tablespoons cornstarch   2 cups milk, boiling

ICING

1 cup confectioners' sugar   1½ tablespoons water
2 tablespoons cocoa

Bake the puffs as in Cream Puffs*.

Filling: Beat the eggs with sugar in a saucepan with a portable mixer. Add cornstarch and vanilla. Beat some more. Add coffee dissolved in milk. Place on low heat and beat at low speed till it thickens. Remove from heat. Beat till cold.

Fill the puffs and spread with confectioners' sugar mixed with cocoa and water.

Yields 25 puffs.

TINY BABAS
Babeczki śmietankowe

DOUGH

¾ cup and 3 tablespoons butter
2¾ cups pre-sifted, all purpose flour
⅔ cup confectioners' sugar
4 egg yolks
1 teaspoon vanilla extract

CREAM

2 eggs	*1 teaspoon vanilla extract*
2 egg yolks	*2 tablespoons cornstarch*
⅔ cup sugar	*1 pint coffee cream, boiling*

To make dough: Cut the butter into the flour and rub in with fingertips. Combine with the sugar, add the egg yolks and vanilla. Knead the dough. Refrigerate for 10 minutes.

Roll out ¼ inch thick. Cut out circles with a tart pan. Fit into individual tart pans. Reserve circles for covering the cups.

To make cream: Beat the eggs and the egg yolks with the sugar for 5 minutes. Add vanilla and cornstarch. Beat some more. Pour in the cream in a thin stream still beating.

Cook on low heat stirring till it thickens. Cool. Fill the cups. Cover with reserved circles.

Bake in a 400° F. oven for 20 minutes until golden.

Yields 15 cream cups.

NUT CUPS
Babeczki orzechowe

Prepare dough as for Tiny Babas*

STUFFING

3 eggs, separated
⅔ cup confectioners' sugar
1 teaspoon vanilla

4 ounces walnuts, ground
½ cup jam

Roll out the dough ¼ inch thick. Cut out circles, fit into individual tart pans. Bake in a 400° F. oven for 10 minutes. Cool.
Beat the egg yolks with sugar and vanilla for 5 minutes. Fold in whipped stiff egg whites and walnuts in small portions alternately, mix slightly.
Spread some jam on the bottom of each cup. Fill with egg mixture. Bake another 15 minutes.
Yields 30 nut cups.

CHOCOLATE SQUARES
Czekoladowe ciastka

BATTER

1½ cups butter
6 ounces baking chocolate
2 cups sugar
2 tablespoons vanilla extract

6 eggs
2 cups flour
½ cup chopped walnuts

SPREAD

2 tablespoons butter
2 tablespoons cocoa

2 teaspoons vanilla extract
Confectioners' sugar

To make batter: Melt the butter with the chocolate, sugar, and vanilla. Cool slightly.
Beat the chocolate mixture, adding gradually the eggs and flour. Add the walnuts.

Bake in a buttered 8½ ×12-inch pan in a moderate 375° F. oven for 45 minutes. Cool, remove from the pan.

To make spread: Mix the butter with the cocoa and vanilla, adding as much confectioners' sugar as needed for a sour cream consistency. Spread over the cake. Refrigerate for ½ hour. Cut into 32 pieces.

Yields 32 squares.

ALMOND SQUARES
Migdałowe ciastka

BATTER

2 eggs	1½ teaspoons baking powder
1 cup sugar	¼ cup butter
1 cup flour	½ cup milk

SPREAD

½ cup peeled slivered almonds
¼ cup butter
¼ cup sugar
1½ teaspoons instant flour
¼ cup coffee cream

To make batter: Beat the eggs with the sugar for 5 minutes. Add the flour and baking powder, mix.

Melt the butter in the hot milk. Pour hot milk into the batter. Beat for 5 minutes. Bake in a moderate 350° F. oven for 35 minutes in a 9-inch square pan, buttered and sprinkled with bread crumbs. Cool slightly.

To make spread: Put the almonds, butter, sugar, flour, and cream in a saucepan. Simmer for a few minutes, mixing. Pour over the cake, spread evenly. Place the cake under broiler for 2–5 minutes, or until golden. Cool. Cut in the pan into 16 pieces.

Yields 16 squares.

EASTER BABA
Babka wielkanocna

DOUGH

2 *envelopes dry yeast*
⅔ *cup sugar*
1 *cup coffee cream, tepid*
4 *cups sifted, all purpose flour*
6 *egg yolks*
1 *tablespoon vanilla extract*
1 *teaspoon almond extract*
1 *tablespoon grated lemon rind*
¼ *pound butter, melted*
⅓ *cup raisins, steamed*

ICING

1 *cup confectioners' sugar*
1 *tablespoon lemon juice or rum*
1 *tablespoon water*

Place the yeast in a small bowl. Add 2 tablespoons sugar and the cream, stir, and let stand for 5 minutes. Add 1 cup flour, stir, and let stand in a warm place until doubled in size.

Beat the egg yolks with the rest of the sugar very well. Add the rest of the flour, the yeast mixture, vanilla and almond extracts, and the lemon rind. Knead the dough for 5 minutes, add butter in small portions. Knead another 5 minutes until smooth. Add the raisins and knead some more.

Place in 2 baba pans, buttered and sprinkled with flour. Place in oven heated to 100° F. Cover with a clean towel, leave the oven door half open. Let stand for 1 hour or until it at least doubles in size.

Bake in a moderate 350° F. oven for 45 minutes. Cool, remove from the pan.

Mix the icing ingredients well. Spread over the cakes, let drip on the sides.

This cake freezes very well. Freeze before icing.

Yields 2 babas. Serves 20.

POPPY SEED YEAST CAKE
Placek drożdżowy z makiem

DOUGH

1 ounce yeast
⅔ cup sugar
4½ cups all purpose flour
1 cup milk, tepid
1 egg
3 egg yolks
1 teaspoon vanilla extract
1 teaspoon grated lemon rind
¼ pound butter, melted

SPREAD

1 pound poppy seed pastry filling
1 tablespoon grated lemon rind
½ cup raisins

CRUMBS

¾ cup flour
3 tablespoons butter
1 teaspoon vanilla
⅓ cup confectioners' sugar

Prepare the dough as in Easter Baba*. Place in oven heated to 100° F. Cover with a towel, leave the oven door half open. Let stand until it doubles in size.

Spread the dough over a 9×12 baking pan, buttered and sprinkled with flour. Spread poppy seed filling combined with lemon rind and raisins. Return to the oven till it doubles in size.

Combine the ingredients for the crumbs. Grate and sprinkle over the cake. Bake in a moderate 350° F. oven for 40 minutes.

Yields 1 9×12 cake. Serves 20.

CHEESE YEAST CAKE
Placek drożdżowy z serem

Prepare dough as for Poppy Seed Yeast Cake*

SPREAD

3 egg yolks
⅔ cup sugar
1 teaspoon vanilla extract
⅓ cup finely chopped candied orange rind
1 pound farmer cheese or ricotta cheese
2 tablespoons butter

Prepare crumbs as for Poppy Seed Yeast Cake*.
Let the dough rise and spread in the pan as for Poppy Seed Yeast Cake*.
Beat the egg yolks with sugar for 5 minutes. Add vanilla and orange rind. Combine with cheese mixed with butter.
Spread over the cake, let rise again, sprinkle with crumbs, and bake as in Poppy Seed Yeast Cake*.
Yields 1 9×12 cake. Serves 20.

CHEESE BREAD
Strucla z serem

DOUGH

4 cups pre-sifted, all purpose flour
4 teaspoons baking powder
2 eggs
⅔ cup soft butter
⅔ cup sugar
2 tablespoons rum
½ pound ricotta cheese
6 ounces raisins
6 ounces almonds, ground
½ cup finely chopped candied orange rind

SPREAD

3 tablespoons butter, melted
⅓ cup confectioners' sugar

Combine the flour with baking powder, eggs, butter, sugar, rum, and cheese. Knead the dough.

Mix the raisins with almonds and orange rind. Add to the dough. Form a narrow loaf.

Bake on a buttered cookie sheet in a moderate 375° F. oven for 1 hour.

Spread the hot cheese bread with butter and sprinkle with confectioners' sugar through a sieve.

Yields 1 loaf. Serves 20.

COUNTRY CHEESE CAKE
Serowiec

DOUGH

⅓ cup margarine
2¾ cups pre-sifted, all purpose flour
⅔ cup confectioners' sugar
2 teaspoons baking powder
1 egg
1 egg yolk
3 tablespoons sour cream

FILLING

3 eggs
⅔ cup sugar
1 teaspoon vanilla
1 pound farmer cheese, ground, or ricotta cheese
2 tablespoons butter
3 tablespoons finely chopped candied orange rind

SPREAD

1 egg white

To make dough: Cut the margarine into the flour with a knife and rub in with fingertips. Add the rest of the ingredients. Knead the dough for few minutes. Refrigerate.

To make filling: Beat the eggs with the sugar for 5 minutes. Add vanilla, beat some more. Combine with the cheese, mixed with butter and orange rind.

Roll out ⅔ of the dough to fit a 9×12 pan, buttered and sprinkled with bread crumbs. Bake in moderate 375° F. oven for 10 minutes. Cool for few minutes. Spread the filling.

Form thin rolls from the rest of the dough. Place them diagonally crisscrossed on the cake. Spread with egg white.

Bake another 40 minutes. Cool and cut into 2-inch squares in the pan. This cake is best the same day.

Yields 32 squares.

GRANDMOTHER'S CHEESE CAKE
Sernik babci

DOUGH

⅓ cup margarine	1½ teaspoons baking powder
1¾ cups all purpose flour	1 egg
½ cup confectioners' sugar	3 tablespoons sour cream

CHEESE FILLING

5 eggs
2 cups confectioners' sugar
1 teaspoon vanilla extract
1 pound farmer cheese, ground, or ricotta cheese
¼ pound butter
1 cup ground, boiled potatoes
2 teaspoons baking powder
¼ cup raisins
¼ cup grated orange rind

SPREAD

1 egg white

To make dough: Cut the margarine into the flour and rub in with fingertips. Add the sugar, baking powder, and egg mixed with sour cream. Knead the dough.

Roll out ⅔ of the dough to fit a 9×12 pan, buttered and sprinkled with bread crumbs. Bake at 375° F. for 10 minutes.

To make filling: Beat the eggs with the sugar for 5 minutes at high speed. Add vanilla. Combine with cheese mixed with butter, potatoes, and baking powder. Fold in the raisins and orange rind. Spread over the cake.

Form thin rolls from the rest of the dough. Place them diagonally crisscrossed on the cake. Spread with the egg white.

Bake for 1 hour. Cool and cut into 2-inch squares in the pan. Yields 32 squares.

EASTER CHEESE CAKE
Sernik wielkanocny

Prepare dough as for Grandmother's Cheese Cake*

SPREAD

6 ounces raspberry jam

CHEESE FILLING

6 eggs
2¼ cups confectioners' sugar
⅔ cup soft butter
2½ tablespoons instant flour
1½ pounds farmer cheese, ground, or ricotta cheese
1½ teaspoons vanilla extract
2 teaspoons grated lemon rind
¼ cup finely chopped candied orange rind
⅓ cup raisins
1 egg white

Roll out ⅔ of the dough to fit a 9×12 pan, buttered and sprinkled with bread crumbs. Bake at 375° F. for 10 minutes. Cool. Spread with jam.

Prepare the cheese filling, spread over the cake, decorate and bake as in Grandmother's Cheese Cake*.

Yields 32 squares.

CHEESE CAKE FROM KRAKOW
Sernik krakowski

CRUST

1½ cups bread crumbs
½ cup sugar

⅓ cup butter, melted

CHEESE

1½ pounds creamed cottage
  cheese
4 egg yolks
¾ cup cream
1 cup sugar
⅓ cup flour
1 teaspoon vanilla extract

Grated rind 1 orange
½ teaspoon grated lemon
  rind
2 tablespoons lemon juice
1 cup mashed potatoes
4 egg whites, whipped stiff

Mix the ingredients of the crust. Spread over the bottom of a 9-inch spring pan. Bake at 350° F. for 8 minutes.

Beat the cheese with egg yolks and some cream in a mixer or blender. Add the rest of the cream, sugar, flour, vanilla extract, rinds, and juice. Beat some more. Combine with potatoes. Fold in egg whites. Mix slightly. Pour over the crust in the pan.

Bake in a slow 325° F. oven for 1 hour and 15 minutes. Turn off the heat. Leave the cake in the oven with door half closed for another hour.

Yields 1 9-inch, tall cheese cake. Serves 20.

ROYAL MAZURKA I
Mazurek królewski I

1 cup soft butter
1¼ cups sugar
8 ounces almonds, peeled,
  ground

1 teaspoon vanilla extract
Grated rind 1 orange
5 egg whites
1½ cups flour

Beat the butter with the sugar at high speed for 5 minutes. Add the almonds, vanilla, and orange rind. Mix.

Beat the egg whites till stiff. Add the flour and egg whites to the butter mixture alternately. Mix lightly.

Spread over a buttered 9×12 cookie sheet. Bake in a moderate 350° F. oven for 40 minutes.
Cool. Cut into small squares. Remove from the cookie sheet with a knife.
Yields 48 squares.

ROYAL MAZURKA II
Mazurek królewski II

DOUGH

6 eggs
2⅔ cups confectioners' sugar
8 tablespoons boiling water
Juice 1 lemon
3¼ cups flour
4 ounces almonds, peeled, ground
¾ pound butter, melted

SPREAD

1 cup apricot jam

ICING

1 cup confectioners' sugar
2 teaspoons lemon juice

Line 2 baking pans (9×12) with buttered wax paper.
Beat the eggs with the sugar at high speed for 10 minutes. Heat the water with the lemon juice. Add to the eggs in a thin stream. Beat 5 minutes more.
Add alternately in small portions: the flour, almonds, and butter. Mix lightly.
Fold into the baking pans. Bake until golden in a moderate 375° F. oven for 30 minutes.
Cool slightly. Remove from the pans. Cool.
Spread one cake with jam. Cover with the other.
Mix the confectioners' sugar with lemon juice. Spread over the mazurka. Cut into small squares.
Yields 32 squares.

CHOCOLATE MAZURKA
Mazurek czekoladowy

DOUGH

⅔ *cup soft butter*	*1 egg*
2¾ *cups sifted flour*	*1 egg yolk*
⅔ *cup confectioners' sugar*	*3 tablespoons sour cream*
2 teaspoons baking powder	

SPREAD

8 ounces baking chocolate	*1¼ cups sugar*
4 tablespoons coffee cream	*1 tablespoon flour*
4 egg yolks	*12 almonds, peeled, chopped*

To make dough: Cut the butter into the flour with a knife and rub in with fingertips. Add sugar and baking powder, mix. Add the rest of ingredients and knead the dough. Refrigerate in a covered dish for ½ hour.

Roll out thin. Place on a buttered cookie sheet, 12×15. Spread the dough with fingers till the sheet is covered. Bake at 375° F. for 15 minutes.

To make spread: Melt the chocolate with the cream in a warm oven. Beat the egg yolks with sugar until fluffy, add the flour. Mix the melted chocolate with the egg mixture, add the almonds. Spread the chocolate mixture over the slightly cooled cake. Return to the oven. Bake in a warm 300° F. oven for 10 minutes. Cool. Cut into small squares. Remove from the sheet with a knife. A white wafer is often used in Poland instead of the cake bottom. Yields 48 squares.

GYPSY MAZURKA
Mazurek cygański

¾ cup sliced raisins
¾ cup sliced figs
¾ cup sliced dates
¾ cup sliced candied
  orange rind
2¼ cups chopped walnuts

Grated rind 1 lemon
6 tablespoons cornstarch
5 eggs, separated
7 tablespoons sugar
1 teaspoon vanilla extract

Mix the first 6 ingredients with the cornstarch. Beat the egg whites until stiff, add sugar gradually, add egg yolks and vanilla. Fold in the fruit mixture, mix slightly. Spread over a buttered and floured cookie sheet. Bake in a moderate 350° F. oven for 20 minutes. Cut into small squares. Remove from the baking sheet with a knife.
Yields 4 dozen squares.

ALL FRUIT MAZURKA
Mazurek bakaliowy

Prepare dough as for Chocolate Mazurka*, or use a commercial white wafer

FILLING

½ cup chopped candied orange rind
½ cup thinly sliced figs
½ cup thinly sliced pitted dates
½ cup thinly sliced dried apricots
½ cup raisins, steamed
½ cup chopped walnuts
⅔ cup chopped peeled almonds

SPREAD

1 egg
1 egg yolk
½ cup confectioners' sugar
1 tablespoon lemon juice

1 teaspoon vanilla extract
⅓ cup butter, melted
2 ounces almonds, ground
2 tablespoons bread crumbs

Prepare the dough as in Chocolate Mazurka* and bake at 375° F. for 10 minutes.
Mix the fruits with nuts and arrange over the cake.
Beat the egg and the egg yolk with the sugar for 5 minutes. Add the rest of ingredients. Mix well. Pour over the cake evenly.
Bake for another 15 minutes.
Yields 48 squares.

FIG MAZURKA
Mazurek figowy

Bottom layer as in Chocolate Mazurka*, or a white commercial wafer

FILLING

1¼ cups sugar
½ tablespoon vinegar
½ cup water
1½ cups chopped walnuts
8 ounces figs, ground
3 ounces candied orange rind, ground

ICING

2 cups confectioners' sugar
3 tablespoons lemon juice

Bring the sugar with vinegar and water to a boil. Cook for 5 minutes stirring. Add the rest of filling ingredients. Cook for 10 minutes stirring. Cool for a few minutes. Spread the warm filling over the cake. Cool.
Combine the sugar with lemon juice. Spread over the mazurka.
Yields 48 squares.

PRUNE MAZURKA
Mazurek śliwkowy

Bottom layer as in Chocolate Mazurka, or a white
    commercial wafer*

FILLING

*2 cups sugar
½ tablespoon vinegar
½ cup water
Grated rind 1 lemon
1 lemon, peeled from the white skin, diced
14 ounces prunes, pitted, finely sliced
8 ounces almonds, slivered*

ICING   *As for Fig Mazurka**

Prepare the filling as for Fig Mazurka*. Spread it warm over the
bottom layer. Cool. Spread with icing.
Yields 48 squares.

DATE MAZURKA
Mazurek daktylowy

Bottom layer as in Chocolate Mazurka, or a white
    commercial wafer*

FILLING

*1¼ cups sugar
½ tablespoon vinegar
½ cup water
6 ounces walnuts, chopped
8 ounces dates, pitted, ground
2 lemons, ground
6 ounces candied orange rind, ground*

ICING   *As in Fig Mazurka**

Prepare the Date Mazurka as Fig Mazurka*.
Yields 48 squares.

MAZURKA FROM WILNO
Mazurek wileński

Prepare dough as in Chocolate Mazurka, or use a white
commercial wafer*

FILLING

6 egg whites
3¾ cups confectioners' sugar
8 ounces instant chocolate
8 ounces almonds, ground
8 ounces dates, pitted, finely sliced

ICING

2 cups confectioners' sugar
3 tablespoons rum

Prepare dough as in Chocolate Mazurka* and bake at 375° F. for
10 minutes.
Beat the egg whites till stiff. Add sugar in small parts, beating constantly. Beat 5 more minutes. Fold in the chocolate, almonds, and
dates. Spread over the bottom layer. Bake another 20 minutes at
350° F. Cool.
Combine the sugar with rum, spread over the mazurka.
Yields 48 squares.

WALNUT MAZURKA
Mazurek orzechowy

Prepare dough as for Chocolate Mazurka*and bake for 10 minutes in 375° F. oven. Or use a white commercial wafer.

SPREAD

½ cup soft butter
3 egg yolks
Juice 1 lemon
2 cups confectioners' sugar
1 teaspoon vanilla extract
1 cup flour
8 ounces walnuts, ground

MERINGUE

2 egg whites
1 cup confectioners' sugar
1 teaspoon vanilla extract

To make spread: Beat the butter with the egg yolks for 10 minutes, adding gradually the lemon juice, sugar, and vanilla.
Add the flour and the walnuts alternately, mixing with a spoon. Spread evenly over the bottom layer.
To make meringue: Beat the egg whites until stiff, add the confectioners' sugar and vanilla gradually, still beating. Spread over the cake. Bake in a moderate 350° F. oven for ½ hour.
Yields 4 dozen squares.

CINNAMON CAKE
Placek z cynamonem

⅔ *cup soft butter or*
  margarine
1 *cup sugar*
2 *teaspoons vanilla extract*
3 *eggs, separated*
1 *egg yolk*

3 *cups flour*
1 *cup milk*
3 *teaspoons baking powder*
3 *tablespoons sugar*
2 *tablespoons cinnamon*

Beat the butter with the sugar for 3 minutes. Add the vanilla and egg yolks, beat 3 more minutes. Add the flour alternately with milk, add baking powder, beat 2 more minutes. Whip 2 egg whites stiff. Fold in.
Fold into a baking pan (9×12), buttered and sprinkled with bread crumbs. Spread with egg white. Sprinkle with sugar and cinnamon. Bake in a moderate 375° F. oven for 45 minutes.
Yields 1 9×12 cake. Serves 20.

EGG WHITE CAKE
Placek z białek

BATTER

½ *cup soft butter*
1 *cup sugar*
1⅓ *cups flour*

2 *teaspoons baking powder*
1 *cup milk*
4 *egg whites*

TOPPING

¾ *cup flour*
2 *tablespoons soft butter*

1 *teaspoon vanilla extract*
⅓ *cup confectioners' sugar*

To make batter: Beat the butter with the sugar for 5 minutes. Add the flour and baking powder alternately with milk. Beat 5 more minutes. Beat the egg whites stiff. Fold in, mix slightly.
Fold into a baking pan (9×12), buttered and sprinkled with bread crumbs.

To make topping: Combine the topping ingredients. Knead for a minute. Sprinkle the cake with shredded topping crumbs.
Bake in a moderate 375° F. oven for 40 minutes.
Yields 1 9×12 cake. Serves 20.

STRAWBERRY SHORTCAKE
Torcik z truskawkami

DOUGH

¾ cup butter
1¼ cups sugar
1½ teaspoons vanilla extract
3 eggs
1 cup sifted flour
3½ teaspoons baking powder
2 cups graham cracker crumbs
1 cup milk
½ cup chopped walnuts

TOPPING

1½ cups whipping cream
¼ cup sugar
1¼ teaspoons lemon juice
2 pints fresh strawberries

To make dough: Cream the butter with the sugar and vanilla until fluffy. Beat in eggs, one at a time.
Mix the flour with baking powder. Combine with graham cracker crumbs. Add to the egg mixture alternately with milk, beating after each addition. Add the walnuts.
Spread batter in 2 greased and wax-paper-lined, 9-inch square cake pans. Bake in preheated 375° F. oven 30–35 minutes. Cool slightly. Remove from pans to cake rack to cool.
To make topping: Whip the cream with sugar and lemon juice until soft peaks form. Spread on cold cake layers.
Slice 1 pint of strawberries over 1 cake. Top with second layer. Garnish with whole strawberries.
Yields 1 9-inch-square cake. Serves 12.

STRAWBERRY TARTS
Ciastka z truskawkami

DOUGH

1 cup margarine
2 cups all purpose flour
⅔ cup confectioners' sugar
4 egg yolks
1 ounce yeast
1 tablespoon flour

TOPPING

4 tablespoons bread crumbs
2 pints fresh strawberries
4 egg whites
1½ cups sugar

To make dough: Cut the margarine into the flour with a knife and rub in with fingertips. Add sugar, mix. Add egg yolks. Add yeast combined with 1 tablespoon flour. Knead the dough for a few minutes. Spread on a buttered and floured cookie sheet. Bake at 375° F. for 10 minutes. Remove from the oven.
Sprinkle with bread crumbs.
To make topping: Place well-drained strawberries on the cake evenly. Beat egg whites. When soft peaks form, add sugar gradually. Beat until stiff. Spread the egg whites over the strawberries. Return the cake to the oven. Bake at 325° F. for 30 minutes.
Remove from the oven. Cut the warm cake into square tarts. Serve fresh. Yields 32 tarts.

STRAWBERRY TORTE
Tort z truskawkami

BATTER

3 eggs, separated
1 cup sugar
4 tablespoons coffee cream
1½ cups instant flour
3 teaspoons baking powder

TOPPING

2 pints fresh strawberries
⅔ cup confectioners' sugar
1 cup whipping cream
3 tablespoons confectioners' sugar
1 teaspoon vanilla extract

To make batter: Beat the egg yolks with sugar until fluffy, add the cream, flour, and baking powder. Beat for 3 minutes. Beat egg whites until stiff. Add 2 tablespoons of the egg whites to the batter, mix. Add the rest of the egg whites, mix slightly.

Spread the batter in 2 buttered and wax-paper-lined 9-inch round cake pans. Bake in moderate 350° F. oven for 20 minutes or until golden. Cool slightly. Remove from pans and cool. Refrigerate overnight.

To make topping: The next day: wash and slice the strawberries, sprinkle with confectioners' sugar. Leave for 20 minutes.

Whip the cream, add the confectioners' sugar and vanilla.

Sprinkle 1 cake layer with half of the strawberry juice. Cover with ⅔ of strawberries, spread with half of the whipped cream. Top with the second layer. Sprinkle with the rest of the strawberry juice. Spread with the rest of the cream. Garnish with strawberries. Refrigerate for 1 hour. This is a real summer treat.

Yields 1 9-inch round cake. Serves 8.

CHERRY PIE
Placec z czereśniami

DOUGH

¼ *pound margarine*
1¼ *cups flour*
¼ *cup sugar*
2 *egg yolks*
1 *teaspoon vanilla extract*

SPREAD

8 *ounces farmer cheese or ricotta cheese*
½ *cup confectioners' sugar*
1 *teaspoon lemon juice*
2 *tablespoons milk*

TOPPING

⅓ *cup sugar*
2 *tablespoons cornstarch*
½ *cup cold water*
¼ *teaspoon almond extract*
1 *quart cherries, pitted*
2 *tablespoons slivered almonds*

To make dough: Cut the margarine into the flour mixed with sugar. Rub in with fingertips. Add the egg yolks and vanilla. Knead the dough. Spread over a pie pan. Bake in moderate 350° F. oven for 25 minutes. Cool.

To make spread: Combine the cheese with all ingredients and spread over the bottom of the pie.

To make topping: Bring to a boil: the sugar with the cornstarch mixed with ½ cup cold water. Simmer stirring for a few minutes. Add the almond extract and the cherries. Spread over the pie. Sprinkle with almonds.

Similar pie can be made with berries or canned fruits.

Yields 1 9-inch pie. Serves 8.

PLUM CAKE
Placek ze śliwkami

BATTER

3 cups biscuit mix   2 eggs
4 tablespoons butter   ¾ cup milk
1 cup sugar

TOPPING

16 prune plums, cut lengthwise into halves

Combine the ingredients of the dough and beat at medium speed
for 5 minutes. Fold the batter into a 9×12 baking pan, buttered
and sprinkled with bread crumbs.
Place the plums on the batter skin down. Bake in a moderate
350° F. oven for 40 minutes.
Yields 32 squares.

PLUM TARTS
Ciastka ze śliwkami

DOUGH

⅔ cup butter   1 egg
2¾ cups all purpose flour   1 egg yolk
⅔ cup confectioners' sugar   3 tablespoons sour cream
2 teaspoons baking powder

TOPPING

40 prune plums, cut lengthwise into halves

ICING

Juice 1 lemon
Confectioners' sugar
Whipped cream

Cut the butter into the flour and rub in with fingertips. Add the
sugar and baking powder, mix. Combine with the egg, egg yolk,

and sour cream. Knead the dough. Cover and refrigerate for ½ hour.

Roll out thin. Place on a buttered 12×15 cookie sheet. Spread the dough with fingers till the sheet is almost covered. Arrange the prunes in rows, skin down.

Bake in a moderate 375° F. oven for 45 minutes. Cool.

Mix the lemon juice with enough confectioners' sugar to have the thickness of sour cream. Spread over the cake. Cut into 40 tarts. The tarts are best the same day. Serve with whipped cream. Yields 40 tarts.

PEACH TARTS
Ciastka z brzoskwiniami

Prepare dough as for Plum Tarts*
15 freestone medium peaches
½ cup confectioners' sugar

Skin the peaches. Cut lengthwise, remove the stones. Place peach halves on the cake in rows. Bake in a moderate 375° F. oven for 45 minutes. Cool.

Just before serving, sprinkle with confectioners' sugar through a sieve. Cut into 30 tarts.

Yields 30 tarts.

RASPBERRY PIE
Torcik z malinami

DOUGH

1½ cups flour
½ cup butter
1 egg yolk

1 tablespoon confectioners'
  sugar
Grated rind ½ lemon

FILLING

2 envelopes gelatin
2 tablespoons cold water
4 tablespoons boiling water

4 egg whites
1 cup sugar
2 pints raspberries

To make dough: Put all the ingredients in a bowl and knead the dough. Roll out and transfer to a 9-inch pie pan. Pat into the bottom and the sides of the pan. Bake in a hot 425° F. oven for 15 minutes.

To make filling: Soak the gelatin in cold water for 5 minutes. Add boiling water, heat in a double boiler, stirring until dissolved. Beat the egg whites till stiff, add the sugar and gelatin gradually, beat 1 more minute. Add 1½ pints of raspberries, mix with a spoon. Fill the cooled shell, refrigerate until set. Garnish with the rest of the raspberries.

Yields 1 9-inch pie. Serves 8.

ORANGE CAKE
Ciasto pomarańczowe

¾ cup sugar
2 eggs
Grated rind 1 large orange
1½ cups flour

2 teaspoons baking powder
⅓ cup margarine, melted
3 tablespoons milk

ICING

2 tablespoons soft butter
2 tablespoons orange juice
1¾ cups confectioners' sugar

To make dough: Place all the ingredients in a bowl. Beat for 5 minutes at medium speed. Pour into a greased and floured 9×4-inch loaf tin or 8-inch ring cake tin. Bake in moderate 350° F. oven for 45 minutes. Cool slightly. Remove from the tin.

To make icing: Mix the butter and the orange juice with confectioners' sugar. Spread on the cake.

Yields 12 slices.

BLUEBERRY SQUARES
Placek z jagodami

½ pound butter or
  margarine
1¼ cups sugar
4 eggs
2 cups flour

1 teaspoon vanilla extract
2 teaspoons baking powder
1½ pints blueberries
¼ cup confectioners' sugar

Beat the butter with the sugar very well. Add the eggs alternately with the flour, beat 5 more minutes. Add vanilla and baking powder.
Fold into a 9×12-inch pan, buttered and sprinkled with bread crumbs. Sprinkle with blueberries. Bake in a hot 400° F. oven for 45 minutes.
Remove from the oven. Sprinkle with confectioners' sugar through a sieve. Cool. Cut into 32 pieces in the pan before serving.
This is a summertime delight.
Yields 32 squares.

PEACH MERINGUE
Beza z brzoskwiniami

6 egg whites
2 cups sugar
1 teaspoon vinegar
½ teaspoon vanilla extract
6 medium freestone peaches, skinned, sliced
2 cups whipping cream
2 tablespoons slivered almonds

Beat the egg whites until stiff. Add sugar two spoonfuls at a time, still beating; add the vinegar and vanilla, beat for 10 more minutes.
Cut out two 9-inch brown paper circles, place them on baking sheets. Spread the egg white mixture evenly on the paper circles. Bake in a slow 275° F. oven for 1 hour. Turn off the heat and leave the meringue in the oven until cold. Keep in a covered cake dish.

Before serving: place the sliced peaches on tissue paper. Beat the cream until stiff. Remove the paper from one meringue. Place the meringue on a flat plate. Spread half of the cream over it, cover with half of the peaches. Remove the paper from the second meringue and place it over the first. Spread the rest of the cream over it, cover with peaches, sprinkle with almonds. Cut with a thin, sharp knife in 12 pieces.

Yields 12 servings.

PINEAPPLE SQUARES
Ciastka z ananasem

DOUGH

3 cups sifted flour	1 cup margarine
2 teaspoons baking powder	3 egg yolks
3 tablespoons sugar	½ cup milk

STUFFING

4½ cups crushed pineapple
6 tablespoons cornstarch
½ cup sugar

TOPPING

1 egg white
1 cup chopped walnuts

DOUGH: Mix the flour with baking powder and sugar. Cut the margarine into the flour with a knife and rub in with fingertips. Mix the egg yolks with the milk, add to the flour, knead the dough. To make stuffing: Mix the pineapple with cornstarch and sugar. Cook on low heat until it thickens. Cool.

Roll out from the dough 2 rectangles 10×15. Place one in a buttered pan. Spread with the pineapple mixture, cover with the second rectangle.

Beat the egg white until stiff, spread over the cake, sprinkle with the walnuts. Bake in moderate 350° F. oven for 40 minutes. Remove, cool. Cut into 35 squares.

Yields 35 squares.

APPLE SQUARES
Placek z jabłkiem

DOUGH

1 cup margarine
4 cups flour
1 cup confectioners' sugar
4 teaspoons baking powder
2 eggs
1 egg yolk
6 tablespoons sour cream

STUFFING

2 pounds cooking apples
4 tablespoons sugar
1 teaspoon cinnamon
1 teaspoon vanilla extract
½ cup confectioners' sugar

Cut the margarine into the flour with a knife and rub in with finger-tips, add the sugar and the baking powder, mix. Add the eggs, egg yolk, and sour cream. Knead the dough for few minutes. Roll out 2 rectangles, 8½×12. Place one in a pan, buttered and sprinkled with bread crumbs. Bake in a moderate 375° F. oven for 15 minutes. Remove, cover with apples, shredded and mixed with sugar, cinnamon, and vanilla. Cover with the second rectangle. Return to the oven, bake for 45 minutes. Cool slightly, remove from the pan. Sprinkle with confectioners' sugar through a sieve. Cut into 32 pieces.
Yields 32 squares.

APPLE CAKE
Ciasto z jabłkiem

½ cup and 2 tablespoons butter
¾ cup sugar
3 eggs
1¾ cups sifted flour
2 teaspoons baking powder
1 tablespoon grated lemon rind
2 medium baking apples, pared, cored, sliced
2 teaspoons sugar
½ cup apricot jam

Beat the butter with the sugar until creamy. Add eggs one at a time, beating until well blended. Add the flour, baking powder, and lemon rind, beat for 4 minutes. Turn into greased 9-inch spring-form pan.
Arrange the apples on the batter, sprinkle with sugar. Bake 1 hour at 350° F. Remove. Brush apples with jam, cool.
Yields 12 wedges.

CHARLOTTE
Szarlotka

FILLING

2 cups sugar
½ cup water
2 pounds apples, shredded
1 teaspoon vanilla extract
1 tablespoon grated lemon rind
3 ounces candied orange rind, finely chopped

DOUGH

½ pound butter
4 cups pre-sifted, all purpose flour
1 cup confectioners' sugar
1 tablespoon grated lemon rind
5 egg yolks

To make filling: Bring the sugar with the water to a boil. Cook for a few minutes, stirring. Add the rest of the ingredients. Cook on medium heat for 1 hour stirring often. The jam is ready when thick and transparent. Cool.

To make dough: Cut the butter into the flour with a knife, and rub in with fingertips. Combine with sugar and lemon rind. Add the egg yolks, knead the dough. Refrigerate for 15 minutes.

Roll out 2 rectangles to fit a 9×12 pan buttered and sprinkled with bread crumbs.

Bake one rectangle for 10 minutes in a 400° F. oven. Remove from the oven. Cool. Spread with the apple jam. Cover with the second rectangle. Bake another 45 minutes.

Sprinkle the hot cake with confectioners' sugar through a sieve. Cut out in the pan into 2-inch squares.

Yields 24 squares.

APPLE RAISIN CAKE
Ciasto z jabłkiem i rodzynkami

½ pound butter
2 cups sugar
4 eggs
2 cups pre-sifted flour
2 teaspoons cinnamon
1 teaspoon baking soda
¾ cup raisins, steamed
4 cups coarsely shredded apples
1 cup finely chopped walnuts

Beat the butter with the sugar till creamy, add the eggs, beat 5 minutes more. Add the flour, cinnamon, and soda, beat 3 more minutes. Fold in the fruits and nuts.

Place in a high, 9-inch pan with removable bottom, buttered and floured. Bake in a moderate 350° F. oven for 1½ hours.

Yields 1 9-inch tall cake. Serves 16.

POPPY SEED SQUARES
Ciastka z makiem

Prepare dough as for Apple Squares*

FILLING

3 tablespoons butter
1 pound poppy seeds, ground twice (may be purchased ground
    in many delicatessen stores)
1½ cups sugar
1 teaspoon vanilla extract
1 teaspoon almond extract
Grated rind 1 lemon
2 egg whites, whipped stiff
½ cup confectioners' sugar

Heat the butter in a saucepan. Add the poppy seeds, fry for few minutes. Add sugar, vanilla and almond extracts, and lemon rind. Cook 15 minutes, stirring. Remove from the heat. Add the egg whites, mix slightly. Cool.

Roll out the dough, bake, fill, and bake again as in Apple Squares*. Sprinkle with confectioners' sugar.

Cut into 2-inch squares in the pan.

Yields 32 squares.

BEVERAGES

It is not accidental that almost all recipes in this chapter are for alcoholic beverages. Tea and coffee are not different in the Polish cuisine. Tea is seldom taken with milk. Coffee is served after, never during the meal, and preferably strong, in a demi-tasse. We have here on the market so many good fruit juices, frozen or canned, that almost no housewife cares to make her own. But the beverages listed on the following pages cannot be obtained in stores, and although the preparation does not require hours of toil—they are definitely "something different."

Alcohol was never considered an evil in Poland. Polish people have not known prohibition, they believe that a tasty alcoholic beverage adds to the zest of life—if not abused. But nothing is good in this world when used without moderation, not even the most delectable food, or . . . love.

It is not customary in Poland to drink beer in large amounts. It is served with meals in small glasses. Even children are allowed a sip occasionally. A working man, who wants to get high on pay day, drinks straight, clear vodka. Wine is considered an elegant drink for people of refinement, and so are the following beverages.

BEVERAGES	NAPOJE
Hot Wine	*Grzane wino*
Hot Beer	*Grzane piwo*
White Punch	*Biały poncz*
Honey Punch	*Napój z miodem*
Summer Punch	*Poncz letni*
Iced Coffee with Cognac	*Mazagran*
Iced Coffee Polish Style	*Kawa mrożona po polsku*
Lemon Vodka	*Cytrynówka*
Orange Vodka	*Pomarańczówka*
Prune Vodka	*Nalewka na śliwkach*
Chocolate Liqueur	*Likier czekoladowy*
Egg Liqueur	*Likier jajeczny*
Fire Vodka	*Krupnik*

HOT WINE
Grzane wino

1 quart red wine   ½ teaspoon cloves
1 cup sugar   ½ teaspoon cinnamon

Combine all the ingredients and heat well, but do not boil. Serve in tumblers.
Excellent after skiing or other winter sports.
Yields 4½ cups.

HOT BEER
Grzane piwo

1 quart beer   4 egg yolks
½ teaspoon cloves   1¼ cups sugar
½ teaspoon cinnamon

Bring the beer with the spices to a boil. Beat the egg yolks with sugar till thick and creamy. Add the beer in a thin stream, beating all the time. Heat stirring, but do not boil.
Excellent on cold nights or after winter sports.
Yields 5 cups.

WHITE PUNCH
Biały poncz

1 quart light white wine 2¾ cups sugar
½ cup arrack   Grated rind 2 lemons
¼ cup lemon juice   Grated rind 3 oranges
¾ cup orange juice

Combine all the ingredients and bring to a boil.
Serve in punch glasses on winter nights.
Yields 8 cups.

HONEY PUNCH
Napój z miodem

⅔ cup honey
2 egg yolks

2 cups hot, strong tea
Juice 2 lemons

Mix the honey with egg yolks well. Add the tea slowly. Heat, add lemon juice. Serve in tumblers.
Good to overcome a slight cold.
Yields 2¾ cups.

SUMMER PUNCH
Poncz letni

2 oranges, peeled, sliced
2 cups sugar
1 quart white wine

Juice 1 lemon
2 cups soda water

Sprinkle the orange slices with sugar. Cover and refrigerate overnight.
Place the oranges with the juice and sugar in a punch bowl. Add the wine and the lemon juice. Mix. Add soda water and serve immediately with ice.
Yields 8 cups.

ICED COFFEE WITH COGNAC
Mazagran

4 cups strong, cold coffee
8 teaspoons sugar

⅓ cup cognac

Mix the coffee with sugar. Add the cognac. Refrigerate for 2 hours. Serve in tumblers with ice.
Ideal for garden parties.
Serves 4.

ICED COFFEE POLISH STYLE
Kawa mrożona po polsku

4 teaspoons sugar
4 cups strong, cold coffee
1 cup vanilla ice cream
1 cup whipped cream

Add sugar to coffee. Refrigerate for 2 hours.
Pour into 4 tumblers, add ice cream, top with whipped cream.
Serve with fruit tarts. Drink without mixing.
Serves 4.

LEMON VODKA
Cytrynówka

Rind 1 lemon, sliced   *1 quart vodka*
2 teaspoons sugar

The lemon rind has to be cut thin, almost transparent.
Add the lemon rind and sugar to vodka. Let stand for 4 days.
Strain. Serve ice cold with hors d'oeuvres.
Yields 1 quart.

ORANGE VODKA
Pomarańczówka

Prepare as Lemon Vodka*, using orange rind.
Yields 1 quart.

PRUNE VODKA
Nalewka na śliwkach

½ pound prunes, pitted, sliced
6 cups vodka

Add the prunes to the vodka. Let stand 6 weeks. Shake every second day.
Strain through a piece of cotton. Serve ice cold.
Yields 6 cups.

CHOCOLATE LIQUEUR
Likier czekoladowy

5 egg yolks
¾ cup confectioners' sugar
1½ tablespoons chocolate syrup
1⅔ cups vodka
¼ cup heavy cream

Beat the egg yolks with the sugar until thick and creamy. Add the syrup. Add the vodka, mix. Whip the cream. Add to the liqueur. Serve after dinner.
Yields 4 cups.

EGG LIQUEUR
Likier jajeczny

5 egg yolks
2 cups sugar
1 teaspoon vanilla

1 cup milk, boiled and
   cooled
1 cup cognac
1½ cups vodka

Beat the egg yolks with the sugar until thick and creamy. Add the vanilla and milk. Beat a few more minutes.
Add the cognac, beat some more. Mix with vodka. Refrigerate for 4 days. Shake before serving.
Yields 5 cups.

FIRE VODKA
Krupnik

1 cup honey
½ cup water
1 teaspoon vanilla
¼ teaspoon nutmeg
1 tablespoon cinnamon
½ teaspoon cloves
1 teaspoon grated lemon rind
2½ cups vodka

Combine the honey with water, vanilla, spices, and lemon rind.
Bring to a boil, cover, and simmer 5 minutes.
Add the vodka, heat, and serve immediately in juice glasses.
Excellent after winter sports.
Yields 4 cups.

INDEX

Butter:
  Dill, 35
  Mustard, 35
  Onion, 35

Cabbage, 236-40 *(See also* Sauerkraut)
  with Apples, Red, 88
  and Apple Salad, 81
  with Bacon, 238
  with Caraway, Red, 240
  with Caraway, Savoy, 237-38
  and Dill Pickle Salad, 81
  Goose with, 165
  Kulebiak with, 58
  Lamb Pot Roast with, 204-5
  in Mayonnaise, 86
  Pierogi with, 223-24
  Polonaise, Savoy, 230
  Rolls, 76
  Sausage with Savoy, Polish, 180-81
  Soup, 115-16
  with Tomatoes, 237
Cakes, 287-92ff. *(See also* Babas;
  Pastries; Tortes)
  Almond Squares, 312
  Apple, 338
  Apple Charlotte, 338-39
  Apple Raisin, 339
  Apple Squares, 337
  Blueberry Squares, 335
  Cheese, Country, 316-17
  Cheese, Easter, 318
  Cheese, Grandmother's, 317-18
  Cheese, from Krakow, 319
  Cheese, Yeast, 315
  Chocolate Roll, 307-8
  Chocolate Squares, 311-12
  Cinnamon, 327
  Coffee Roll, 308
  Egg White, 327-28
  Fruit, Quick, 292
  Fruit, from Warsaw, Light, 289-90
  Honey, from Warsaw, 287
  Orange, 334
  Pineapple Squares, 336
  Plum, 332
  Poppy Seed Squares, 340
  Poppy Seed Yeast, 314
  Strawberry Shortcake, 328
  Walnut Ring, 291
Calf's Feet, Fried, 61-62
Calf's Liver. *See* Liver

Całuski, 286
Canapés, 32
  Brain, Toasted, 51
  Ham, Toasted, 49-50
  Ham, Tomato, and Cheese,
    Toasted, 53
  Liver, Toasted, 51
  Liver Sausage, Toasted, 50
  Mushroom, Toasted, 52-53
  Sardine, Toasted, 52
  Sausage, Liver, Toasted, 50
  Sausage and Horseradish, Toasted,
    50
Carp, 138
  in Aspic, 41-42
  with Beer, 149-50
  au Gratin with Mushrooms, 154
  in Gray Sauce, 142-43
  in Greek Sauce, 39-40
  in Horseradish Sauce, 40
Carrots:
  and Peas, 234
  Polonaise, 231
Carrot Salads:
  Apple and Horseradish, 84
  Apple and Sauerkraut, 82
  and Rhubarb, 85
Cauliflower:
  au Gratin, 244
  with Ham au Gratin, 71
  Polonaise, 232
  Soup, 118
Charlotte, 338-39
Cheese, 216ff., 222-23
  Baba, Rice and, 260
  Bread, 315-16
  Cake, Country, 316-17
  Cake, Easter, 318
  Cake, Grandmother's, 317-18
  Cake from Krakow, 319
  Cake, Yeast, 315
  Canapés, Ham and Tomato, 53
  Casserole, Cottage, 223
  Cookies, 284
  Croutons, 136
  Dumplings, 222
    Sweet, 265
  Fish with, 147-48
  Noodles with, Sweet, 267
  Pancakes, 222-23
    Sweet, 266-67
  Pascha from Lwow, 269

354   *Index*